The Advaita Vedānta of Śiva Saṁhitā

First Ever Vedantic Exposition

THE ADVAITA VEDĀNTA OF ŚIVA SAṀHITĀ

First Ever Vedantic Exposition

Commentary on the first chapter of Śiva Saṁhitā by

K Kathirasan

Edited by

S. Anuradha

Kannan Krishnasamy

MOTILAL BANARSIDASS PUBLISHERS
PRIVATE LIMITED • DELHI

First Edition : Delhi, 2018

ISBN :978-81-208-4172-7

Also available at

MOTILAL BANARSIDASS
41 U.A. Bungalow Road, Jawahar Nagar, Delhi 110 007
1 B, Jyoti Studio Compound, Kennedy Bridge, Nana Chowk, Mumbai 400 007
203 Royapettah High Road, Mylapore, Chennai 600 004
236, 9th Main III Block, Jayanagar, Bengaluru 560 011
8 Camac Street, Kolkata 700 017
Ashok Rajpath, Patna 800 004
Chowk, Varanasi 221001

MLBD Cataloging-in-Publication Data

The Advaita Vedānta of Śiva Samhitā:
First Ever Vedantic Exposition
by K KATHIRASAN
ISBN : 978-81-208-4172-7
Includes Glossary, Bibliography and Index
I. Philosophy II. Advaita Vedānta III. Hatha Yoga
IV. Śiva Saṁhitā V. Commentary VI. Kathirasan K,
VII. Anuradha, S. VIII. Kannan K.

Published by

Motilal Banarsidass Publishers Private Limited
www.mlbd.com • mlbd@mlbd.com
Printed by Nice Printing Press

CONTENTS

PREFACE

"Let the joy I experienced spread in the world," says Tirumular in Tirumandiram. That pretty much sums up the decision to transcribe and edit the lecture series on *Śiva Samhitā* by Kathirasan K.

Although the knowledge of Self has to be learnt directly from a teacher, this first ever exposition on the first chapter of the *Śiva Samhitā* will be very beneficial for the seekers. The chapter is unique as it explains how a seeker can attain total freedom by understanding his true nature. The chapter is also priceless because it organizes the teaching of *Sanatana Dharma* ahead of explaining the nature of Self.

Kathirasan has explained each verse in detail and supported the teachings with references from *Upanishads*, *Bhagavad Gītā* and other *Vedānta* texts. The communication style is also simple making it easy for a reader and seeker to understand the meaning of this great text.

My respects to the teaching tradition starting from *Īśvara* to the anonymous author of *Śiva Samhitā* to Kathirasan that has made this knowledge available to seekers.

I am also grateful to the Hindu Centre, Singapore, under whose aegis these lectures took place in 2010-2011.

S. Anuradha
Singapore, 2017

ACKNOWLEDGMENT

I would like to thank my teacher, Śri Swami Satprakashananda Saraswati of Atma Vidya Vanam for teaching and introducing me to traditional *Vedānta* and for showering me with his grace, compassion and for always inspiring me through his commitment to the *Vedānta Sampradāya*. More than anything else I am very indebted to him for permanently changing my worldview through his formal and informal teachings. Without these new pair of lenses, I would not have been able to teach and share this knowledge. The commentary on the *Śiva Samhitā* would not have been possible without the precious knowledge gained through him and the *parampara* he belongs to.

INTRODUCTION

Śiva Samhitā has come to be known as one of the three source texts for the *Haṭha Yoga* tradition. The other two being *Haṭha Yoga Pradīpikā* and the *Gheranḍa Samhitā*. However, it is strange that many do not appreciate the *Śiva Samhitā* for its clear exposition of the subject of *ātmajñāna* or Self-Knowledge as taught by the *Upaniṣad*-s. While it may be considered as one of the traditional *Haṭha Yoga śāstra*, the truth is that this text is not only a *Haṭha Yoga śāstra*, but a *Vedānta-Haṭha Yoga* text as well. This is due to it being profoundly influenced by *Advaita Vedānta* unlike any other known *Haṭha Yoga śāstra*-s. The significant departure from the teachings of the *Haṭha Yoga* tradition will be obvious to anyone who studies the first chapter in its entirety.

The teachings of the first chapter of the *Śiva Samhitā* is very much rooted in the *Advaita Vedānta* tradition popularised and organised by *Śaṅkarācārya*. And modern scholars like James Mallinson do not consider it a unitary text, but a compilation of teachings. Mircea Eliade attributed a Buddhist influence on *Śiva Samhitā* which I would disagree with. It is my view that scholars get confused by words such as *śūnya* (void) thinking it to be a Buddhist invention, when such words and ideas are also found and used in the *Vedānta* tradition[1] but interpreted differently.

The other interesting point is that the classification of *Śiva Samhitā* being a *Haṭha Yoga śāstra* had made it oblivious to the *Vedāntin*-s. But having gone through every verse of the first chapter, I realised that this is a rare *Vedānta* teaching where the organisation of the subject is unparalleled. I would venture to conclude that the first chapter of this text is complete in its coverage of the key teachings of *Vedānta*. I am yet to encounter a *Vedānta* text which is as organized and structured as this one. It has systematised the *Vedānta* teachings such that it is consistent with the tradition of *Advaita Vedānta* as taught in the *Upaniṣad*-s.

Another unique feature of the *Śiva Samhitā* is that the teachings of *Sanātana Dharma* (or Hinduism) are found to be organised into two lifestyles – ethics, securities and pleasure (*pravṛtti mārga*) and liberation (*nivṛtti mārga*). The text has distinguished these two lifestyles very clearly and systematically. This is quite rare as most *Vedānta* texts do not present *pravṛtti mārga* as a subject before introducing Self-Knowledge or *Brahmavidyā* (knowledge of *Brahman*), which is usually done after a brief discussion of the *sādhana*

1 see Brahma Sūtra Bhāṣya 1.4.15

catuṣṭayam (four-fold qualifications of a seeker of *mokṣa*). This urgency in almost all *Vedānta* texts could be attributed to the author's assumption that the reader is a qualified person, traditionally a renunciate (*saṇnyāsin*). On the other hand, the *Śiva Samhitā* takes pains to organize the teachings of *Sanātana Dharma* viz *pravṛtti mārga* and *nivṛtti mārga*.

Among its five chapters, the first chapter of the *Śiva Samhitā* is comprehensive about *Vedānta*, within the larger context of *Sanātana Dharma*. It is truly a blessing to any seeker who wishes to embark on *Vedāntic* study using the *Śiva Samhitā*'s first chapter.

I stumbled on the *Śiva Samhitā* during my independent research on *Haṭha Yoga śāstras*. As I was perusing the verses of its first chapter, the verses caught my rasp attention and I was stunned by the clarity of each verse in presenting the teachings of *Vedānta*.

I have used the 1914-15 edition of the *Śiva Samhitā* published by the Panini Office (Allahabad). I have edited a few of the verses where needed using the critically edited version by Kaivalyadhama S.M.Y.M. Samiti published in 2009. The translations used were from the revised edition of the former publication by Dr G.P. Bhatt in 2004, published by Motilal Banarsidass. The critically edited version was also used to improve the translation where necessary. I have also further improved the translation of the verses where necessary.

The book that you are holding in your hand covers each and every verse of the first chapter of the *Śiva Samhitā* with an elaborate commentary based on the *Advaita Vedānta* tradition as taught by *Śaṅkarācārya*. However, the purpose of this unfoldment is to present the teachings of the verses such that you appreciate the vision of *Vedānta* and the nature of your being, Self. But this book does not aim to substitute the requirement of a teacher to instruct this knowledge in a traditional manner. The *Upaniṣad*-s state that *Vedānta* must be learned by approaching a living qualified teacher and there is no substitute for that need,

ācāryavān puruṣo Veda

one who has a teacher knows[2]

tadvijñānārthaṃ sa gurumevābhigacchet
samitpāṇiḥ śrotriyaṃ brahmaniṣṭham

2 Chāndogya Upaniṣad 6.14.2

For knowing that Reality he should go, with sacrificial faggots in hand, only to a teacher versed in the *Vedas* and established in *Brahman*.[3]

In the process of studying this book, you may also appreciate the core teachings of *Sanātana Dharma* which is the discovery of happiness through one of the two lifestyles mentioned above.

The word *Śiva* in *Śiva Samhitā* refers to either Lord *Śiva* or 'auspiciousness' itself, *Śivam*. The word *Śivam* also refers to the *ātman*, Self.[4] *Samhitā* means a collection of hymns or knowledge. The term *samhitā* is also quite common for texts within the *tantra* or the *āgama* traditions. In some of manuscripts of the *Śiva Samhitā*, the opening verse begins with the line "*Īśvara uvāca*" which means that the teaching is from Lord *Śiva* himself thereby indicating that the knowledge is not authored by any human agent and hence *apauruṣeya*. Therefore, it is worthy of being placed under the category of *āgama* or *tantra*. As in most *Śaiva āgamas*, the teaching takes place as a dialogue between *Śiva* and *Pārvati*.

The *Śiva Samhitā* has a total of five chapters and the subjects within are as follows:

Chapter 1 – *Advaita Vedānta* (96 verses)

Chapter 2 – *Haṭha Yoga* & *Advaita Vedānta* (57 verses)

Chapter 3 – *Haṭha Yoga* (115 verses)

Chapter 4 – *Haṭha Yoga* (111 verses)

Chapter 5 – *Haṭha Yoga* & *Advaita Vedānta* (260 verses)

The assimilation of the teachings found in the first chapter would be very helpful to know the Self clearly. In my opinion, the study of the other chapters is futile unless the assimilation of Self-Knowledge is prevented by the lack of mental fitness due to many reasons including the desire and value for ethics, securities and pleasure (*pravṛtti mārga*). In such a situation, the practice of *Haṭha Yoga* (or *Karma Yoga*) taught in the other chapters may prove to be useful in making the mind fit for the assimilation of Self-Knowledge. The text *Aparokṣānubhūti* confirms this pedagogy,

ebhiraṅgaiḥ samāyukto rājayoga udāhṛtaḥ
kiñcitpakvakaṣāyāṇāṃ haṭhayogena saṃyutaḥ

Thus has been described *Raja Yoga* (Self-Knowledge) consisting

3 Mundaka Upaniṣad 1.2.12

4 Māṇḍūkya Upaniṣad 7

of these steps. With this is to be combined *Haṭha-Yoga* for (the benefit of) those whose desires are partially attenuated.[5]

The *Aparokṣānubhūti* states that if the Self-Knowledge has not been assimilated, then the practice of *Haṭha Yoga* becomes necessary. We can infer from this instruction that the role of *Haṭha Yoga* is to prepare and prime the seeker to be able to assimilate Self-Knowledge. The relation between *Haṭha Yoga* and *Vedānta* (Self-Knowledge) is that the former prepares one in the assimilation of the latter. *Vedānta* is a *jñāna sādhana* (discipline of knowledge), while *Haṭha Yoga* is the means or spiritual practice (*sādhana*) to obtain purification of the mind (*cittaśuddhi*) and attain the competence (*adhikāra*) to undertake the *jñāna sādhana*.

Haṭha Yoga is a more complex system to developing *adhikāra* and *cittaśuddhi* because it prescribes more disciplines than the traditional *Vedic* method of *Karma Yoga* as taught in the *Bhagavad Gītā*. *Haṭha Yoga* advocates both the performance of one's duties and the conditioning of the body-sense-mind complex in an integrated manner, which you do not find in other Hindu traditions. In that sense it is highly systematic and complete in its purpose of preparing a seeker for the assimilation of the Self-Knowledge. However, one should not erroneously conclude that *Haṭha Yoga* is the only available path to developing *adhikāra* and *cittaśuddhi*. In *Sanātana Dharma* there are numerous disciplines that can be observed to achieve this goal. The *Bhagavad Gītā* enumerates a couple of them too.[6]

Modern scholars of *Haṭha Yoga* have speculated that the *Śiva Samhitā* could be a compilation of discrete *Haṭha Yoga* and *Vedānta* teachings. This could be attributed to its first chapter which appears to be unrelated to its other chapters. But this could be a premature conclusion because the traditional methodology, as discussed above, is such that the *Vedānta* could also be taught to a seeker to gauge his readiness. If he happens to be unready, then other disciplines can be introduced to develop this readiness. This approach can also be found in the *Kena Upaniṣad* where symbolic meditations are taught for unprepared seekers after having taught Self-Knowledge.

In the hands of a teacher who knows the intention of the text (*tātparya*) and the *Vedāntic* teaching methodology (*sampradāya*), the *Śiva Samhitā* will not look like a compilation of contradictory teachings.

5 Aparokṣānubhūti 143

6 Bhagavad Gītā 4.25-31

You may find apparent contradictions in most scriptures (*śāstra*) but it can be reconciled if you knew the fundamentals of methodology of *Vedānta* well.

Another value the *Śiva Samhitā* creates is that it shows the connection between *Haṭha Yoga* and *Vedānta* traditions. That also means that *Haṭha Yoga* which is now perceived as an independent teaching tradition, is compatible with *Vedānta* if one uses its practices and not its philosophical position (*siddhānta*). It is therefore not antagonistic to Self-Knowledge. In the *Śiva Samhitā*, the *Haṭha Yoga* teachings which was born in the *Nātha* tradition[7] co-exist with *Vedānta*.

The current dating given to the *Śiva Samhitā* is around 15th century CE and according to James Mallinson, it was supposedly committed to writing in *Vārāṇāsi*, India which is also known as Benares or Kashi. While the text could have been composed in 15th century CE, the content of the teaching is timeless and beginning-less (*anādi*). Any truth that is timeless is always relevant and ever fresh to all people always, at all places and in all circumstances. Such is the nature of Self-Knowledge. For example, regardless of whether you lived five thousand years ago or five thousand years later, one thing which is certain is the desire for happiness above everything else. So, any teaching that brings you to this happiness is indeed timeless. It is universal and relevant always. That is the meaning of *Sanātana Dharma*, a 'teaching that is always fresh'.

One unique feature of *Śiva Samhitā* is that it encourages *grhastha*-s[8] or householders to take up *Haṭha Yoga* while most of the other texts assume that the practitioner is a *saṇnyāsin* (renunciate).

Suppose we subscribed to the view that this text had an author (*pauruṣeya śāstra*), then we must conclude by inference that the author must have been a great *mahātma*, so great that he did not even leave his name behind on the manuscript. The tradition of *Sanātana Dharma* has this noble value that knowledge is everyone's birthright and hence there is no copyright on spiritual works. We should appreciate the fact that the text has come from the pen of a great *mahātma* who knew how to bring these two traditions together.

---

7 a partial list of teachers in the Nātha tradition can be found in Haṭha Yoga Pradīpikā 1.4-8

8 verse 5.210

As a reader, it is good to note that this book was transcribed from a series of discourses and hence it has retained both the first person and objective points of view in presenting the knowledge. It is my firm belief that the confluence of the theoretical world and the world of personal experience will meet both the needs of the seekers and scholars. This has been the approach of traditional scholarship of *Vedānta* teachers. However, as stated above, in no way will this book replace the need of a living teacher.

Do also note that the words Self, *Brahman*, Consciousness, *caitanya* and *ātman* have been used interchangeably and hence to be treated as synonyms, unless qualified otherwise. Likewise do the words *mukta*, *jñāni* and *jīvanmukta* possess the same meaning.

There is a glossary at the end of the book for those who are not familiar with the popular jargons used in *Vedānta* and Vedic literature.

1

CONSCIOUSNESS ALONE EXISTS

ईश्वरउवाच
एकं ज्ञानं नित्यमाद्यन्तशून्यं नान्यत् किञ्चिद्वर्तते वस्तु सत्यम् |
यद्भेदोस्मिन्निन्द्रियोपाधिना वै ज्ञानस्यायं भासते नान्यथैव || १

Īśvara uvāca
ekaṃ jñānaṃ *nityam*ādyantaśūnyaṃ nānyat kiñcidvartate vastu satyam |
yadbhedosminnindriyopādhinā vai jñānasyāyaṃ bhāsate nānyathaiva || 1

God spoke
There is One Eternal Consciousness without beginning or end. No other real entity exists. The diversity which is found in this universe is nothing but the Consciousness but varied due to the sense perceptions as limiting adjuncts.

This opening verse is the grand statement of *Vedānta*. This is what every *Upaniṣad* teaches – 1. the knowledge of the supreme reality and 2. the simultaneous destruction of ignorance and its effects through that knowledge. This is a very important point, for it snows what is truth (*sàtyam*) and what is untruth (*mithyā*).

Īśvara uvāca means 'God speaks'. And what does he speak about? In the context of the text, *Īśvara* (God) talks about his nature and if you look at the whole universe (*jagat*) as *Īśvara* then you are also included in it. So, when *Īśvara* teaches about his nature, he is also talking about your nature. Any subject that you may learn is nothing but analyzing an aspect of *Īśvara*. For example, through chemistry you only understand the chemical composition of *Īśvara*. Anything that you put your finger on is an aspect of god. If you look at every teaching as a branch to understand *Īśvara*, then any pursuit is a sādhana (spiritual practice), not a chore and every student should ideally enjoy the learning process. You enjoy understanding and appreciating the creation which is not different from the creator. When you look at it that way, is there anything called secular knowledge? This is the reason why in *Sanātana Dharma* there is no difference between secular knowledge and religious knowledge. Everything is therefore spiritual alone. That is why *Sanātana Dharma* is called a way of life.

In the context of *Vedānta* when *Īśvara* talks, he reveals himself and by revealing himself he reveals your Self (*ātman*). The first word of the verse is '*ekam*'. What does *ekam* mean? Does it mean 'one' or 'one without a second'? How do we understand it? We usually use the word 'one' to distinguish one from the other. But one could also mean – 'only one, no other'. A good illustration is a goldsmith shop where there are many different gold ornaments but when it comes to gold, there is only 'one' gold and nothing else. From the standpoint of the ornaments on display there, the number of ornaments will continue to increase in terms of its design and function over time. But from the standpoint of gold, there is only gold which pervades all ornaments. Similarly, this word '*ekam*' means not just one but 'one without a second'. That means if this 'one' is understood, it is as good as understanding everything in this universe. The 'one without a second' is hence called non-dual (*advaita*).

This *ekam* is the only reality and it pervades the floor, wall, country, earth, space, universe, you, and whatever that you know and do not know. And that *ekam* is *Īśvara* or *Brahman*. From the standpoint of *ekam* there cannot be a second thing. Everything is contained in this 'one' and nothing else is worthy of being called 'one'. We call it 'one' for the sake of our understanding. From *Īśvara*'s point of view he does not really need to care because he is totally complete without your interpretation, appraisal or perception. We are the ones who attempt to limit *Īśvara* by our definitions, descriptions and illustrations although he is limitless.

Now that we know what *ekam* indicates, what is the nature of this *ekam*? The verse proceeds further to define this *ekam* as the nature of knowledge (*jñānaṃ*). What is knowledge? In this context, it does not mean knowledge in a conventional way. In the conventional definition of knowledge there is always a separation between the object you know and the knower. For example, you are now holding this book and the book is the object of your knowledge and you are the knower of the book. Between you and the book there is a separation. You are not the book and the book is not you.

In *Vedānta*, knowledge refers to the reality that makes any knowledge possible. This may sound cryptic so let us see what does this mean? Let us look at a typical example. If I place a flower in front of you, you see this flower because of your eyes. However, you will not be able to see this flower if the lights are switched off. Similarly, every knowledge you have is always about a mental or physical object. Like the light that makes your perception of the flower possible, there is this consciousness that makes you conscious of every knowledge or thought of an object possible. If that consciousness is not there, then you will not be even reading this book. This Consciousness is referred to as *jñānaṃ* or knowledge in the context of this verse.

That is why when we say that *Īśvara* is *jñānasvarūpa* it does not mean the knowledge as we know it conventionally. It means that *Īśvara* is the Consciousness that makes everything knowable to you. If not you will not be conscious of a second thing apart from your being. The traditional word for this Consciousness or knowledge is *caitanya* or *śuddha caitanya* which means pure Consciousness. It is not as if there is something called 'impure' consciousness. It means that it is not an 'object related consciousness' but is an 'independent consciousness' not dependent on anything else.

It is not easy to understand this *jñānaṃ* or Consciousness due to its subtlety. Because *Vedānta* as a philosophy works only if it is taught to you as an instruction (*upadeśa*) such that you pursue it as a spiritual commitment. As an academic subject, it will not be as effective, and will remain as one of the many theories you already know. You may just appreciate it as a textbook subject and when you wake up the next day you are the same ignorant person (*ajñāni*). *Vedānta* works only if is taught to a qualified seeker because the subject matter is very subtle and hence requires a relentless pursuit to realise it.

Here is another example to understand consciousness; let us suppose you have an image projector which has projected an image on a white screen. If you removed the white screen, the projection may land on the wall behind the screen. Suppose you removed that wall too, where would the image fall on? You would have realised by now that an image projection needs a static surface to be projected on and ideally it must be a clean, white and static background. The projected images can be moving like frames in a movie, but the background remains static. So, in any projection two things are required. One is the static substratum, and the other is the projection which depends on the static substratum. The conclusion that we can draw here is that all the moving images in a projection are only seen if there was a static substratum. Similarly, the image projections are our thoughts (*vṛtti*) and the static background is the Consciousness that makes it all possible for you to be conscious of those thoughts. If there was no Consciousness, you will not be able to function as you are and you will not be experiencing the world. Where there is a projected image there must be a screen but where there is a screen, there need not be a projection. The screen can exist independent of a projection but the projected image cannot exist without a screen. Where thoughts are, Consciousness is; but Consciousness can exist without thoughts. For example, in your deep dreamless sleep state, you are conscious but you have no thoughts. You were conscious that there were no thoughts. It is like eyes that 'see' nothing when lights are switched off, yet 'seeing' without seeing anything.

Consciousness lights up both thoughts and the absence of thoughts, just like the projection screen. The beauty is that thoughts reveal to you the existence of Consciousness, which is your Being. Where there is thought, there is Consciousness. In sleep when I do not have thoughts, I am Consciousness. The truth is that with or without thoughts I am always Consciousness without a second, '*ekam jñānaṃ*'. Is there a moment when I am not this Consciousness? No. So, I am worthy of being called jñānasvarūpam, of the nature of Consciousness. Because of Consciousness everything else becomes evident to me. If not for this Consciousness there would be nothing called perceptions. If you are not here, it is as good as nothing is evident to you. If you were not Consciousness, there is no *brahmavidyā* (knowledge of *Brahman*) to seek. If you are not conscious, does it matter whether this book you are holding in your hands existed or not? That part of you which makes everything conscious to you is *jñānaṃ*, which is also called *Īśvara* or *Brahman*. This Consciousness is indeed *Brahman*.[1] It is this Consciousness which is *ekam jñānaṃ nityam ādyantaśūnyam* as stated in the first verse.

The next word in the verse is *nityam* which means eternal, changeless or that which has no beginning or end. The word 'changeless' is very important because something that has no beginning and end can still be subject to change. So, the word *nityam* means both eternal and implies changelessness. In summary, *nityam* means that which does not change in the three periods of time (*trikāla abādhitam satyam*).

Is the universe *nityam*? No! It changes all the time. It is the opposite of *nityam* which is impermanent (a*nityam*). So, what is *nityam*? *Nityam* is that thing which is jñānaṃ. The whole universe is changing, so where is the reality in it? The illustrations to appreciate *nityam* are the clay - pot, ocean - waves and golden ornaments. In these examples, the forms (pot, wave and ornament) change but the respective substance (clay, water and gold) remains the same.

From my standpoint, what is it that changes in me? In fact, everything from the body to my thoughts change. However, Consciousness remains the

1 Aitareya Upaniṣad 3.3

same in spite of my changing body-sense-mind complex. Consciousness serves as the substratum of these changes. Hence the body-send-mind complex is a*nityam* (non-eternal) but consciousness is *nityam*. How old is this consciousness? It is eternal. Can you put a date of birth on it? Can we put a place of birth to it? Can you put a gender to it? The answer is No. You cannot put an age to this Consciousness. The concept of age is born along with your thoughts. In deep sleep you do not have such thoughts that you are a seventy-year-old or a five-year-old. Hence this Consciousness which is your being, is ageless, eternal, changeless and primordial.

So now you have two realities to grapple with. One is the changing world which is experienced through your body-sense-mind complex and the other is the Consciousness that is 'one without a second', changeless and eternal. Which one is you? Your response will depend upon the knowledge that you have about yourself. If you identify yourself with the body-sense-mind complex then definitely you are changing and subject to birth and death. But if you know that you are that Consciousness that makes this body-sense-mind complex possible, then you are that changeless and eternal reality.

This Consciousness as it has been discussed is equated to *ātman*, Self with a capital 'S'. This *ātman* is of the same nature as God (*Brahman*). Hence *Brahman*, *ātman* and Consciousness are referring to the same reality. From the standpoint of Consciousness all thoughts do not have independent reality. Similarly, the changing world too is not independent from *Brahman* as it depends on *Brahman* for its existence like the way thoughts depend on Consciousness. This Consciousness which is the core of your being is of the same nature as *Brahman* which is the essence of the universe. Hence the essence of yourself and the essence of the universe is one and the same. Therefore, you are not separate from the universe.

However most of the time our thoughts about ourselves are based on the judgements that "I am tall, I am short; I am angry, I am happy, I am dying" etc. In fact, every thought of yours defines what you are not, instead of what your true essence is. Every thought only reveals a limited personality of yourself. On the other hand, *Vedānta* states that you exist in spite of your thoughts. With or without a thought, you are certainly that Consciousness. There are some philosophies that deny the very existence of an eternal and changeless Consciousness. For example, the Buddhists contend that the Consciousness we are talking about is like a chariot (an illustration from the Buddhist teacher *Nāgārjuna*) which is a composite, made up of parts. If you kept dismantling each part of the chariot, there will be no chariot in the end. Buddhism's view is that consciousness can be broken down because it is in the form of thoughts. The consciousness they are referring to is what we call as cognitive consciousness which are but thoughts. Hence, they claim that consciousness is always about an object and if the object is removed the consciousness ceases. *Vedānta* refutes this by using the same example of the chariot, saying that consciousness is like the ground on which the dismantled parts of the chariot are laid, hence forming the substratum for the chariot be it assembled or dismantled. In fact, *Vedānta* removes the erroneous understanding by differentiating cognitive consciousness from Consciousness (with a capital C).

The Buddhist argument is straightforward. They claim that without an object there cannot be knowledge, therefore, consciousness depends upon an object. So, if the object is demolished, your consciousness gets demolished and if your consciousness can be demolished, it is then a*nityam*. Because prior to the 'object consciousness' there was no consciousness, when the object is absent, consciousness too is absent. *Vedānta* counters this by stating that the Consciousness that is taught by the *Upaniṣad*-s is not the same as the object centred consciousness. The *Upaniṣad*-s teach about the Consciousness that makes even the consciousness of the objects possible. It also states that the obsession with thoughts as consciousness should be abandoned. And that the focus should be the removal of erroneous knowledge about the world, God and Self. If you had one thorn in your foot, you take a second thorn to remove and dislodge the first one eventually discarding both away. This means that you do not correct wrong thinking with non-thinking, but with right thinking. Both are thoughts nevertheless. That Consciousness which is eternal and pure (*śuddha*) has to be seen very clearly with the help of *śāstra* and *guru*.

The next word in the verse is '*ādyantaśūnyam*' which is combination of three words (*ādi* + *anta* + *śūnyam*). The word '*ādi*' means 'beginning', '*anta*' means 'end' and '*śūnyam*' means 'devoid of'. This word means that Consciousness is devoid of beginning and end in terms of time and space. It is therefore infinite. The *Upaniṣad* states,

īśāvāsyam idam sarvam

Īśvara (or Consciousness) pervades everything.[2]

2 Īśāvāsya Upaniṣad 1

The word *śūnyam* does not refer to the Buddhistic *śūnyam*, which means void or emptiness. Here *śūnyam* means devoid of a beginning and end. The definition of *Brahman* found in the *Upaniṣad*,

satyam jñānam anantam brahma

Brahman is eternal, Consciousness and limitless[3]

The first verse of *Śiva Samhitā* is very similar to the above verse. The words satyam means *nityam*, *jñānam* is *jnānam* and *anantam* is the same as *ādyantaśūnyam*. The teaching in this verse is the *Upaniṣad* teaching indeed. *Īśvara* pervades everything including you. If you are not included in this equation then God is not complete. You alone make *Īśvara* complete and you attain your highest goal which is *Mokṣa* or freedom when you understand this fact very clearly.

This compound word *ādyantaśūnyam* is very important to better appreciate the word *ekam* as 'one without a second'. Sometimes people claim that "there is only one god and that god is mine" or that the God belonging to a particular faith is the only real one. One guy will say *Kṛṣṇa*, another will say *Śiva* and another will say something else. Whether the gods are fighting in the heavens to establish their supremacy or not, one thing appears to be certain and that is we are fighting over it. When you say, "there is only one god" there is still room for contention because you have not defined that god as ekam, *jñānam*, *nityam*, *ādyantaśūnyam*. With this definition, there is no scope for conflict as there is no possibility of God having a second reality apart from it. Therefore eliminating the very question of a Supreme God existing apart from another God.

Vedānta's strength lies in defining a reality such that it cannot be improved further. The very final definition resolves into the very reality that you are trying to understand. It is like a salt doll trying to measure the ocean. When it tries by entering the ocean, it dissolves in it. When you try to understand the Consciousness from your point of view, the distinctions vanish immediately. All these ideas and concepts that we talk about are not separate from the essence of your Self or the world. All the thoughts resolve into that reality.

You cannot find this teaching as explicitly stated in any tradition except in *Upaniṣad*-s. You can find passing statements of these in scriptures of other faiths but you will not have an unbroken teaching tradition as in the case of *Vedānta*. So, having this knowledge is one thing and being able to teach

3 Taittirīya Upaniṣad 2.1.1

it is another thing. Even if a civilisation had this knowledge but if there was no teaching tradition available, then it is as good as any dead civilisation belonging to the pages of a history textbook. *Vedānta* states that one must have earned a lot of puṇya (merits) to encounter this perennial wisdom.

That rare is the birth in which you come to know about this knowledge called *Vedānta*. The *śāstra* implies this,

Īśvara anugrahāt eva pumsād advaita vāsanā

Through *Īśvara*'s grace that the desire for non-duality (Advaita) arises.[4]

There are so many people out there who do not have access to this knowledge. Somehow, a few of us would be led to this knowledge due to some good deeds we committed in the past. Honestly if you are born in this tradition and have encountered this wisdom, you are indeed extremely fortunate.

The *Upaniṣad* states that a person who dies without knowing this *Īśvara* or *Brahman*, is like committing suicide (*ātmahana*).

asuryā nāma te lokā andhena tamasāvṛtāḥ
tāṃste pretyābhigacchanti ye ke cātmahano janāḥ

Verily, those worlds of the *asura*-s are enveloped in blind darkness; and thereto they all repair after death who are suicides.[5]

Why is he considered a suicide (*ātmahana*)? Because *Brahman* is as close to you as what water is to a wave. The separation is only notional with just a thought away. The potential to understand *Īśvara* is just a thought away and hence this ignorance, termed as demon (*asura*), is called a suicide.

You must be fortunate if you have the desire to know your Self in this life itself. You are even more fortunate if you attained the knowledge having desired it. As the *Bhagavad Gītā* states:

manuṣyāṇāṃ sahasreṣu kaścidyatati siddhaye
yatatāmapi siddhānāṃ kaścinmāṃ vetti tattvataḥ

Scarcely one out of thousands of persons strives for *Mokṣa*. Scarcely one among those successful strivers truly understands Me.[6]

---

4 Avadhūta Gītā 1.1
5 Īśāvāya Upaniṣad 3
6 Bhagavad Gītā 7.3

This is further summarised in the *Vivekacūḍāmaṇī*:

jantūnāṃ narajanma durlabhamataḥ puṃstvaṃ tato vipratā
tasmādvaidikadharmamārgaparatā vidvattvamasmātparam
ātmānātmavivecanaṃ svanubhavo brahmātmanā saṃsthitiḥ
muktirno śatajanmakoṭisukṛtaiḥ puṇyairvinā labhyate
durlabhaṃ trayamevaitaddevānugrahahetukam
manuṣyatvaṃ mumukṣutvaṃ mahāpuruṣasaṃśrayaḥ

For all beings, a human birth is difficult to obtain, more so is a male body; rarer than that is *Brāhmana*-hood; rarer still is the attachment to the path of *Vedic Dharma*; higher than this is erudition in the scriptures; discrimination between the Self and not-Self, Realisation, and continuing in a state of identity with *Brahman* – these come next in order.

(This kind of) Mukti (Liberation) is not to be attained except through the well-earned merits of thousands of births. These are three things which are rare indeed and are due to the grace of God – namely, a human birth, the desire for liberation, and the refuge of a liberated person.[7]

With just one statement – *ekam jñānam nityam adyantaśūnyam*, the highest knowledge of the *Upaniṣad*-s has been unfolded. This shows that with minimal words, a subtle and profound subject can be revealed. This is the strength of the teaching tradition of *Vedānta*. As the *Upaniṣad* states,

śravaṇāyāpi bahubhiryo na labhyaḥ
śṛṇvanto'pi bahavo yaṃ na vidyuḥ
āścaryo vaktā kuśalo'sya labdhā
āścaryo jñātā kuśalānuśiṣṭaḥ

He who cannot even be heard of by many, whom many,
even hearing, do not know, wondrous is he who can teach
and skillful is he who finds (Him) and wondrous is he
who knows, even when instructed by the wise.[8]

How can we protect this teaching tradition? And where is this tradition? The tradition resides in the mind of the person who practices it and then teaches it. If you desire to protect this tradition, you must practice it, teach it and most importantly, also protect the person who is practicing and teaching this wisdom. For without teachers the tradition will cease to exist.

7 Vivekacūḍāmaṇī 2-3
8 Kaṭha Upaniṣad 1.2.7

That is why the teaching is important, and part of the teaching is also to correct all the misunderstandings that have taken place in the tradition. By doing this you are protecting a great tradition, a tradition that teaches the means to happiness and peace for all creatures. Here is a concise story from the concluding chapters of *Mahābhārata.*[9]

At the end of the war the *Pāṇḍavā*-s took a vow called *mahāprasthāna* in which you walk towards the northern direction without food. On the way, a dog follows them. One by one the *Pāṇḍavā*-s drop dead due to the severity of the vow. Finally, only *Yudhiṣṭhira* and the dog are left. There is something about animals – they are faithful and do not bite the hand that feeds. At that moment, a chariot came from heaven with Indra in it and he said to *Yudhiṣṭhira*, "I am impressed by your penance (*tapas*), you can enter heaven alive." *Yudhiṣṭhira* agreed to jump along with the dog but *Indra* refused as there was place only for one. *Yudhiṣṭhira* said to *Indra* that he would rather die than forsake the dog which had been faithfully following him.

Dying is not easy and to enter heaven painlessly is a rare opportunity. Yet *Yudhiṣṭhira* chose compassion and gratitude instead of pleasure in heavens. This story teaches us to show gratitude to any being that has placed trust and loyalty to us. This is the indeed the vision of *Sanātana Dharma* which teaches us to love, respect and have gratitude towards every creature.

This *Vedic Dharma* urges everyone to first find happiness around them and then within oneself. It starts with simple values such as extending your respect and gratitude to all, including animals and other beings. This is the reason why the *Dharma* makes the worship and respect of nature, and living beings a daily duty.

Here is the summary of the discussion thus far. The four words *ekam, jñānam, nityam, ādyantaśūnyaṃ* which form one part of the first verse, are instrumental in presenting what *Brahman* is. In fact, the key word among the four words is *jñānam*, which is Consciousness. The rest of the words (*ekam, nityam, ādyantaśūnyaṃ*) help in bringing more clarity to what Consciousness is. The whole intention of *brahmavidyā* is to know *Brahman*. These four words are like definitions. Every *śāstra* has a model or methodology (*prakriyā*) to teach. If these four words are assimilated to be the nature of your Self, it is as good as understanding *Brahman*. And knowing *Brahman* is *Mokṣa*,

9 in the Mahāprasthānika Parva

brahmavid āpnoti param

The knower of *Brahman* attains the highest.[10]

The *Upaniṣad* states that the word *ekam* needs to be qualified to gain more clarity,

ekam eva advitīyam

certainly, one without a second[11]

The 'one' is qualified by 'without a second'. There is only one Consciousness and there is nothing second to it. A goldsmith shop illustration would help us to better understand this teaching. There is only gold but many ornaments in the shop. Every ornament is pervaded by gold. If you were to have won a lucky draw that allows you to choose just one item from the goldsmith shop, what would that be? I would choose gold. The one who sees only gold owns the whole shop; the one who chooses an ornament owns only that. In the same way, if you understand Consciousness as the whole creation, then you and the creation are not different. This is the subject matter of 'one without a second'.

The second word is *jñānam*, absolute Consciousness; this Consciousness serves like a blank screen on which a projection takes place. If there is no blank screen there cannot be a projection. Similarly, if there is no consciousness, there is no universe as you experience it.

The third word is *nityam* which means eternal and existing in all three periods of time (past, present and future). Consciousness is eternal. It was there before creation, existing during creation and does not cease to exist even after the creation dissolves.

The fourth word is *ādyantaśūnyaṃ*: devoid of beginning and end. This means that Consciousness is omnipresent or limitless. The limitlessness would also mean that Consciousness is present in everything that is in space.

Understanding these four words properly will provide a firm foundation that cannot be shaken by the views of other philosophies and doctrines. It is a knowledge that cannot be improved further because improvement implies an inherent deficiency. This knowledge is the final word and cannot be improved further. That is why it is called *Vedānta*. '*Veda*' means knowledge and '*anta*' means final. If this knowledge is understood properly,

---

10 Taittirīya Upaniṣad 2.1.1

11 Chāndogya Upaniṣad 6.2.1

there is nothing more to be known.

śaunako ha vai mahāśālo'ṅgirasaṃ vidhivadupasannaḥ papraccha
kasminnu bhagavo vijñāte sarvamidaṃ vijñātaṃ bhavatīti

Śaunaka, well known as a great householder, having approached *Angiras* duly, asked, 'O adorable sir, (which is that thing) knowing that by which everything else is known[12]

Does that mean that a liberated person (*jīvanmukta*) would not desire to know anything? For example, would he not ask someone, "how are you?" or "how was your day?" Is there anything left to be known for him? In fact, there are so many things not known to him, but that does not rob his knowledge of the Self. The *jīvanmukta* is not a knower of all the details (*sarvavit*) but someone who knows that everything in this universe is not separate from Consciousness (*sarvajña*) in a generic sense. Like the gold in the goldsmith shop, you do not need to know every ornament in the shop to know gold. But knowing gold it is as good as knowing everything in the shop. This is sufficient as the need to discover the details of the universe will take one into the exploration of objects which further lends reality to the changing and impermanent world. Any new knowledge or lower knowledge (*aparāvidyā*) cannot negate the absolute knowledge (*parāvidyā*) of Consciousness. For instance, the knowledge of ring cannot negate the knowledge of gold, due to the former depending on the latter for its existence. Even an unknown object made of gold cannot take away your knowledge of gold. Similarly, something may appear unknown to a *jīvanmukta* but that does not unsettle his Self-Knowledge.

12 Muṇḍaka Upaniṣad 1.1.3

2

DIVERSITY IS DUE TO THE SENSES

Let us discover the remaining parts of the first verse, '*yadbhedosminnindriyopādhinā vai jñānasyāyaṃ bhāsate nānyathaiva*', which means 'diversity which is found in this universe is nothing but the Consciousness but varied due to the sense perceptions as limiting adjuncts'. The second part of the verse is a confirmation of the earlier four key words. The second part of the verse reassures that there is no other reality except Consciousness in this universe. And that diversity we see in this world is the result of sensory perceptions. This diversity constitutes how we see the world through the five sensory organs: sight, taste, touch, sound and smell. All that we see as the universe comes through these five sensory organs. The other important message of this sentence is that the sensory perceptions are dependent on Consciousness for its existence, just like how the wave depends on water for its existence. In fact, what the sensory organs report is not apart from Consciousness.

The notion that there is diversity in the universe is rooted in duality, and scriptures present that duality to be caused by *māyā/mithyā/avidyā* (creative power/dependent reality/ignorance). We can use any of these three words, despite them being different words. We will discuss these terms in the chapters to come.

The verse states that sense organs (*indriyā*-s) are the reason for this duality. The limitations we see are also caused by these sense organs. The explicit reference to sense organs being the cause for diversity implies that the *Śiva Samhitā* undertakes the enquiry from oneself rather than from the external world. It urges to look at creation from your standpoint.

In *Vedānta* there are two well known ways of approaching Self-Knowledge. The first is called 'subjective creation' (*dṛṣṭi-sṛṣṭi-vāda*) and the other is called 'objective creation' (*sṛṣṭi-dṛṣṭi-vāda*). A '*vāda*' means a position. '*Sṛṣṭi*' means creation while '*dṛṣṭi*' means vision.

Objective Creation assumes that the creation is there for me to see it. In this position one assumes that there is a creation before me, and I see it. This approach proceeds from the belief that creation existed before me and will go on after me. Here *māyā* is seen as the cause of creation and as a power of *Brahman*. Creation is nothing but *nāma* and *rūpa* (name and form) and the *jīva* (individual) is also a *nāma - rūpa*. I see myself as one of the many individuals, all of them as real as I am. Between you and I there is no difference too, because we are part of the same reality. This approach uses the creation as the starting point for the enquiry to arrive at Self-Knowledge. *Brahman* is used in an objective sense because it pervades the whole universe and everything is resolved into *Brahman*. I can know myself to be *Brahman* (or Consciousness) because I am part of *Brahman*. In the Objective Creation approach one takes the 'external inward' direction to conclude that "I am *Brahman* or Consciousness".

The Subjective Creation on the other hand is different. This position takes the view that 'creation exists because I see it'. Because I exist therefore creation exists. The creation is evident to me because of my ignorance (*avidyā*). In the Subjective Creation approach, the starting point of the Self-enquiry is that there is no reality apart from me. In my perception and in my presence alone the universe exists. If I do not experience the universe, it is as good as the universe being non-existent.

In Subjective Creation, you are the creator (*Brahmā*), sustainer (*Viṣṇu*) and destroyer (*Śiva*).

svayaṃ brahmā svayaṃ viṣṇuḥ svayamIndraḥ svayaṃ śivaḥ
svayaṃ viśvamidaṃ sarvaṃ svasmādanyanna kiñcana

The Self is *Brahmā*, the Self is *Viṣṇu*, the Self is *Indra*,
the Self is *Śiva* - the Self is this entire universe.
Indeed, nothing exists apart from the Self.[13]

It is difficult to accept this view because the notions that "I am one among the many people" and that "I am this body" are very strong and deep seated. Therefore, this methodology is not recommended to 99% of the seekers. This is the reason why almost all of the *Vedānta* texts adopt the Objective Creation approach, and only a rare few use Subjective Creation. Only a handful of texts are known to adopt the view of Subjective Creation because this methodology should be taught one-on-one because of its subtlety. It is best not to assume this approach to be the mainstream approach, because it can be very confusing without a teacher to guide. The reason being that most of us operate on the premise that there are multiple individuals and all of them equally the same as I am.

---

13 Vivekacūḍāmaṇī 389

Śaṅkarācārya's grand-guru (*Govindapāda's guru*) *Gauḍapāda* takes the Subjective Creation approach in his *Māndukya Kārika*. *Śaṅkarācārya* has written a commentary on the *Kārika*-s to make this approach easier to understand. *Gauḍapāda* takes the view that there is no creation.[14] And if there was no creation, the very idea about the cycle of births and deaths (*samsāra*), and even *Mokṣa* become irrelevant. This is a very extreme view, therefore, a renunciate (*saṇnyāsin*) is the best candidate for this teaching, as he or she does not have to deal with the world of transactions as much as the common man does. The student in this path needs to be closely guided as though he is walking on a tightrope. In fact, there are only a couple of books dealing with this methodology. One such text is *Vedānta Siddhānta Muktāvali* by *Prakāśānanda*. *Aṣṭāvakra Gītā*, *Avadhūta Gītā* and parts of *Vivekacūḍāmaṇī* teach based on this methodology too.

The *Śiva Samhitā* initially adopts the Subjective Creation approach. It states that the diversities are caused by the sense organs. If you do not have the sense organs, you will not see this world of diversity. If you note carefully, you do not have to prove diversity; your sense organs are already diversified. What one sense organ perceives, the other sense organs cannot prove. They are all independent means of knowledge. The world that I see as a diverse reality is not an illusion; it is a dependent reality because the sense organs report it to me. The sense organs are the basis of this diversity. The five sense organs provide five different dimensions to the world. The verse states that all duality that you see is because of your sense organs. If you did not have these sense organs, you would not see duality. Or if you had one more sense organ, you may probably experience another dimension. A good example is the deep sleep state where all sense organs go to sleep, and the universe becomes undifferentiated. In that deep sleep you do not see a second reality. Only when you wake up, you see the universe with its diversities.

The next question is whether you willfully became ignorant, or are you naturally disposed to it? This enquiry leads us to not judge our ignorance as a curse. We were born with these sense organs and hence, there is no need to say that the world is a curse or an illusion. Many use these sense organs to enjoy the world. Traditionally, *Vedānta* was taught only to eligible or qualified individuals. Ideally it should not be taught to everyone indiscriminately although it is taught liberally today, and that tends to sap the lives of many, instead of destroying ignorance. This happens due to a

---

14 Māndukya Kārika 2.28

lack of appreciation for the seeker's qualifications and its role in *Vedānta*. Teaching this knowledge indiscriminately can upset people's lives, hopes, ambitions, blissful ignorance and zest for life. A verse attributed to the *Yoga Vāsiṣṭha* states the following:

ajnasya ardha-prabuddhasya sarvam brahmeti yo vadet
mahānaraka jāleṣu sa tena viniyojitaḥ

He who preaches to the ignorant and the half-learned that everything is *Brahman*, verily entangles him in a mesh of horrible hells.

This is the reason why Sanātana Dharma presents two lifestyles for human beings,

sukhābhyudayikaṃ caiva naiḥśreyasikam eva ca
pravṛttaṃ ca nivṛttaṃ ca dvividhaṃ karma vaidikam

The acts prescribed by the *Veda* are of two kinds. One which promotes the acquisition of Prosperity and Happiness known as *Pravṛtti*; and the other which leads you to *Mokṣa*, known as *Nivṛtti*.[15]

pravṛttaṁ ca nivṛttaṁ ca dvi-vidhaṁ karma vaidikam
āvartate pravṛttena nivṛttenāśnute 'mṛtam

The works of the *Veda*-s are two-fold – those that relate to *Pravṛtti* and those that leads to *Nivṛtti*. *Pravṛtti* brings you rebirth and *Nivṛtti* leads you to *Mokṣa*.[16]

In summary the two lifestyles are:

1. a life of activity pursuing ethics, securities and pleasure (*pravṛtti mārga*), and
2. a life cf renunciation (*nivṛtti mārga*) that leads you to freedom, *Mokṣa*.

These two lifestyles have been distinguished very clearly. Hence there is nothing wrong in being ignorant of the Self, and choosing to continue to be so if you happen to belong to the first lifestyle (*pravṛtti mārga*). Let people stay where they are, for *Īśvara* knows when and how to guide everyone through either of the lifestyles. If *Īśvara* is seen all knowing (*sarvajña*), he would know how and when to guide a person towards Self-Knowledge. You do not have to play God; the one who plays God, is the one who disturbs the natural flow of life because he thinks he is greater than everyone else, and that he assumes to be the chosen one to do this.

15 Manu Smṛti 12.88

16 Bhāgavata Purāṇa 7.15.47

This pursuit of Self-Knowledge requires renunciation in one form or another, which is the characteristic of the second lifestyle (*nivṛtti mārga*). The one who truly knows oneself to be God or *Brahman* will not disturb the stability and pursuits of others. That person would only exhibit non-threatening traits such as calmness, tranquility and humility,

adveṣṭā sarvabhūtānāṃ maitraḥ karuṇa eva ca
nirmamo nirahaṅkāraḥ samaduḥkhasukhaḥ kṣamī
santuṣṭaḥ satataṃ yogī yatātmā dṛḍhaniścayaḥ
mayyarpitamanobuddhiryo madbhaktaḥ sa me priyaḥ

He who never hates any being, who is friendly and compassionate,
who is free from the feelings of I and mine, who looks upon
all pain and pleasure the same as and who is forgiving;
He who is content, who is ever contemplative and is self-
restrained and who is firm in his convictions, who has his
mind and reason dedicated to Me - he is dear to Me.[17]

If the perceptions and diversities caused by sense organs are a problem, then how do we overcome this? How does this diversity cease? Is it a physical removal of diversity? For example, would you see the world dissolve and disappear when you know Consciousness? Some popular traditions teach of a superconscious state (*samādhi*) that would supposedly remove these perceptions and diversities. If the world dissolves into nothingness, who was the one who witnessed the dissolution? So many questions can be asked to demolish such irrational beliefs. Such an experience will not pass the test of experience as you would know that the liberated persons (*jīvanmukta*-s) live and walk this world amongst us, sharing the same space and time with us. So, the experience of a superconscious or transcendental state is not what the *Upaniṣad*-s teach.

The *Upaniṣad*-s present a far more realistic and rational means to overcome the challenges of diversity. The solution lies in just understanding the content of the diversity for it to be removed. It is like knowing that the ornament is gold, the pot is clay or the wave is water. By knowing the content or the essential nature of a thing, one can appreciate the difference between what changes and what does not.

So, a *jīvanmukta* resolves the universe of diversity into himself. This happens when he knows his true nature. So how is it possible to resolve this universe into myself? Is it a physical dissolution or is it a dissolution by

17 Bhagavad Gītā 12.13-14

understanding? It is the latter. For example you do not have to destroy the pot to understand that it is clay. Before it became a pot, it was clay, when it was a pot it was clay, and after the pot is destroyed it is still clay. If clay exists in all three periods of time then it is as good as the pot is resolved. Similar is the case with the universe. Before creation it was Consciousness (*Brahman*), during the creation it was also Consciousness and after the dissolution it is still Consciousness. It is *Brahman*, the Consciousness in all the three periods of time. So, know that it is only *Brahman* that exists.

Now let us discuss the wave-water illustration. Before a wave became a wave, it was water; even while being a wave it was still water, and remains as water after the wave merges into the ocean. The wave does not have to change its state to know that it is water. Similarly, in sleep, "I am Consciousness", in waking state "I am Consciousness", and in dream state "I am Consciousness". You are Consciousness in all three states and hence you cannot be just one single state! You are *ekam jñānam nityam ādyantaśūnyaṃ.* You are beyond the three experiential states of waking, dreaming and sleeping. In fact, you are not beyond it, but pervading the three states invariably. So, you are that Consciousness regardless of what state you are in.

Then why do we think that we have a state of existence? Because I take myself, the Consciousness, to be the sense organs, therefore I see the states. I see the states because I am ignorant of this Self-Knowledge. When I am anchored in this knowledge, this diversity will not exist for me but that does not mean that the sense organs will not report diversity to me. It is in knowing that you are Consciousness in spite of diversity.

The point of the first verse is to prove that there is only one reality without a second. The teaching (*siddhānta*) of the text is stated in the first verse. All the other verses are just a commentary and elaboration on the first verse. This first verse is an axiomatic statement (*māhāvākya*) which has the capacity to directly remove ignorance, when one conducts the enquiry with a traditional or qualified teacher.

3

ĪŚVARA IS THE FIRST TEACHER

अथ भक्तानुरक्तोऽहं वक्ष्ये योगानुशासनम् |
ईश्वरःसर्व भूतानाम् आत्म मुक्तिप्रदायकम् || २

atha bhaktānurakto'haṃ vakṣye yogānuśāsanam |
Īśvaraḥ sarva bhūtānām ātma muktipradāyakam || 2

Therefore, I, Īśvara, who is the attached to my devotees, and the giver of mokṣa to all creatures, shall expound the teaching of Yoga.

Having presented the essence of the *Upaniṣad*-s in the first verse, the text now moves on to present *Īśvara* (God) as the teacher of *Vedānta* or *Yoga*. *Īśvara* is the lover of devotees (*bhakta*) and attaches himself to his devotees who seek him. The distance between *Īśvara* and a devotee is not one of physical space but entirely dependent on either knowledge or ignorance. A *bhakta* is one who recognises *Īśvara* as the creator, sustainer and dissolver of the Universe. The *bhakta* is born the moment he recognises *Īśvara* as such, similar to the way a father is born when a child is born - simultaneously.

Īśvara is the expounder of *Yoga* which means that *Īśvara* is the source of *Yoga*. The word '*Yoga*' in this verse means the 'knowledge through which one knows the Self' (*yujyate anena iti Yogaḥ*). In the tradition of *Sanātana Dharma*, anything that cannot be created by human endeavour is always attributed to a greater being, i.e., by *Īśvara*. Any knowledge that reveals realities that are beyond the senses, cannot be created by a human being. All products that humans create are limited by their limited knowledge and understanding based on limited sensory experiences. Hence a limited human being cannot create a limitless being, nor the knowledge of the limitless being. Hence *Īśvara* alone can expound this knowledge of the limitless because it is about Himself. This is the reason why all traditions of *Sanātana Dharma* will trace their teachings to *Īśvara*. This is also why we chant the following traditional verse to salute *Īśvara* as the first *guru* before the study of *Vedānta*:

sadāśiva samāraṃbhāṃ śaṅkarācārya madhyamām
asmadācarya paryantāṃ vande guru paramparām

Salutation to the lineage starting with Lord Śiva, with *Śaṅkarācārya* in the middle and continuing up to my immediate teacher

Īśvara alone grants liberation (*mokṣa*) by revealing the knowledge which is not separate from him. He bestows it to the one who seeks it. It is like saying that the sun shines on all objects but gets reflected only on certain objects. *Mokṣa* does not happen without you actively pursuing it. A sincere seeker is a suitable surface on which the knowledge will reflect. However, one should not misconceive that *Īśvara* literally 'gives' *Mokṣa* to his devotees without the latter putting any effort. The idea of 'giving' refers to the knowledge that finds its source in Him.

त्यक्त्वाविवादशीलानांमतंदुर्ज्ञानहेतुकम् ।
आत्मज्ञानायभूतानामनन्यगतिचेतसाम् ॥ ३

tyaktvā vivādaśīlānāṃ mataṃ durjñānahetukam |
ātmajñānāya bhūtānām ananyagaticetasām || 3

In the Yoga are discarded all those doctrines of the disputants, which lead to false knowledge. Self-Knowledge is for those minds that have surrendered to him.

Disputants are persons who are good at debating against this knowledge. A dispute also indicates that you have not understood Self-Knowledge well. However, when this knowledge is known there can be no disputant. The knowledge of the *ātman* (*ātmajñāna*) will destroy those who debate against it, by taking away ignorance or false knowledge (*mithyā jñāna*).

False knowledge is destroyed for people who exclusively pursue this knowledge and who have surrendered to *Īśvara*, and not for those who follow other interests with the same intensity. It does not mean that you should have no other interests while pursuing this knowledge. You may still need to make a living. Even a sannyāsin must beg to sustain his body. It just means that this knowledge should be the primary interest and pursuit of your life.

Surrendering to *Īśvara* is a total reliance on *Īśvara* or having a vision that sees *Īśvara* as the Supreme Being.

sarvadharmānparityajya māmekaṃ śaraṇaṃ vraja ।
ahaṃ tvā sarvapāpebhyo mokṣayiṣyāmi mā śucaḥ ॥

Abandoning all forms of rites and duties, take refuge in Me alone.
I shall free you from all sins. (Therefore) do not grieve.[18]

18 Bhagavad Gītā 18.66

For the seekers of *mokṣa* (*mumukṣu*), no matter what he or she does, at the back of their minds there is only one goal – *mokṣa*. If someone were to not have *mokṣa* as his or her goal, then there is no reason for that person to feel bad about it. Because people get pressurised by their peers to seek this Self-Knowledge because *Vedānta* has become a mainstream and popular topic today. So, it is perfectly alright not to seek *mokṣa*.

The *Bhagavad Gītā*, makes a pertinent point when it states that there are two lifestyles for people – 1. a lifestyle to seek securities and pleasure and 2. a lifestyle to seek *mokṣa*.

loke'smin dvividhā niṣṭhā purā proktā mayānagha
jñānayogena sāṅkhyānāṃ karmayogena yoginām

In this world, as I have said, there is a twofold path, O Sinless One! There is the *Yoga* of Knowledge for those who are contemplative, and the *Yoga* of Action for those who are active.[19]

Hence one need not assume that *mokṣa* is the only goal of life. One also needs to appreciate the role of one's disposition (*svabhāva*) in choosing one's lifestyle and goals.

Lord *Kṛṣṇa* in the *Bhagavad Gītā* tells Arjuna that he must recognise his nature to be that of a warrior (*kṣatriya*), and so he must fight.[20] And that he should not take on the role of another person.[21] Similarly, the desire for *mokṣa* is determined by one's disposition. If you approach Self-Knowledge merely because you are curious, it may squeeze the juice out of your life, leaving you high and dry. It will kill your passion and zest for life. The doer-knower conflict will dominate your life. In the external world, you may talk about Self-Knowledge but internally, you may be thinking about the enjoyments that you are missing. This could make you physically and mentally divorced. These feelings indicate that you are not prepared for this Self-Knowledge. It is here that the teacher intervenes to direct the person to the right path, which is to enjoy life but with *Dharma* as the basis (*pravṛtti mārga*). And there is nothing wrong about this, as we do need such people to maintain the world and its functions.

This knowledge will work only for those persons who have no other primary goals except that of *mokṣa*. There are others who may have this *jñāna* but they may not get the fruit of the knowledge (*jñānaphala*) i.e.,

19 Bhagavad Gītā 3.3
20 ibid 2.31-37
21 ibid 3.35

mokṣa. This is the category of people known as pundits and professors of *Vedānta* in educational institutions. They may know about *Vedānta* but not about the *ātman*. The subject matter of *Vedānta*, is not *Vedānta* philosophy but Self-Knowledge. While the scholars can help us in our appreciation of the knowledge, no real inner progress is made by just studying this subject academically.

This misplaced curiosity I stated earlier can be very damaging in *Vedānta* studies. In today's *Vedānta* circles, many people are studying *Vedānta* because of peer pressure, curiosity and misconceptions about the benefits accrued. Your body-mind-sense complex may tell you otherwise, but you would still be seeking *Vedānta* because someone told you that the goal of our life is *mokṣa*. So, you could have blindly believed this to be a universal truth. All our scriptures clearly state that *mokṣa* is not the only goal. We can follow any of the two lifestyles (*pravṛtti mārga* or *nivṛtti mārga*). Most scriptures however will refer only to *pravṛtti mārga*. In *Ramāyāna*, most of the references are to *Dharma*; in Mahābhārata, only occasionally *mokṣa* is taught. Only those who are not interested in *dharma*, *artha* and *kāma* as their primary goals will seek *mokṣa*.

4

THE FOUR-FOLD CONSIDERATIONS

Having appreciated the nature of this text, it is now important to study the *anubandha catuṣṭayam* – four-fold considerations which set the tone and direction for anyone desiring to study a text. In the case of the *Śiva Samhitā* the four considerations are as follows:

1. The <u>subject</u> of the text (*viṣaya*): The subject of *Śiva Samhitā* is Self-Knowledge (*ātmajñāna*).

2. The <u>purpose</u> (*prayojana*) of the text: The purpose is liberation of the self (*ātma mukti* which is another term for *mokṣa*)

3. The person <u>competent</u> to study it (*adhikāri*): A *mumukṣu* is qualified to study the text. The text uses the term '*ananya gati cetasām*' for a *mumukṣu*.

4. The <u>relationship</u> between the above three (*sambandha*): The *mumukṣu* gains *mokṣa* through *ātmajñāna*.

The conclusion of the four-fold considerations is that a *mumukṣu*, by gaining *ātmajñāna* will attain *mokṣa*. All traditional teachers will analyze the text in this manner. The text is worth studying only if the four considerations have been successfully addressed. This is how you measure the integrity of a text. It is best if you could use the words from the very text, to address these considerations.

5

NATURE OF KARMA

The text now shifts gear to refute all the views opposing this Self-Knowledge. In today's context, it means dismissing all the different products available in the spiritual supermarket.

Before we go into that, let us recollect the fundamental workings of action (*karma*) and its results. When a person does an action, there will be a reaction or a result. There are two aspects to this result (*karmaphala*) – seen result (*dṛṣṭa phala*) and unseen result (*adṛṣṭa phala*). For example, I hit someone and the pain is visible. The seen result is the joy that I may derive from hurting that person. The unseen result on the other hand emerges from the intention behind the action. The unseen result is further divided into two groups,- demerit (*pāpa*) and merit (*puṇya*). *Pāpa* is earned when the intention is contrary to *Dharma* and *puṇya* is earned if it is consistent with *Dharma*. *Pāpa* and *puṇya* for a given action can come either in this life or the next. Every day we do countless actions, and it is the intention that counts.

The role-based duty (*svadharma*) is one of the key ways through which one can accrue of merit and demerit. If an action is done consistent with one's *svadharma*, we get *puṇya*. An action done contrary to one's *svadharma*, will earn you *pāpa*. Doing someone else's duty even when done well, will get us *pāpa*. The *Bhagavad Gītā* states:

śreyānsvadharmo viguṇaḥ paradharmātsvanuṣṭhitāt
svadharme nidhanaṃ śreyaḥ paradharmo bhayāvahaḥ

One's own duty, performed imperfectly, is better than
another's duty well performed. Destruction in one's own duty
is better, for to perform another's duty leads to danger.[1]

Both merit and demerit produce comfortable and uncomfortable situations respectively. Every comfortable situation is a product of right action (*satkarma*), and an uncomfortable situation is a product of wrong action (*vikarma*). Both are impelled by intentions alone.

Every one of us keep doing actions all the time, and thereby creating

1 Bhagavad Gitā 3.35

opportunities for future experiences of merits and demerits. Then how will merits and demerits exhaust? Can we exhaust them through *karma*? More *karma* will only create more to the merits and demerits. Even while meditating we are doing a mental action (*mānasa karma*), which will produce future experiences. Therefore, meditation cannot be a means to *mokṣa* as it creates more merits (*puṇya*). And to experience these results, more births are needed.

You cannot use *karma* to beat *karma*. You cannot fight fire with fire. Both merit and demerit will produce experiences, and you must be born again to experience them - this is the cycle of births and deaths (*samsāra cakra*). The only difference is that it could be either a lower birth or a higher birth. A higher birth could be you being born as a celestial being (*deva*) and the lower could be an ordinary living thing (*prāṇi*). Human birth is hence a mix of both *pāpa* and *puṇya*.

So, whether you like it or not, the more *karma*-s you do, no matter how great the actions are, they will produce a result. This includes meditation practices. And these fruits will bring you to another birth. As long as *karma*-s are done, *samsāra* does not end and therefore *mokṣa* is not achievable.

सत्यंकेचित्प्रशंसन्तितपःशौचंतथापरे।
क्षमांकेचित्प्रशंसंतितथैवशममार्ज्जवम्।४

satyaṃ kecitpraśaṃsanti tapaḥ śaucaṃ tathāpare |
kṣamāṃ kecitpraśaṃsaṃti tathaiva śamamārjavam || 4

Some praise truth, others purity and austerity; some praise forgiveness, others equanimity and straightforwardness.

People, who praise truth claim that they do not have to do anything but speak the truth to attain *mokṣa*. Some people think that *tapas* or austerities such as meditation, fasting and *Yoga* will get you *mokṣa*. All kinds of extreme practices are called *tapas* in this verse.

Some praise cleanliness (*śaucam*), while some claim forgiveness (*kṣama*) to be the means to *mokṣa*. There are people who claim compassion to be adequate to attain *mokṣa*. Some praise equanimity or mastery of the mind (*śama*) and there are those who praise straightforwardness (*ārjavam*). Many people also take the view that following simple values are sufficient to lead one to *mokṣa*. The fact is that simple do-not's and do's (*yama* and *niyama*-s) are enough to lead a good life but not enough to attain *mokṣa*. The *Śiva Samhitā* is disputing all such views.

केचिद् दानं प्रशंसन्ति पितृकर्म तथापरे |
केचित् कर्म प्रशंसन्ति केचिद् वैराग्यम् उत्तमम् || ५

kecid dānaṃ praśaṃsanti pitṛ*karma* tathāpare |
kecit *karma* praśaṃsanti kecid vairāgyam uttamam || 5

Some praise charity; others laud the rituals performed for one's departed ancestors; some praise action; others think dispassion to be the best.

Some praise charity (*dānam*). Service (*sevā*) is also a form of charity, and many assume that by serving others or the needy one can gain *mokṣa*. With *dānam*, the text has covered all the values listed in the *yama-niyama*-s.[2] It has dismissed them as being not a valid means to *mokṣa*. They may produce merits but still bind you by creating opportunities for future births and experiences.

Next comes offerings to ancestors (*pitṛ karma*). This *karma* is one of the five daily duties of a Hindu (*nitya karma*)[3]. Some claim that by pleasing *pitṛs* you can attain *mokṣa*. Yes, you may join them after death but that is not *mokṣa*. Some praise *karma*, which here means following one's duties (*svadharma anuṣṭhānam*). *Svadharma* comprises the *nitya karmas* and other role-based duties, but it cannot confer *mokṣa* either. Some praise dispassion (*vairāgyam*) which helps as a pre-requisite, but by itself does not confer *mokṣa*. Sometimes dispassion is overemphasised in *Vedānta*, but it is only one among the four pre-requisite requirements for embarking on Self-Knowledge and not a direct cause of *mokṣa*.

केचिद् गृहस्थकर्माणि प्रशंसन्ति विचक्षणाः ।
अग्निहोत्रादिकं कर्म तथा केचित् परम् विदुः ॥ ६

kecid gṛhasthakarmāṇi praśaṃsanti vicakṣaṇāḥ ।
agnihotrādikaṃ *karma* tathā kecit param viduḥ ॥ 6

Some wise persons praise the duties of householders; others say that all types of fire sacrifices are the best.

Some people praise the duties of a householder (*gṛhastha*). The householder does five daily duties – worship of god, worship of teacher, worship of ancestors, serving human beings and serving other living beings.[4]

---

2 yama-niyama-s are ethical guidelines

3 a householder is expected to perform five daily rituals as per the Vedic tradition

4 see Manu Smṛti 3.67

The society thrives due to the economically active people like the householders. The householders should support the students (*brahmacāri*), forest dwellers (*vānaprasthi*) and the renunciates (*sannyāsin*).

The *mīmāmsaka*-s, the followers of the *mīmāmsa* school of Vedic philosophy, prescribe the highest status to rituals and particularly uphold marriage, because without being married you cannot perform fire rituals (*agnihotra*). The verse states that some praise fire rituals, but that too will not confer *mokṣa* as it will create numerous births due to the accrued results of *karma*.

मन्त्रयोगंप्रशंसन्तिकेचित्तीर्थानुसेवनं।
एवंबहून्उपायांस्तुप्रवदन्तिहिमुक्तये॥७

mantrayogaṃ praśaṃsanti kecit tīrthānusevanaṃ |
evaṃ bahūn upāyāṃstu pravadanti hi muktaye || 7

Some praise mantra yoga; others pilgrimage to sacred places. Thus diverse are the ways which people declare as leading to mukti.

Some praise *mantra yoga* which includes regular chanting, and repeated chanting of a deity's name (*japa*) and pilgrimage (*tīrthānusevanam*). People believe that such practices will confer *mokṣa*, but the verse claims that such beliefs and practices will not be effective. It states that diverse are the ways to *mokṣa* peddled by the world. But all the means stated above are not the effective means to attaining *mokṣa*.

This text was purported to be recorded in the 15th century CE, but the situation has not changed even today. You go to one teacher and he states that by chanting the *Bhagavad Gītā*, you can attain *mokṣa*; another one states that you should do breathing practices (*prāṇāyāma*), and yet another teacher prescribes *yoga* postures. And finally, there are those who praise social service or *sevā* as a means to *mokṣa*. Perhaps there is a better chance of you attaining *mokṣa* if you had not met such teachers. Yet another one will tell you to go find a teacher (*guru*) and that you will certainly attain *mokṣa*. In fact, your stress levels and that of those around you will worsen, upon you finding a *guru*. That is the reason why you do not look for a *guru*, but let the *guru* find you. You should not be hunting for a *guru*, but you should hunt for knowledge. And your sincere prayers too, will land you the right *guru* who must be a qualified teacher. This will be discussed later in this book.

When you hunt for a *guru*, there are higher chances of you being disappointed. Because there is so much hype about the supposed *guru*-s, you may mistake the hype for competency and authenticity. People you meet may set your expectations so high, that you may go away disappointed after meeting such *guru*-s. I have met a couple of them in my life where their charisma and their fine ability to teach, have been mistaken to be the hallmarks of an authentic *guru*. Most often the best *gurus* are ones that do not seek attention, fame and prominence. These teachers are like oxygen which nourishes you, but rarely in your perception. It is also good to keep in mind that your chosen *guru* may not be the *guru* for everyone else that you know. A *guru* and seeker relationship is a personal one. The close guidance a *guru* provides is meant for you alone, and not for the people around you.

Of course, there could be many other paths, techniques, practices and beliefs that are sold in the spiritual market that is not covered in this text. But you can add all that and conclude that they are all wrong, because it is knowledge alone that confers *mokṣa*.

tapo vidyā ca viprasya niḥśreyasakaraṃ param
tapasā kilbiṣaṃ hanti vidyayā'mṛtamaśnute

For a wise man, austerities and knowledge are the highest means to *mokṣa* (*niḥśreyasa*). Austerities remove impurities and knowledge gives immortality (*mokṣa*)[5].

The *Śiva Samhitā* has dismissed all the popular views on attaining *mokṣa*, such as the various *sādhana*-s or *karma*-s. The text will henceforth categorize the diverse schools of thought, and then dismiss them all in the following verses.

एवंव्यवसितालोकेकृत्याकृत्यविदोजनाः ।
व्यामोहमेवगच्छंतिविमुक्ताःपापकर्मभिः ॥ ८

evaṃ vyavasitā loke kṛtyākṛtyāvido janāḥ |
vyāmohameva gacchanti vimuktāḥ pāpa*karma*bhiḥ || 8

People who are not certain about right and wrong though free from demerit remain deluded only.

Prior to this verse, the following types of actions were dismissed - do's and do not's, austerities, role-based duties, daily duties, chanting, fire rituals, dispassion and pilgrimages. All these are usually praised as a valid means to *mokṣa* by the world, but this has been refuted. All *karmas* be they physical (*kāyika*), mental (*mānasika*) or verbal (*vācika*), will produce results and hence rebirth.

5 Manu Smṛti 12.104

The verse states that even people, who know what is right and wrong are equally deluded and not exempted from being ignorant. Actions cannot get you out of *samsāra* yet many seekers of *mokṣa* are still engaging in *karma*, or have been asked to engage in *karma* by their *guru*-s. Such people are bewildered as they find themselves not making any progress in their spiritual path. Bewilderment also implies the continuous performance of *karma*-s, despite knowing that *pāpa* and *puṇya* do not get exhausted through *karma*.

Then what is the value of *karma*? *Bhagavad Gītā* states clearly that those who do *karma* will get caught in samsāra, but those who perform *karma* as a *Yoga* (*Karma Yoga*), are able to overcome it.[6] Hence *Karma Yoga* is a lifestyle that aids you in Self-Knowledge through mental purification. While *Karma Yoga* does not confer *mokṣa*, it does purify your mind adequately to assimilate Self-Knowledge.

na hi jñānēna sadṛśaṅ pavitramiha vidyatē
tatsvayam yōgasamsiddhaḥ kālēnātmani vindati

There is no greater purifier in this world like knowledge. He who is perfected in *Karma Yoga* finds it (knowledge) in the Self in time.[7]

Veda Vyāsa, the author of *Bhagavad Gītā*, is indeed a compassionate sage because he has provided an alternative lifestyle for *mokṣa*, to those who are desirous of it but are unable to or could not abandon their duties. For these people, *Karma Yoga* is prescribed.

The *Śiva Samhitā* may appear harsh because it states that even being free from *pāpa*, does not make you wise or free. But that is the truth. *Swāmi Vivekānanda* said that if *pāpa* is the thorn that pricks us, *puṇya* is the crown of thorns.[8] From afar it may look like a crown but only to the one who wears it, knows otherwise.

एतन्मतावलम्बी यो लब्ध्वा दुरितपुण्यके ।
भ्रमतीत्यवशःसोऽत्र जन्म मृत्युपरम्पराम् ॥ ९

etanmatāvalambī yo labdhvā duritapuṇyake |
bhramatītyavaśaḥ so'tra janmamṛtyuparamparām || 9

---

6 Bhagavad Gītā 3.9

7 ibid 4.38

8 quoted in Sri Ramakrishna - The Great Master by Swami Saradananda

The person who follows such doctrines incurs merit and demerit, and wanders helplessly here in this world through a series of births and deaths.

This verse is beautiful as it defines (*lakṣaṇa*) of *samsāra*. It defines it as the series of birth and death (*janmamṛtyu paramparā*) which means "I am born", "I die", and "I am born" again and "I die" again, and so forth. One who follows the doctrine of *karma* by observing his *svadharma* i.e., live a life following the *yama*-s and *niyama*-s and doing all the daily duties, will go through this *janmamṛtyu paramparā*. The text is sarcastic when it refers to the cycle of birth and death as *janmamṛtyu paramparā*, for usually we refer to the word *paramparā* in a positive way as in *guru śiṣya paramparā* (the tradition of a teacher and student).

Because I am ignorant of the fact that *karma* and *karma*-based doctrines will not give *mokṣa*, I am again and again driven into *samsāra* as though by dire necessity. This delusion will impel me to do *puṇya karma*-s if I am pure (*sattva*), and *pāpa karma* if I am lethargic (*tāmasic*).

At this point, I would like to ask people who call themselves *mumukṣu*-s, "Why is it that you are after *mokṣa*?" There could be many answers, and one of them could be that "it is the goal of life." Most often than not, people who pursue *mokṣa* without examining if it was the goal of their lives, are probably pursuing it because someone had told them so. It is like following the trend in the name of being a good Hindu or spiritual person. This is the first group of *mumukṣu*-s.

The second group of *mumukṣu*-s which is likely the predominant group, are usually quite unhappy with life. They have problems with their mother-in-law, father-in-law, wife, husband, bosses, friends, relatives, job and politics. These unresolved issues make them unhappy and because someone had told them that *mokṣa* is the way out, they go for it. They assume that *mokṣa* is going to give them a type of happiness by neutralising all the problems in their lives.

Both these groups of *mumukṣu*-s have misunderstood *mokṣa*. The truth is that if you have a problem in life, *mokṣa* cannot solve it for you. *Mokṣa* is like removing the head as a solution for a headache. These groups of people are seekers of enjoyments (*bhubukṣu*) but unable to solve the problems of life. If suppose your mother- in-law was perfect, father-in-law was perfect, boss, father and everyone else were to be perfect, will you still seek *mokṣa*? This is a very important question that you must ask yourself. Do you want to remove your sorrows? or do you want to remove both happiness (*sukha*) and sorrow (*duḥkha*)? Because today we think that the removal of *duḥkha* is *mokṣa*. This is not true; for to attain *mokṣa*, you must renounce the value for both happiness and sorrow as both are but emotional states that bind us. The *Bhagavad Gītā* states,

yaṅ hi na vyathayantyētē puruṣam puruṣarṣabha
samaduḥkhasukham dhīram sōmṛtatvāya kalpatē

O leader of men, he to whom sorrow and happiness are the same and do not affect - that wise man alone is worthy of immortality (*mokṣa*)[9].

9 Bhagavad Gītā 2.15

6

FALSE DOCTRINES ABOUT THE SELF

अन्यैर् मतिमताम् श्रेष्ठैः श्रुत्यालोकनतत्परैः ।
आत्मानो बहवः प्रोक्ता नित्याः सर्वगतास् तथा ॥ १०

anyair matimatām śreṣṭhaiḥ śrutyālokanatatparaiḥ ।
ātmāno bahavaḥ proktā nityāḥ sarvagatās tathā ॥ 10

Others, best among the wise, preoccupied with the Veda-s declare that selves are many, eternal and omnipresent.

The *Śiva Saṃhitā* had earlier stated that those who were doing *karma* are subject to the *janmamṛtyuparamparā*. Now the text is addressing the various schools of thought or *siddhānta*-s. It is intent on negating the dualistic (*dvaita*) philosophies which state that God is separate from the Self, and that there are many *jīvātma*-s (individual selves) everywhere, which are eternal and omnipresent. The moment I utter these three words - many, eternal and omnipresent, contradiction presents itself because that which is eternal and omnipresent cannot be many. *Śiva Saṃhitā* is basically disarming the proponents of duality and negating the idea of *mokṣa* as going to another realm, and living there with one's favourite deity.

kāmātmānaḥ svargaparā janmakarmaphalapradām.
kriyāviśēṣabahulāṅ bhōgaiśvaryagatim prati

Filled with desires, having heaven as their destination, leading to more births as the result of their *karma*-s, and prescribe various *karma*-s, for the attainment of enjoyment and power.[1]

These are the seekers who want to go to heaven and enjoy their life there too by performing the ritualistic injunctions in the *Veda*-s. They are basically *bhubukṣu*-s or seekers of enjoyments because that is all that they think about.

However, there is nothing wrong with being a *bhubukṣu* but not for the one who is seeking *mokṣa*, for the *mumukṣu* is not intent on even enjoying in heaven. The desire for enjoyment only reinforces the fact that the seeker is disposed for *pravṛtti mārga*.

1 Bhagavad Gītā 2.43

यद्यत्प्रत्यक्षविषयंतदन्यन्नास्तिचक्षते ।
कुतःस्वर्गादयःसन्तीत्यन्येनिश्चितमानसाः ॥ ११

yadyatpratyakṣaviṣayaṃ tadanyannāsti cakṣate |
kutaḥ svargādayaḥ santītyanye niścitamānasāḥ ||11

Some, asking where things such as heaven etc are to be found, are convinced that there is nothing apart from the object of direct perception.

This verse tackles those who do not look at the scriptures as valid. There are two ancient materialist philosophies called the *Cārvāka* and *Lokāyata*. They look at the universe as just matter and nothing beyond that. The materialists use only perception (*pratyakṣa*) and inference (*anumāna*) as means of knowledge (*pramāṇa*). They do not rely on scriptural teachings (*śabda*). Their philosophy is to be happy at all costs. They have no concept of *pāpa* or *puṇya*. Hence, they are also called nihilists. They have their own texts (*nāstika śāstra*), in Sanskrit too, to counter the Hindu scriptures (*āstika śāstra*) and see no value in the latter. People like these live amidst us even today, and at times they end up behind bars if they are unable to appreciate basic universal ethics. At one point in time in ancient India, these philosophies were very influential and hence the *Śiva Samhitā* records them.

The *Śiva Samhitā* states that these propounders were charismatic and good at debating (*vivādaśīlānām*). Sometimes when you are good at debating, even untruth can appear as truth. So, do not mistake charisma and logic for wisdom.

ज्ञानप्रवाहइत्यन्येशून्यंकेचित्परंविदुः ।
द्वावेवतत्त्वंमन्यन्तेऽपरेप्रकृतिपूरुषौ ॥ १२

jñānapravāha ityanye śūnyaṃ kecitparaṃ viduḥ |
dvāveva tattvaṃ manyante'pare prakṛtipūruṣau ||12

Others believe the world to be a series of thoughts; some proclaim the void as the greatest. Still others believe in two ultimate realities, matter (prakṛti) and God (puruṣa)

The *Śiva Samhitā* now turns its gaze to Buddhism. I am going to spend some time on this verse because it is good to know the subtleties of opposing views, especially when it closely resembles Self-Knowledge.

There were two main philosophical schools of Buddhism in ancient India which were the schools of *jñānapravāha*, also known as *kṣaṇikavāda* and *śūṇyavāda*. There were also other early Buddhist philosophies such as the *yogācāra*, *vijñānavāda* and *mādhyamika*. But these were the two primary schools which traditional *Vedāntin*-s like *Śaṅkarācārya*, spent their energy refuting them in their written works. In fact, *Śaṅkarācārya* took great effort in refuting these schools in his *Brahma Sūtra Bhāśya*. These two schools are directly in conflict with *Vedānta* because of the way they define Consciousness or *caitanya*.

Jñānapravāha or *kṣaṇikavāda* defines Consciousness to be a succession of thoughts or thoughts with no permanence. This philosophy is taught and alive till today. On the other hand, *Vedānta*'s definition of reality is that Consciousness has no beginning or end. The *Vedāntic* Consciousness pervades your thoughts and does not depend upon your thoughts. It is there in the states of dream, deep sleep and waking. It 'was', 'is' and 'will be' at the time of birth, life and death. Body does not condition Consciousness; Consciousness also does not condition the body because conditioning the body would imply change, and that implies that Consciousness is also changing.

What is the relationship between the 'changing' and the 'changeless' then? The changing depends upon changeless but changeless does not depend upon the changing. The body depends upon Consciousness but Consciousness does not depend upon body. Consciousness does not condition the body, dream, sleep and thought. But all the changes depend upon Consciousness for its existence. This Consciousness is called *caitanya* or *jñānam* as stated in the opening verse of the *Śiva Samhitā*.

The *kṣaṇikavāda* of the Buddhists teach 'the theory of momentary existence' and the argument of this philosophical school of Buddhism is that the whole universe that you see does not have absolute consciousness or permanence. The individuals do not have absolute consciousness but only momentary consciousness. Contrary to the teachings of the *Upaniṣad*-s, they hold that the *ātman* or Self, is not absolute consciousness. To them *ātman* is not *ekam, nityam, adyantaśūṇyam*. They claim that there is no such *ātman* and that consciousness is only momentary thoughts. Hence Buddhism is sometimes also called *anātmavāda*.

An illustration would better present their position: I enter a restaurant. Before I entered the restaurant, the thought about pizza was in my mind. Once I entered it, my eyes fell on the new lasagna dish that was on their poster, and the thought of the lasagna replaced the thought of the pizza. After seeing that lasagna, I proceeded to the washroom and the thought of the washroom replaced the thought of the lasagna. Like this we have several minute thoughts, each replacing the other and hence the *kṣaṇikavādi*-s (propounders of *kṣaṇikavāda*) conclude that this is what you are and that you nothing else. According to them, your reality is nothing but successive thoughts. If you ask the question where do the thoughts rest on, they would say "why bother to even ask this question." Every thought changes, every thought is dependent upon the object of thought – lasagna thought depended upon the lasagna poster, etc. Every thought's content rests in some object. When the next thought comes, it replaces the current thought. They claim that reality is only in dream and waking states and there are no thoughts in deep sleep. According to them, a state without thoughts is not worthy of investigation. To them there is nothing in deep sleep except nothingness. Even the talk about sleep occurs only after you wake up.

The second school of Buddhism which is *śūṇyavāda*, does not interest itself about momentary consciousness as much as it is interested in concluding the whole universe to be *śūṇya* (void or emptiness). They say that nothing in this world lasts eternally. *Śūṇya* here does not mean a void but rather being devoid of any permanent character. The whole universe is resting on nothing. They give the illustration of the chariot, as discussed in one of the previous chapters, which comprises an axle, wheels, canopy, reins, seat and pillars. If you take away the parts, there will not be a chariot. According to *śūṇyavadis*, the chariot is a figment of your imagination. The chariot has two wheels, an axle and a chair. And when we dismantle it, the two wheels, axle and a seat still exist but we do not call it a chariot. That means the chariot is essentially in the mind.

The argument is that the whole universe is made up of parts which are not held together by anything. In turn each part is made by several other parts and so on till it arrives at nothingness or emptiness. Everything is held together by the mind and thoughts.

Vedānta's arguments against these philosophical positions are many but I will share two of them. The first argument is that if you removed the parts of the chariot, it must be placed in some space. For the chariot to first exist, there must be a base. And that base or substratum on which anything is put together is the Consciousness as taught in the *Upaniṣad*-s .

Vedānta also dismisses the Buddhist contention that the whole universe came from nothing (void). According to *Upaniṣad*-s, something can come out of something, for example, ghee or clarified butter from milk; but nothing can come out of something, as in milk always remains milk unchanged. However, something cannot come out of nothing. Ghee cannot come out of nowhere like a 'son of a barren woman', an oxymoron.

The Buddhist position of something coming from nothing is like that of 'flowers in the sky'. A man told that he saw a nice bouquet of flowers in the sky. He looked at all the flowers and found a pretty red one, and decided to pluck it. He then gave that to his wife who decided pin it on her tresses and he loved how she looked with that flower. In this story, the first illogical point about having found a bouquet of flowers in the sky was completely overtaken and forgotten by the subsequent points in the story. This is how we get distracted from illogical positions. The starting point may be illogical but because the story was built on the first erroneous premise, it distracts you into the details of what had happened afterwards and the story starts to sound real and interesting. Most creation theories are fraught with this flaw.

The *Vedāntin*-s find the Buddhist position untenable, because it appears to build all its teachings on the premise of emptiness or void which is itself of unsound reasoning.

I shared two ways with which *Vedānta* refutes the conclusions of the few Buddhist schools discussed in the text. The reason why the Buddhists came to such conclusions is due to the lack of the means of knowledge called *śabda pramāṇa* viz the *Veda* and *Upaniṣad*-s. They depended primarily on perception (*pratyakṣa*) and inference (*anumāna*) for understanding the universe.

The second part of the *Śiva Samhitā* verse being discussed tackles the philosophical position that there are two eternals – *prakṛti* and *puruṣa*. This philosophical school is called the *Sāṅkhya* and its principal teacher (*ācārya*) is *Kapila*. This is not an entirely atheistic (*nāstika*) school of thought like Buddhism and Jainism, as *Sāṅkhya* depends on the *Veda*-s too for its philosophy.

Sāṅkhya teaches that there is the changing *prakṛti* or *māyā* and changeless *puruṣa* (*Brahman*) which are both eternal. They preached duality. If someone states there are two eternals, you should ask which of the eternals is real. How can the changing reality be called eternal? Do these two realities occupy the same space? Also from which reality did the thing that differentiates the two come from? When you have two fundamental realities, then you must postulate a third which is 'space' because they cannot exist separately without space. That would lead to another question: Is the space superior to the two fundamental realities? Could space be the third reality?

By asking such questions *Sāṅkhya* gets invalidated. The arguments against *Sāṅkhya* are immense but what I shared is the gist. Among the Vedic philosophies, *Sāṅkhya* is the most popular and comes closest to *Vedānta* in terms of its metaphysics. Refuting *Sāṅkhya* would be as good as defeating all other philosophical schools (*darśana*-s) that had used the *Veda*-s as its means of knowledge. For example, if you beat the current heavyweight champion in the boxing match, you become the number one automatically without having to beat all those who have been defeated by your opponent. As a result, the *Śiva Samhitā* only demolishes *Sāṅkhya* and does not bother about the other *āstika* or *Vedic* philosophical schools.

Sāṅkhya is also similar to another philosophy that exists today - *Śaiva Siddhānta*[2], which is an extension of the metaphysics of *Sāṅkhya*. *Puruṣa* is called *pati* and *prakṛti* is *pāsam*. Within *prakṛti* there are *jīva*-s or individuals called *paṣu*. All of them are seen as eternals in *Śaiva Siddhānta*. The nature of *pati* is not the same as *Brahman* as taught in *Vedānta*, because *Śaiva Siddhānta* talk about three distinct realities. If 'two' eternal realities are untenable then 'three' is naturally an aberration as it creates more diversity. Why do people subscribe to it then? We must look at this from a psychological angle why such *sampradāya*-s are born.

People generally have certain biases that are lodged in their sub-conscious mind. Our mental makeup, likes and dislikes, childhood baggage and issues are rooted in this subconscious mind. So naturally, certain religious ideas that talk about love or a loving god will resonate with certain types of minds. For example, a person who was deprived of love in his or her childhood may get attracted to a *sampradāya* that looks at God as someone who loves his children. Likewise, there can be innate tendencies (*vāsanā*) in our minds that may make a *sampradāya* look very appealing. However, *Vedānta* unlike any other philosophical school is a unique *sampradāya* that considers the sub-conscious biases and anticipates possible issues. It encourages one to be objective and ruthless in one's discrimination. There is no room for your emotional issues when it comes to inquiry into realities. While there is a time and place for such issues, it is not to be brought into the laboratory of Self-Knowledge.

2 a popular philosophy among the Tamils of Tamil Nadu and the Tamil diaspora

अत्यन्तभिन्नमतयः परमार्थपराङ्मुखाः |
एवमन्ये तु सञ्चिन्त्य यथामति यथाश्रुतम् || १३
निरीश्वरमिदं प्राहुः सेश्वरञ्च तथापरे |
वदन्ति विविधैर्भेदैः सुयुक्त्या स्थितिकातराः ||१४

atyantabhinnamatayaḥ paramārthaparāṅmukhāḥ |
evamanye tu sañcintya yathāmati yathāśrutam || 13
nirīśvaramidaṃ prāhuḥ seśvarañca tathāpare |
vadanti vividhairbhedaiḥ suyuktyā sthitikātarāḥ ||14

Holding very different beliefs, some people thus shun the Ultimate Reality and, thinking in accordance with their beliefs and what they have heard, they say that there is no God in the universe. Others say that there is God. Those uncertain of their position cleverly argue diverse opinions.

After refuting the various schools, the *Śiva Samhitā* now makes a summary statement. Some say that there is no God, others say that there is God while some sit on the fence. These positions were based on solid arguments and reasoning alone. But is your reasoning good enough to create a philosophy or *siddhānta*? Our minds are limited, so why should we base our convictions on solely reasoning? Also, just because these arguments sound good, can they be assumed to be right? Right and wrong are not subjective while good and bad are. The feel-good factor is not a good gauge for what is right. For example, drugs will make one high on the feel-good factor but are they right for you? On the other hand, medicine is always bitter but does its job. *Vedānta* is also bitter when it comes to reasoning but it does its job. *Vedānta* will not work when you have preconceived notions. For a person who has built a defence system based on his or her beliefs, no amount of teaching will work. This could be the reason why the *Śiva Samhitā* adopts a methodology to present Self-Knowledge so that the assimilation is systematic and well founded. First it refuted karma, then the various philosophical schools and finally concludes that all these are based on reasoning alone, without the support of scriptures and therefore to be discarded.

एते चान्ये च मुनिभिः सङ्ज्ञाभेदाः पृथग्विधाः ।
शास्त्रेषु कथिता ह्येते लोकव्यामोहकारकाः ॥ १५
एतद् विवादशीलानां मतं वक्तुं न शक्यते ।
भ्रमन्त्यस्मिञ्जनाः सर्वे मुक्तिमार्गबहिष्कृताः ॥ १६

ete cānye ca munibhiḥ saṅjñābhedāḥ pṛthagvidhāḥ ।
śāstreṣu kathitā hyete lokavyāmohakārakāḥ ॥ 15
etad vivādaśīlānāṃ mataṃ vaktuṃ na śakyate ।
bhramantyasmiñjanāḥ sarve muktimārgabahiṣkṛtāḥ ॥ 16

These and various other ideas have been taught by sages in the scriptures and they confuse people. One cannot fully explain those doctrines of people devoted to debates. Everyone loses their way in them and is driven away from the path to Mukti.

The *Śiva Samhitā* states that sages (*munayaḥ*) who are respected by many people also create confusion (*vyāmohakārakās*). Suppose your understanding is that *Brahman* alone is real and that everything else in the universe is apparent (*brahmasatyam jaganmithyā*); You then visit a local temple and the priest states, "Your Self cannot surely be *Brahman* because you were not the creator of the universe, let alone your own parents", and this gets you doubtful over your own convictions. The priest you met was respectful and could have even authored Sanskrit texts; or perhaps he has miraculous powers (*siddhi*-s) and therefore you are automatically taken in. Hence the *Śiva Samhitā* warns that even charismatic sages and teachers have the potential to delude you.

People who can debate very well can also delude us. Many new traditions are born when their philosophical position or *Siddhānta* is not clear and they derail you from the pursuit of Self-Knowledge. However, having stated that, we should not disrespect these teachers because they could be sincere or could have done great austerities. But just because they have done austerities does not mean that their Self-Knowledge is clear. Do not always equate the two; A person who has done austerities (*tapasvi*) is not necessarily a teacher familiar with the teaching methodology (*śrotriya*) or a person established in Self-Knowledge (*brahmaniṣṭha*).

Modern *Yoga* and other new age spiritual teachers are also contributors to this delusion. In fact most of them do. They claim that by stretching your limbs you can get *mokṣa*. The truth is that you will feel lighter if you did *prāṇāyāma* and even acquire some powers (*siddhi*-s), but not *mokṣa*. The confusion in the modern *Yoga* schools is so bad to the point of not being able to differentiate *haṭha yoga* from *aṣṭāṅga yoga*. Some teach *aṣṭāṅga* yoga as a means to *mokṣa* without even reading a single *sūtra* of the source text, the *Yoga Sūtra*. A lot of them teach meditation as a means to *mokṣa* too. Meditation is a mental action which will produce results and to enjoy the result I must be reborn. So, there is no question of *mokṣa* through meditation.

The key argument against meditation as a means to *mokṣa* is that meditation is a mental action, and it cannot generate new knowledge. Some schools claim that by meditating you can create new knowledge. Insights (*pratibhā*) may arise due to meditation but new knowledge is not possible. This is how new cults are created claiming that meditation is the means to end all your problems. This is popularly called *Rāja Yoga* in today's world, which is a gross misinterpretation of the meditative and contemplative practices found in the *Veda*-s and *Tantra*. These teachings mislead people into thinking that meditation is sufficient to solve all of life's problems. Such teachings are highly damaging to the human mind as it does not stand the test of reason or your own experience.

The *Śiva Samhitā* has now completed the discussion on the various erroneous *siddhānta*-s, covering both the *āstika* and *nāstika* schools. The one thing that I like about *Śiva Samhitā* is that it does not mince words. We must cultivate such courage in ourselves to understand the true purport of scriptures, or else we will become victims of those who delude us.

7

YOGAŚĀSTRA: THE HIGHEST KNOWLEDGE

आलोक्यसर्वशास्त्राणिविचार्यचपुनःपुनः ।
इदमेकंसुनिष्पन्नंयोगशास्त्रंपरंमतम् ॥ १७

ālokya sarvaśāstrāṇi vicārya ca punaḥ punah |
idamekaṃ suniṣpannaṃ yogaśāstraṃ paraṃ matam || 17

Having studied all the scriptures and having anaylsed them repeatedly, this one consummate teaching of Yoga is held to be supreme.

Having repeatedly analyzed the scriptures, the Yogaśāstra is declared to be the ultimate knowledge. The Śiva Samhitā claims that this knowledge is called supreme knowledge (*param matam*) because it cannot be corrected or improved further, as it is complete. One of the traditional ways to verify the completeness is by examining if its teachings opposed your logic (*yukti*) and experience (*anubhava*). This *Yogaśāstra* is indeed Self-Knowledge.

This scrutiny must be done respectfully but ruthlessly. You must be ruthless like a weed cutter, who gets rid of weed quickly and completely. If your reasoning is not ruthless then your understanding will be murky.

यस्मिन्ज्ञातेसर्वमिदंज्ञातंभवतिनिश्चितम् ।
तस्मिन्परिश्रमःकार्यःकिमन्यच्छास्त्रभाषितम् ॥ १८

yasmin jñāte sarvamidaṃ jñātaṃ bhavati niścitam |
tasminpariśramaḥ kāryaḥ kimanyacchāstrabhāṣitam || 18

One should work hard at knowing that by which everything is known. There is no need to bother with what is taught in the other scriptures.

The verse, whose first line is very similar to the *mantra* from the *Upaniṣad*[1] has important points which are splendid advice for a *mumukṣu*. The thing which is to be known i.e., *Yogaśāstra*. This *Yogaśāstra* is the one through which everything else is known. There is nothing left to be known or experienced, as everything is as good as accomplished when you know the *Yogaśāstra*. And hence it is not needed that you go through other texts.

Suppose you go to a gold jewellery shop, and you look at the many ornaments made of gold. There will be many different types of jewellery for you to choose from, but suppose you choose gold, then the whole shop

1 Muṇḍaka Upaniṣad 1.1.3; Bṛhadāraṇyaka Upaniṣad 4.5.15

is yours. Likewise, if you know the reality that is also *ātman* or *Brahman*, it is as good as knowing the Universe or being everything. This is a very important point because sometimes, we forget to include ourselves in the universe.

When I say that the universe is not apart from Consciousness, I am also not apart from that same Consciousness. When you know *Brahman*, the universe and your individuality gets resolved. And what is left is *Brahman* alone. If that *Brahman* alone remains, is there any name or form that can bind you? Do you have to become free, or are you already free? The idea of being bound or free is entirely notional, because even as you are reading this book you are that *Brahman*. It is just that you do not know it or yet to establish your understanding in it.

Some people take the view that knowing *Brahman* is not enough, but experiencing the reality is more important. Such a view is not tenable in this teaching because 'knowing is experiencing'. All experiences are either known correctly or erroneously. Sometimes you may experience something without even knowing what it is. For example: the rising of the sun in the eastern horizon, tasting something that you do not know, seeing the railway tracks merging at the distant end, the earth being flat. Hence, experience does not guarantee you valid knowledge.

Once *Brahman* or *ātman* or Consciousness is known, it is known for good and there is no room for future error. Experience has its limits and this is where all our modern *Yoga* traditions have gone wrong. In fact, this is where many teachers, even the popular ones get it wrong too. They want to convince you that you must experience this reality in order to attain *mokṣa*, when you have never been apart from that Consciousness, ever. Some good illustrations to present this point are the story of 'The Tenth Man' and 'The Beggar Prince'.

Tenth Man Story

"Ten ignorant people crossed a river by swimming and reached the other shore safely. They began to count themselves to see whether all had reached the shore. One man counted all the nine persons and forgot to count himself, the tenth person and began to weep bitterly. He thought that one man had been drowned. The other nine persons also counted in the same manner each man forgetting to count himself and began to weep when the tenth man was missing. When one man wept, all the nine persons joined with him in weeping. A bystander who was noticing their folly pointed out, "O man, no one is missing. There are ten men here. Tenth man is yourself. You have failed to count yourself."[2]

The Beggar Prince

"There was a prince who was lost when he was very young. He was brought up by the beggar and the child thought he was a beggar. He was totally ignorant of his true identity as a prince and hence went through the misery of a beggar. One day, one of the ministers saw the child's birthmark and took him to the palace as a prince. Now that he knew he was a prince, the distress felt as a beggar was gone."[3]

In these stories, upon realisation the tenth person and the prince understood that they were 'already that'. It is the accomplishment of the already accomplished (*prāptasya prāptiḥ*). You only need to 'know', and it is only a notional change. You were always the tenth man, but you were not aware of this; it is as simple as that.

The next line of the verse states that by knowing this reality, you will know everything; then why should you care about the other schools of thought? Why should you care if someone is teaching something new three shophouses down the road? For a *mumukṣu*, these offerings from other teachers or philosophies are of no value. But to arrive at this conviction, you must first be convinced that this *Yogaśāstra* is the supreme knowledge. Until you are convinced, you will continue to graze for different experiences, teachers and congregations. Instead of seeking the eternal, you will become an eternal seeker. Because there is no conviction, people will easily usurp your mind. When a person has not rationalised enough, it is easy to shake the person's beliefs. The *śāstra* states that when that Consciousness is understood, you will graze no more.

However, the conclusion that this *Yogaśāstra* is the *param matam* must not be a belief. Belief is something that is pending verification. For example, the existence of heaven is purely a belief, and any spiritual product that cannot be attained becomes the most marketable product. Even this Self-Knowledge can become like that, if you do not have the proper appreciation, with respect to its veracity and tenacity. Hence the verse states that one should work hard at it.

Even the choice of words we use to understand this knowledge is important. This Consciousness is referred to in many spiritual circles as 'oneness' or

---

2 story as told by Swāmi Sivananda

3 story as told by Shashank Katti in his book 'My Humble Understanding of Spirituality'

'divinity'. A very popular statement in these circles is that you are 'divine'. I ask, "Why do you have to be so obsessed with one's divinity? Are you implying that the other objects of the world are not divine?" Divinity is only with relation to something that is not divine. If the whole universe is *Brahman*, is there a place or thing which is not divine? Then drop the word 'divine'. There is no need to call anything divine. A reality is to be seen as it is. The attempts to call it divine are a superimposition but a good marketing tool though.

This conclusion that *Yogaśāstra* is the supreme knowledge cannot be a belief. If it is a belief, then it has to be converted into a tenable knowledge system. Whether you realise it or not, depends on the next stage of your effort. But first, you must understand it clearly and rationally. From my experience in teaching this knowledge to students I realized that what may initially seem clear, after a day or two, will become hazy and doubt-filled.

When something sounds very nice, analyse it further because niceness is not the key indicator of valid knowledge. Knowledge may be bitter because it does not depend or appeal to our likes and dislikes. Our own superimpositions are nice because they are based on our likes and dislikes. But knowledge is not like that. If you think this teaching should appeal to your likes and dislikes, then your expectations are wrong. Teaching should not cushion you; *Vedānta* is not to cushion you, but to prick you and keep you alert so that you can see yourself clearly. It may make you uncomfortable, but that is the nature of knowledge. Call it a rude awakening, because that is how it is. You should not think that the teaching should conform to your petty belief systems and values. If that is the case, then you should bid farewell to this Self-Knowledge.

There must be a razor-sharp enquiry in which everything that can be objectified can be negated, using analysis supported by scripture. If that shakes your foundation, then it is the right teaching. If it does not and you feel insecure, then maybe you are in the wrong place for learning.

Beliefs have to be converted into a rational conviction, and you need the faith to take this journey. You must be convinced that what you are aiming for, is the greatest and highest goal that you can ever attain. Otherwise you will keep changing teachers or philosophies, and finally you may completely renounce spirituality too.

Why then, does a seeker constantly go from one text to another? People do this because humans are a curious lot. We want to know what others are teaching.

Secondly, you go looking at other texts or teachings because sometimes you have doubts which have not been resolved. That is a genuine reason. When you have doubts about who you are, then clarify it. You should not graze everywhere, but should go to the right place for clarity. Even the different jargons for the same reality used in different traditions can confuse you. For example, in each tradition the word 'consciousness' can be used differently. That is why the tradition encourages that you not learn this knowledge from a book. This knowledge should also not be taught to a big congregation because in such an environment there is a higher chance of misinterpretation. In group teaching this is an inevitable risk.

The third reason could be the lack of qualification which gives this illusion that another text may solve the problem of non-assimilation.

8

QUALIFICATIONS OF A SEEKER

योगशास्त्रमिदंगोप्यमस्माभिःपरिभाषितम् ।
सुभक्तायप्रदातव्यंत्रैलोक्येचमहात्मने ॥ १९

yogaśāstramidaṃ gopyamasmābhiḥ paribhāṣitam |
subhaktāya pradātavyaṃ trailokye ca mahātmane ||19

This teaching of Yoga, taught by me, succinctly defined is to be secret and given to the man in the three worlds who is a true devotee and a noble person.

This verse, states that this *Yogaśāstra* is a secret (*gopyam*) and if it is so, then it should be revealed to someone you trust and who meets the requirements. Such a person is called great soul (*mahātman*) in this verse. The great soul referred to here is indeed an *adhikāri*, a qualified seeker.

idaṃ te nātapaskāya nābhaktāya kadācana ।
na cāśuśrūṣave vācyaṃ na ca māṃ yo'bhyasūyati ॥

Never should this be told by you to one who is not
austere, who is not a devotee, nor to one who has no wish
to listen, nor certainly to him who mocks Me.[1]

What are the requirements of the qualified seeker? He must be great devotee (*subhakta*) and not just an ordinary devotee (*bhakta*). He is a *bhakta* who is clear about his goal in life. The knowledge is such that you must know exactly what you want. If you do not know what you want, then you are going to be lost.

He should also possess exemplary values. By just looking at him, you will be inspired to teach him. When you meet some students, you feel confident that they will learn this successfully and there are others with whom you do not want to share this knowledge with.

The seeker of this knowledge should have observed all the values, – *yama* and *niyama*-s. Even if you have not accomplished them, then at least you should have value for them.

1 Bhagavad Gītā 18.67

This rule is applicable to even *Indra*, a prominent *Vedic* god. Even if *Indra* comes to learn this knowledge, you must assess if he is qualified. There is an episode in the *Upaniṣad*[2] where *Brahmā* asks *Indra* to stay with him for many years before teaching him the knowledge. A teacher must teach well but only after assessing the student. Teaching indiscriminately to anyone is not supported by the *Vedānta* tradition.

There are also other qualifications required of a seeker. These will be discussed in another chapter.

2 see Chāndogya Upaniṣad 8.7.1 to 8.12.6

9

TWO PARTS OF VEDA – ACTION AND KNOWLEDGE

कर्मकाण्डंज्ञानकाण्डमितिवेदोद्विधामतः ।
भवतिद्विविधोभेदोज्ञानकाण्डस्यकर्मणः ॥२०

karmakāṇḍaṃ jñānakāṇḍamiti vedo dvidhā mataḥ |
bhavati dvividho bhedo jñānakāṇḍasya karmaṇaḥ || 20

There are two parts of the Vedas - Action (karmakāṇḍa) and Knowledge (jñānakāṇḍa). There is a further two-fold division for knowledge and action sections.

The *Śiva Samhitā* explains in this verse how the *Veda* is structured. It is very interesting to note that the text does not plunge into the subject of Self-Knowledge immediately. It is setting the tone to introduce the subject matter systematically. This is how the traditional teaching works. You introduce the subject in such a way, that you prevent or reduce future possibilities of confusion about the methodology of the *Veda*.

There are two parts to the *Veda*-s –

1. *Karmakāṇḍa* - Action
2. *Jñānakāṇḍa* - Knowledge

The further divisions of each are the *Samhitā* (portion of the *Veda*-s pertaining to hymns) and the *Brāhmana* (portion of the *Veda*-s pertaining to rituals) of the *Karmakāṇḍa*. The *Āraṇyaka* (portion of *Veda*-s pertaining to meditation techniques) and *Upaniṣad* (portion of the *Veda*-s pertaining to Self-Knowledge) are the source of *jñānakāṇḍa*.

There are *Vedāntin*-s who ridicule rituals to be ineffective in attaining *mokṣa* but the truth is that you need these hymns and rituals to make yourself fit for learning Self-Knowledge. Lack of observance in *karmakāṇḍa*, can lead to obstacles while pursuing Self-Knowledge. Traditional *Vedānta* teaching tells you exactly where the obstacles to knowledge are and how you can overcome them. Unfortunately, modern or neo-*Vedānta* suffers from this deficiency of not knowing the methodology of teaching.

The *jñānakāṇḍa* of the *Veda*-s deals with primarily meditations and Self-Knowledge. Technically, only the Self-Knowledge portion is called *Vedānta*.

Many of us take the short cut to this part of the Veda without going through *karmakāṇḍa*. The proper approach is for one to have observed *karmakāṇḍa* before entering the world of *jñānakāṇḍa*.

द्विविधं कर्मकाण्डं स्यान्निषेधविधिपूर्वकम् |
निषिद्धकर्मकरणे पापं भवति निश्चितम् |
विधिना कर्मकरणे पुण्यं भवति निश्चितम् || २१

dvividhaṃ karmakāṇḍaṃ syānniṣedhavidhipūrvakam |
niṣiddhakarmakaraṇe pāpaṃ bhavati niścitam |
vidhinā karmakaraṇe puṇyaṃ bhavati niścitam || 21

The two-fold Action section comprises prohibitions and injunctions. By doing what is prohibited, demerit (pāpaṃ) occurs. By doing what is sanctioned, merit (puṇyaṃ) takes place.

Karmakāṇḍa can also be divided in another way into two primary subjects – prohibitions (*niṣedha*) and injunctions (*vidhi*). It is knowing what you should do (*vidhi*) and should not do (*niṣedha*). *Vidhi* is based on *svadharma*. Doing *niṣedha karma* brings *pāpa*, and observation of *vidhi* gets you *puṇya*. *Śaṅkarācārya* states in his *Bhagavad Gītā Bhāṣya*[1] that *puṇya* leads to knowledge and memory retention. Therefore, if you want knowledge of the *śāstra* you must do your duties well. The greatest fruit of *puṇya* is knowledge (*vidyā*) and memory (*smṛti*). It is this memory that saves you from great perils. Discretion is unavailable by the loss of memory.[2] Memory is the seat of knowledge and hence, one needs to strengthen this with effort.

त्रिविधो विधिकूटः स्यान्नित्यनैमित्यकाम्यतः |
नित्येऽकृते किल्बिषं स्यात्काम्ये नैमित्तिके फलम् ||२२

trividho vidhikūṭaḥ syānnityanaimittyakāmyataḥ |
nitye'kṛte kilbiṣaṃ syātkāmye naimittike phalam ||22

The injunctions are threefold – obligatory (nitya), occasional (naimittika) and optional (kāmya). By the non-performance of nitya or daily rites demerit accrues. The observance of occasional and optional rites brings merits.

The injunctions can be divided into three – daily duties (*nitya*), occasional rituals (*naimittika*) and rituals for specific outcomes (*kāmya*). The non-performance of daily duties accrues *pāpa*, while the performance of occasional rituals and rituals for specific outcomes confers *puṇya*. By not doing daily rituals, obstacles will be created for the person. You may not

1 Bhagavad Gītā Bhāṣya 15.15

2 Bhagavad Gītā 2.63

know where problems in your life come from, and the simple solution to these problems is to observe the five daily duties, known as *pancamahāyajña*. By doing these five daily duties, you do not positively generate *puṇya* but it neutralises the *pāpa* that is accrued from the five accidental injuries (*pancasūnā*) and *pāpas* that are ready to unfold. All the *pāpa* and impurities (*mala*) that you brought from previous births can be neutralized by the performance of the *pancamahāyajña*.[3]

Not doing the daily rituals will not generate new *pāpa*. But rather it does not create a means to neutralize the *pāpa*-s ready to unfold. This omission of duties is called *pratyavāya doṣa*. Therefore, doing *nitya karma*-s cancels the *pāpa*-s of the past as that is its prime purpose.

If suppose not doing *nitya karma*-s will accrue *pāpa*, then those who are ignorant and non-Hindus will also incur *pāpa*. These people will incur *pāpa* because by orthodoxy they do not have access to the *Veda*-s. Hence, such a view is untenable and therefore the *Śiva Samhitā* addresses this point.

Śaṅkarācārya also confirms that the non-performance of *nitya karma* does not accrue fresh *pāpa*[4] but neutralises the past impurities and demerits. If I am facing a lot of obstacles and uncomfortable experiences in my life then doing *nitya karma*-s could be a possible solution. You would have seen your life change internally and externally, if you had constantly performed your *nitya karma*. You will also look at things differently; your worldview changes and your responses to experiences too would have changed. That is how *nitya karma* works. You are the testimony to that and you do not need the *śāstra* to prove that to you. Despite all the difficulties you may face in your life, you may still be able to sport a smile through it all. You can accept adversity with a little grace because you have *Īśvara*'s grace. We cannot dismiss the value of prayer and rituals.

Naimittika karma-s are rites of passage performed to invoke the grace of *Īśvara* at the different stages of an individual's physical and mental growth. It starts with *garbhādhāna* (ritual of impregnation) and ends with *antyeṣṭi* (the funeral rites). All of which generates *puṇya* for the individual.

Kāmya karma-s are optional rituals done for the fulfillment of specific desires such as the obtainment of a child, for getting rains or wealth etc. These *karma*-s also generate *puṇya*.

---

3 Manu Smṛti 3.67-71

4 see Taittiriya Upaniṣad bhāṣya intro, 1.11, Bhagavad Gītā bhāṣya 4.18, Chāndogya Upaniṣad bhāṣya 4.2.2

द्विविधम् तु फलं ज्ञेयं स्वर्गो नरक एव च |
स्वर्गो नानाविधश्चैव नरको'पि तथा भवेत् || २३

dvividham tu phalaṃ jñeyaṃ svargo naraka eva ca |
svargo nānāvidhaścaiva narako'pi tathā bhavet || 23

Be it known that fruits of action are twofold – heaven or hell. The heavens are of various kinds and hells are also diverse.

The fruits that we obtain from doing *karma*-s, other than *nitya karma* will transform into experience of heaven (*svarga*) or hell (*naraka*). *Puṇya* leads you to heaven and *pāpa* to hell. Heaven is a place where pleasures are experienced and hell is the opposite. There are *Purāna*-s that depict the details of these experiences. The *Garuḍa Purāṇa* has very vivid depictions of Hells.

पुण्यकर्मणि वै स्वर्गो नरकः पापकर्मणि |
कर्मबन्धमयी सृष्टिर्नान्यथा भवति ध्रुवम् ||२४

puṇyakarmaṇi vai svargo narakaḥ pāpakarmaṇi |
karmabandhamayī sṛṣṭirnānyathā bhavati dhruvam ||24

Heaven results from meritorious actions, hell from wrong actions. Indeed creation is full of binding actions and nothing else.

Three conclusions are made in this verse which are:

1. Heaven is attained by *puṇya*
2. Hell is attained by *pāpa*
3. *Karma* is a bondage because it binds you to either Heaven or Hell.

Hence, the whole creation can be divided into pleasant, unpleasant and indifferent experiences. The whole universe is a product of *karma* and it is in my hands to make it hell or heaven. By right actions I make my living a pleasant one and by wrong ones, sorrowful and painful. However, it should be noted that not all of us will consider *karm*a-s as bondage because some of us may prefer to go to heaven and *karma*-s are the means to it.

जन्तुभिश्चानुभूयन्ते स्वर्गे नानासुखानि च ।
नानाविधानि दुःखानि नरके दुःसहानि वै ॥ २५

jantubhiścānubhūyante svarge nānāsukhāni ca ।
nānāvidhāni duḥkhāni narake duḥsahāni vai ॥ 25

Creatures enjoy many pleasures of various kinds in heaven; many intolerable pains are suffered in hell.

In heaven there are many types of enjoyments. What you call hell or heaven is nothing but experiences. Two people can be in the same place but one can be miserable and the other happy. Suppose I go to heaven after death and I see two of my friends Mohan and Ravi also there. But I am happy to see Mohan because he got me a job in my early years. Ravi on the other hand is unhappy to see Mohan because he fired Ravi and gave his job to me. Such is the nature of happiness and sorrow in the subtle worlds.

पापकर्मवशादुखं पुण्यकर्मवशात्सुखम् |
तस्मात् सुखार्थी विविधं पुण्यं प्रकुरुते ध्रुवम् || २६

pāpakarmavaśāddukhaṃ puṇyakarmavaśātsukham |
tasmāt sukhārthī vividhaṃ puṇyaṃ prakurute dhruvam || 26

Through the power of wrong actions there is sorrow; through the power of meritorious actions happiness. Therefore, one who desires happiness must perform meritorious actions.

Every man is a pursuer of happiness (*sukhārthi*) and not a pursuer of sorrow (*dukhārthi*). It is a hint that there is something inside me, regardless of who I am, that likes and seeks only happiness. For that happiness alone I value *puṇya*. Do we choose to pursue happiness or are we programmed to pursue happiness? We naturally seek happiness, and do not like anything that opposes it. This is a very good point the *Śiva Samhitā* makes and we need to recognise it. And also, it is good to know that one arrives at Self-Knowledge through right action viz *puṇya* alone not *pāpa*.

पापभोगावसाने तु पुनर्जन्म भवेत्खलु ।
पुण्यभोगावसानेऽपि नान्यथा भवति ध्रुवम् ॥ २७

pāpabhogāvasāne tu punarjanma bhavetkhalu ।
puṇyabhogāvasāne'pi nānyathā bhavati dhruvam ॥ 27

When the sufferings for wrong actions are over, one is born again; when the rewards of right action are exhausted, the very same thing is sure to happen.

Both *pāpa* and *puṇya* get exhausted in hell or heaven. Once this is exhausted, a person is back to square one, which is another birth. Even if you take any role, it will have a beginning and an end. Similarly, *pāpa* also gets exhausted. If *pāpa* is likened to be thorns, then *puṇya* is only a crown of thorns as stated previously. Both *pāpa* and *puṇya* bind by creating more births, and hence they are not that different from each other.

स्वर्गेऽपिदुःखसंभोगःपरश्रीदर्शनादिषु ।
ततोदुःखमिदंसर्वंभवेन्नास्त्यत्रसंशयः ।२८

svarge'pi duḥkhasaṃbhogaḥ paraśrīdarśanādiṣu |
tato duḥkhamidaṃ sarvaṃ bhavennāstyatra saṃśayaḥ || 28

Even in heaven one experiences pain by seeing the higher enjoyment of others, so everything in life is sorrowful. There is no doubt about this.

Even in heaven there is pain because you could see others enjoying greater happiness than you. Your worst enemy could also be in heaven massaging Lord *Śiva*'s legs while you are 200 metres away and unable to even see the Lord's crown. Even in heaven there is gradation and as a result, unhappiness. So why seek it? Is heaven worth seeking? Yes, it is worth seeking if you know there is nothing greater than heaven. If you knew there is something greater than heaven, then heaven becomes miserable. Even in hell you can be happy because there could be others who could be suffering more than you. Happiness is relative. That is why the *Śiva Samhitā* states "*tato duḥkhamidaṃ sarvaṃ*" like what the Buddha proclaimed as the first noble truth. Everything is suffering because nothing can satisfy you always. This feeling is called dispassion or *vairāgya*. But do not impose this feeling of yours on the rest of the population, because the common man will not feel the same way as you do.

The first noble truth of Buddhism about the world being sorrowful (*sabbe sankhāra dukkha)*[5] is consistent with *Vedānta*. In contrast, the *Upaniṣad* states an additional statement that views the universe as *Brahman* (*sarvam khalvidam brahma*)[6]. One of the reasons for Buddhism to have taken a path of its own was the non-reliance on the *śabda pramāṇa* and instead it solely relied on perception and inference. What the senses perceived were taken to be valid, and what they inferred from what was perceived as the truth. They created great logicians as a result but that also ended up creating many different schools of Buddhism with varied perceptions of the four noble truths, all within the first thousand years of Buddha's death.

In the game of logic, he who debates the best wins, and not necessarily he who knows. That is why in *Sanātana Dharma* mindless debates are not encouraged. A point which is a fact, an evident truth, cannot be debated. Can you debate about gravity? You cannot because it is evident. Only a truth that is not evident can be debated. In *Sanātana Dharma* we have dialogues (*samvāda*) but not the kind of debate seen in academic circles. *Samvāda* is conducted for the sole purpose of ascertainment of truth (*tattva nirṇayam*).

5 this is in pāli

6 Chāndogya Upaniṣad 3.14.1

तत्कर्मकल्पकैः प्रोक्तं पुण्यं पापमिति द्विधा|
पुण्यपापमयो बन्धो देहिनां भवति ध्रुवम् || २९

tatkarmakalpakaiḥ proktaṃ puṇyaṃ pāpamiti dvidhā|
puṇyapāpamayo bandho dehināṃ bhavati dhruvam || 29

Teachers have divided karma into two parts; meritorious (puṇyaṃ) and demeritorious (pāpam) actions. As a result of karma, embodied selves are bound by the chain of right and wrong deeds.

This verse summarizes what we have already discussed. The experiences of *pāpa* and *puṇya* are successive products of one's *karma*. That is why, you can be happy now and after five minutes, may not be so and so on. The actions that are fated will unfold in succession and cannot be stopped. One has no choice but to experience them. If one happens to be a *mumukṣu*, one should not even entertain the notion that one can escape it. The only thing one can do is to tolerate or endure it and focus on the five daily duties and meditation. The only valid 'escape' is through *jñāna* and not *karma*.

10

RENUNCIATION: SANNYĀSĀ

इहामुत्र फलद्वेषी सफलं कर्म सन्त्यजेत् |
नित्यनैमित्तिकं सङ्गं त्यक्त्वा योगे प्रवर्तते ||३०

ihāmutra phaladveṣī saphalaṃ karma santyajet |
nityanaimittikaṃ saṅgaṃ tyaktvā yoge pravartate ||30

Those who are not desirous of enjoying the fruits of their actions in this or next world, should renounce all reward oriented actions. Having similarly discarded the attachment for the obligatory and occasional acts one should employ oneself in the practice of Yoga.

The *Śiva Samhitā* ends the subject on *karma* with another wake up call. The very things that have been taught earlier are to be now renounced, and one must now embark on *Yogaśāstra*. It means that you renounce all the things that bind you and take *sannyāsā* (renunciation). If you cannot take up *sannyāsā* then one is encouraged to take to internal *sannyāsā* (*antaraṅga sannyāsā*).

In the mode of internal *sannyāsā*, you renounce by accepting whatever accrues as a result of your actions (*prasāda*). One should renounce the fruits which will accrue here and hereafter. For some it is easier to renounce what is here but not hereafter. Such people will kill themselves and others to enjoy in heaven. Although it does not make sense, people believe in it because they have been indoctrinated. You can be indoctrinated too, to such an extent that you lose all sanity.

Your goal is to know that by which you know everything. You can either take *sannyāsā* or if you have binding reasons you can stay where you are, do your duties and renounce the fruits. A *Karma Yogi* is one who has taken internal *sannyāsā*. The text *Jīvanmuktiviveka* allows for such an alternative to *sannyāsā* if you are unable to take it due to binding duties:

brahmacārigṛhasthavānaprasthānāṃ,
kenacin nimittena sannyāsāśramasvīkāre pratibaddhe sati,
svāśramadharmeṣv anuṣṭhīyamāneṣv api Vedanārtho mānasaḥ
karmādityago na virudhyate, śrutismṛtīihāsapurāṇeṣu loke
ca tādṛśāṃ, tattvavidāṃ, bahūnām upalambhāt

When, for whatever reason, *Vedic* students, householders, and forest-dwellers are prevented from entering *sannyāsā*, there is nothing to prevent the mental renunciation of rites and the like for the purpose of knowledge, even while they remain performing the duties of their own order, because we see many such knowers of truth in the *śruti*-s, *smrti*-s, *itihāsa*-s, and *purāna*-s.[1]

कर्मकाण्डस्य माहात्म्यं ज्ञात्वा योगी त्यजेत्सुधीः |
पुण्यपापद्वयं त्यक्त्वा ज्ञानकाण्डे प्रवर्तते ||३१

karmakāṇḍasya māhātmyaṃ jñātvā yogī tyajetsudhīḥ |
puṇyapāpadvayaṃ tyaktvā jñānakāṇḍe pravartate ||31

The wise yogi, having examined the truth of karmakāṇḍa (action), should renounce them; and having left both puṇya and pāpa, he must engage in jñānakāṇḍa (knowledge).

This is the final statement on *karmakāṇḍa* before paving way for *jñānakāṇḍa*. The *Śiva Samhitā* sarcastically states that after knowing the greatness of *karmakāṇḍa*, its greatness is that it is not that great after all. Therefore, one should renounce it. A similar mantra appears in the *Upaniṣad*,

parīkṣya lokānkarmacitānbrāhmaṇo
nirvedamāyānnāstyakṛtaḥ kṛtena

Having scrutinised the worlds won by works,
let a *brāhmaṇa* arrive at non-attachment. The (world)
that is not made is not (won) by what is done.[2]

Traditionally, you renounce it by taking *sannyāsā* through which you renounce both action and results, which is exactly the purport of the *Śiva Samhitā* verse. But this is not possible for someone who is not ready for *sannyāsā*. For such a person, the *Bhagavad Gītā* recommends that he or she renounces the results of one's actions which are *puṇya* and *pāpa*. How does one do that? This is done by observing *Karma Yoga*, viz *prasāda buddhi* or accepting any result that accrues from an action as a gift from *Īśvara*. Here are two verses from the *Bhagavad Gītā* which explain such an attitude.

yogasthaḥ kuru karmāṇi saṅgaṃ tyaktvā dhanañjaya
siddhyasiddhyoḥ samo bhūtvā samatvaṃ yoga ucyate

O *Dhananjaya*! Established in the *Yoga*, perform actions, abandoning attachment, remaining even-minded in success and

1 Jīvanmuktiviveka 1.1.14
2 Muṇḍaka Upaniṣad 1.2.12

failure; for, the even-mindedness is said to be the *Yoga*.[3]

buddhiyukto jahātīha ubhe sukṛtaduṣkṛte
tasmādyogāya yujyasva yogaḥ karmasu kauśalam
karmajaṃ buddhiyuktā hi phalaṃ tyaktvā manīṣiṇaḥ
janmabandhavinirmuktāḥ padaṃ gacchantyanāmayam

Whosoever is endowed with determining faculty, he casts off both of these viz., the good action and the bad action. Therefore strive for *Yoga*; *Yoga* is discretion in action. By renouncing the fruit, born of action, the intelligent ones endowed with determining faculty and freed from the bond of birth, go to the place that is devoid of illness.[4]

Renouncing action is easy, but renouncing *puṇya* and *pāpa* is not. Even a *jñāni* must face the fruits of action in the form of *prārabdha karma*. *Prārabdha* is the portion of the past *karma* which is responsible for the present body. Having accepted the laws of actions and fruits, you should endure them by accepting them gracefully. The moment you stop fighting, mitigating or opposing what comes, it is as good as renouncing.

However, renunciation should not be without a purpose. If you renounce without a purpose, you are not an *āstika* or *vaidika*. One should sacrifice actions for the sake of Self-Knowledge. There is only one purpose for which you renounce actions, which is for *ātmajñāna*. The *jñānakāṇḍa* used in this verse is the same as *Jñāna Yoga*. I can renounce *karmakāṇḍa* for *jñānakāṇḍa* alone and this is what is meant by renouncing with a purpose.

However, a *brahmacāri*, *gṛhasthā* or a *vānaprasthin* can renounce as an *antaranga sannyāsin* as mentioned earlier with the support from *Jīvanmuktiviveka*. He is also none other than a *Karma Yogi*. The *Karma Yogi* does not renounce actions, but only the results of action. He will accept results as they come gracefully. In our case, we can interpret this verse to be referring to both *sannyāsā* and *Karma Yoga*.

Renunciation of action is only for the *sannyāsin*. I want to emphasise this or else you may think you can renounce action. However, doing action is important for a *Karma Yogi*. And he is no smaller than a *sannyāsin*. *Kṛṣṇa* states in the *Bhagavad Gītā*:

sannyāsaḥ karma yogaśca niḥśreyasakarāvubhau ।
tayostu karmasaṃnyāsātkarmayogo viśiṣyate ||

3 Bhagavad Gītā 2.48

4 Bhagavad Gītā 2.50-51

> Both renunciation and the *Karma Yoga* effect *mokṣa*. But, of these two, *Karma Yoga* is better than renunciation of action.[5]

However, one should not downplay the role of *sannyāsā* in the pursuit of Self-Knowledge. It is this mode of *sannyāsā* that is ideal for *Jñāna Yoga* due to its conducive lifestyle. Only a *sannyasin* can dedicate his life to *Jñāna Yoga* with total renunciation of *karma*-s and its results. The qualification of *uparati* indeed refers to this mode of *sannyāsā*. It is also worth to note that the teaching tradition of *Vedānta* has been kept alive over hundreds of years by the *sannyasin*-s alone, with the sole exception of a few teachers who were non-*sannyasin*-s. Most of the *Vedānta* literature were also authored by the *sannyasin*-s.

With this understanding, let us enter the subject of *jñānakāṇḍa*. From verse 33 onwards, a great number of verses will describe the nature of the *ātman*, which is the main subject of *Śiva Samhitā*.

5 Bhagavad Gītā 5.2

11

KNOWLEDGE OF THE SELF: ĀTMAJÑĀNA

आत्मा वा'रे तु द्रष्टव्यः श्रोतव्येत्यादि यच्छ्रुतिः |
सा सेव्या तु प्रयत्नेन मुक्तिदा हेतुदायिनी ||३२

ātmā vā're tu draṣṭavyaḥ śrotavyetyādi yacchrutiḥ |
sā sevyā tu prayatnena muktidā hetudāyinī || 32

The Vedic mantra that "the self is to be seen and heard etc" is liberating; serving the cause, it alone should be perused consistently with all effort.

The *Śiva Samhitā* quotes the *śruti*, the revealed scripture, for the first time by stating the following - *ātman vā'retu draṣṭavyaḥ śrotavyetyādi* i.e one should hear about the *ātman*, analyse it and abide in it. The word *śruti* refers to the *Veda* and its constituents. This statement is almost the same as a *mantra* from the *Upaniṣad*,

ātmā vā are draṣṭavyaḥ śrotavyaḥ mantavyaḥ nididhyāsitavyaḥ

The *ātman*, should be realised – should be heard of, reflected on and meditated upon.[1]

Why is the verse quoting the *śruti*, especially since all this while it did not quote any other scripture? What is the value of *śruti* in the context of *ātmajñāna* or Self-Knowledge? To understand that, we should discuss the topic called *pramāṇa* or the 'valid means of knowledge'.

In the *Vedānta* tradition, there are a total of six *pramāṇa*-s.[2] But the six can be broadly classified into three, which are – perception (*pratyakṣa*), inference (*anumāna*) and revelation (*śabda*). Perception is a means of knowing things that you can perceive through the sense organs. It refers to all that can be seen, felt, heard etc.

The second means of knowledge is inference. Inference depends on perception for its function, for example – when we see smoke on the mountain, we can infer there is a heat source or fire. In this illustration, the smoke was perceived while the fire as the cause was inferred.

For most of us perception and inference are something already known to

1 Bṛhadāraṇyaka Upaniṣad 2.4.5

2 a complete exposition of the six pramāṇa-s can be found in the text Vedānta Paribhāṣā by Dharmarāja Adhvarīndra

us. In fact we live our lives using these two *pramāṇa*-s daily.

What then is the value of the third *pramāṇa* which is *śabda*? Here the word *śabda* refers to the *Veda*. *Śabda* is a body of literature which has great value because it reveals what perception and inference cannot reveal. For example, when you read about a conflict between North Korea and South Korea in the newspaper – this information is not available for perception or inference. It comes to you from the newspaper and reveals something that is outside my perception and inference. Without it, I would not come to know about the conflict. Hence the newspaper becomes a valid means of knowledge or *pramāṇa* to know about something beyond the range of my perception and inference.

In metaphysics, we talk about realities which exist but can never be known through perception and inference. However, these realities can be known only through *śabda*. Without the *śabda* or *śruti* I will never come to know that '*ātmā vā are draṣṭavyaḥ śrotavyaḥ mantavyaḥ nididhyāsitavyaḥ*'.

Therefore, of the three *pramāṇas*, the *śruti pramāṇa* or *śabda pramāṇa* is the only means to know the *ātman*. I have no other option available and hence would have to depend upon this body of knowledge to know the Self. The *Veda*, along with its other texts written by human beings (*smṛti*) help us gain this Self-Knowledge. That is why scriptural knowledge is indispensable. The *śruti* reveals realities such as God, *dharma*, *karmaphala*, *punarjanma*, *mokṣa*, *puruṣārtha*, *svarga-naraka*, *ātman*, etc.

Without these revelations, I can never come to know about these realities. Even if Einstein were to state that there is God, it is only speculation as far as it goes.

Is the revelation then a belief system? Not entirely. A revelation to be valid, it must be in line with logic and experience, and should not oppose them. For example, I can accept the existence of heaven because that will not contradict my experience. And neither can you prove nor disprove the existence of heaven. But suppose someone states that there is an eternal heaven then it cannot be accepted, because we all know that any place subject to creation must undergo destruction too. The *Śiva Samhitā* had earlier explained the limitations of heaven.

Within the domain of what the *śāstra* reveals, there are some things that can be proven and some which cannot be proven. For example, heaven cannot be proven but its knowledge can improve the way some people live their lives. Some of the things mentioned by the *śāstra* we take with faith and whatever you take with faith you cannot immediately prove them. These teachings are called indirect knowledge (*parokṣa jñāna*). This is the first of the two types of teachings of the *śāstra*.

The second type are teachings that can be experienced and proven immediately. These are called direct knowledge (*aparokṣa jñāna*). *Mokṣa*, *ātman* and *Brahman* fall within this category. Of course, it also depends upon what kind of god you believe in! *Mokṣa* comes under the category of direct knowledge. You can get to realise the knowledge and prove the words of the *śāstra*-s instantaneously if your mind is prepared. I know "I exist" but I need the *śāstra* to help me know my true nature, like a mirror that allows you to see your own eyes. The eyes do not have the ability to see itself without the help of a mirror. Similarly, the *śāstra*-s help us to 'see' our true nature clearly. Therefore, it is a *pramāṇa* for Self-Knowledge.

The *Śiva Samhitā* is using the *śruti* to reveal the *ātman*. Now, we come to the next question. How does one come to know this *ātman*? What is the process? The *Bṛhadāraṇyaka Upaniṣad* uses four words to explain the process. They are:

Drṣṭavyaḥ – The *ātman* is to be seen and here the word 'seen' means seeing through the eyes of knowledge and not literal seeing. The three steps to see the *ātman* are:

1. *śrotavyaḥ* which is the same as *śravaṇam* and it means listening to the words of the *śruti* through a qualified teacher;
2. *mantavyaḥ* or *mananam*, which means analysis on the Self-Knowledge, obtained from *śravaṇam* to remove doubts; and
3. *nididhyāsitavyaḥ* or *nididhyāsanam* which means to abide in the knowledge of Self.

Ātman cannot be known without a *pramāṇa* and among the three steps, *śravaṇam* is crucial. This first step is the listening to the teaching of *śruti*. There is no other way, except to listen to the words of the *śāstra* from a living *guru*. You do not listen to some audio player. It is through the words of the teacher that you gain the knowledge of something that you previously did not know. Sometimes we may have the same knowledge in books but there may not be a tradition to teach it, to refine it and make it into a pedagogy. I have heard people of other faiths quoting a few random verses on non-duality from scriptures, but what they lack is a 'tradition' to teach this effectively. In contrast, a Hindu in a remote village in India would not be surprised if you were to tell him that he is god. This is because in the tradition of *Sanātana Dharma* the fact that god is within me is accepted as common knowledge. Hence this method of Self-Knowledge has evolved through an unbroken tradition over more than two thousand years to very sophisticated levels. Hence, the traditional methodology is very robust and effective.

After gaining the knowledge, you must analyse or do *mananam* to remove the doubts (*samśaya*). This can be done either with the aid of a teacher or unaided. Between the two, the aided approach is a safer one. This analysis may also take place while doing the *śravaṇam*. Most *Vedānta* texts will usually present the analyses in anticipation of the doubts.

Having removed the doubts, you must now remove all the opposing or contrary tendencies (*viparīta bhāvanā*). What are these opposing tendencies? For example, the *śāstra* has told you that you are *Brahman*. You disbelieved initially but are convinced after some time as you kept listening to the teachings. However, still some opposing thoughts will come to you from time to time. These contrary thoughts and tendencies are neutralised in *nididhyāsanam*. This can be done aided or unaided. Most of the time *nididhyāsanam* is done unaided. After conceptually understanding *ātman*, you have to now see 'it' as your very 'Being' in that internal space of the mind which no one can do for you. Yes, sometimes the *guru* can help, but you have to do it yourself. These three steps are usually successive but not always. Sometimes they can take place simultaneously.

Although there are three steps, one is primary and the other two are secondary. *Śravaṇam* or listening is primary (*aṅgi*) while *mananam* and *nididhyāsanam* are secondary (*aṅga*-s). It is only upon listening can you do *mananam* and *nididhyāsanam*. Both *mananam* and *nididhyāsanam* depend on *Śravaṇam*. *Śravaṇam* is the one that does the job – or rather, the knowledge gained in it does it. No amount of independent religious practices or *sādhanas* can help a seeker (*sādhaka*) in this pursuit except that of knowledge viz *śravaṇam*, *mananam* and *nididhyāsanam* .

As a *sādhaka* it is good for you to know this. Some people argue that the means of knowledge is also impermanent so why give it so much importance. It is a good argument but *śāstra* is needed because that alone does the job, like the ladder which helps you up to the next level of a platform. And after one reaches the next level with the help of the ladder, you discard the ladder. After it has fulfilled its purpose, the ladder is not needed. After the knowledge becomes established, the three steps, the *śāstra* and the knowledge all become useless. But until you achieve it, they are essential, for without them you cannot achieve any progress in Self-Knowledge.

The first part of this verse shows us that the *pramāṇa*, without which we cannot understand the *ātman*, comes from the *śruti*. *Īśvara* is the revealer of the *śruti*. So, this is *Īśvara*'s knowledge about *Īśvara* himself.

Sā sevyā means worship and this act of worship is nothing but the process of *śravaṇam*, *mananam* and *nididhyāsanam*. This worship means that you do nothing else but this *śravaṇam*, *mananam* and *nididhyāsanam*. You must look upon it as something you cannot dispense with because there are no other means to attain this Self-Knowledge. Without the *śāstra*, there is no way to know yourself. A similar point is made in the *Brahma Sūtra*[3] that the *śāstra* is the source of this knowledge.

The whole teaching of *Vedānta* rests on *Bhagavad Gītā* (representing *smṛti*), *Upaniṣad* (representing *śruti*) and *Brahma Sūtra* (representing logic or *nyāya*), which are collectively called the *prasthāna traya*. *Brahma Sūtra* adopts the logical approach in establishing the knowledge of the *śruti* and the *smṛti*. Without *śāstra*, there cannot be this Self-Knowledge and without it, you will be eternally lost. If you do not understand this point properly you will look for perceptual truth or inferential truth. You will go to various *sampradāya*-s and *guru*-s, hoping someone will show you the truth. You might also look for a teacher who will show you the truth via the experiential way, for example, *samādhi*, or some 'void' experience. That is why this verse is very important. The *śravaṇam*, *mananam* and *nididhyāsanam* cannot be employed without the knowledge of the *śāstra*.

Śravaṇam cannot be done on your own but only through listening to a teacher. There could be a few rare exceptions like *Ramaṇa Mahāṛṣi*, although the matter is debatable. The tradition states that this learning cannot be accomplished on your own. *Śaṅkarācārya* affirms this point in many of his commentaries. This is because our mind sees what it likes to see, and that too based on its likes and dislikes. Our likes and dislikes become obstacles because knowledge and truth are quite independent of our likes and dislikes

There is a specific episode in the *Upaniṣad*[4] where *Indra* and *Virocana* approach *Brahmā* to know the Self. *Brahmā* initially describes the Self inaccurately to test their ability to discriminate. This is an authentic

3 Brahma Sūtra1.1.3 (śāstra yonitvāt)

4 see Chāndogya Upaniṣad 8.7.1 to 8.12.6

method of teaching where sometimes a teacher will teach you a wrong idea or a lower truth, to test you and to make you work harder. The purpose is primarily to test the capabilities of the student before instructing.

The *śravaṇam* takes place aided and not unaided. That is why it is stated here as *śravaṇam* and not self-study (*svādhyāya*). The teaching takes place in the form of a dialogue. The teacher wields the knowledge of the *Upaniṣad*-s for the *śravaṇam* to take place. *Śravaṇam* is done on what the teacher is sharing. You take that back and do *mananam* and *nididhyāsanam*. It is also possible that the teacher aids the *mananam* and *nididhyāsanam* during the *śravaṇam*.

Now the qualifications of the teacher should also be discussed and this comes from the *Muṇḍaka Upaniṣad*,

tadvijñānārthaṃ sa gurumevābhigacchet
samitpāṇiḥ śrotriyaṃ brahmaniṣṭham

For knowing that Reality he should go, with sacrificial faggots in hand, only to a teacher who is a *śrotriya* and *brahmaniṣṭha*.[5]

The first qualification needed is that the teacher should be a *śrotriya* and a *brahmaniṣṭha*. A *śrotriya* is someone who knows the *śruti* and the *smṛti*, and this also implies that he knows the teaching methodology of *Vedānta*.

The teacher should also know the intention (*tātparya*) of the scripture. If he does not know it, then he will interpret it in any way that he likes. Without knowing the intention of the scripture, one will not know how to prioritise the themes of *bhakti*, meditation (*dhyāna*) and *jñāna* in texts that one may encounter. You may end up choosing that which appeals to you. Fortunately, or unfortunately, the way to ascertain the intention of a given text is found only in the teaching tradition or *sampradāya* of *Vedānta*. Hence it is important that a teacher come from a proper *sampradāya*.

The teacher must know the traditional methodology of teaching. He must know how to use the words of the scriptures. It is a skill that one has to learn for another *śrotriya*. If you do not know how to use the words, you can confuse, delude and mislead the seekers.

The next qualification of the teacher is that he must be a *brahmaniṣṭha*. There are two meanings to this word. The first meaning is a liberated person (*mukta*). The second meaning is a person committed to *Brahman*. *Niśtha* literally means 'commitment'. The person who fits the second meaning is a

5 Mundaka Upanisad 1.2.12

unique person. He is a person who is convinced that the 'Self is *Brahman*' but is yet to assimilate it. Such a person is perhaps someone who has done *śravaṇam* and *mananam* but *nididhyāsanam* is something in progress. Hence, he has not seen himself as *Brahman*.

Ideally a *brahmaniṣṭha* is a *mukta* but the second category of teachers also exist and can be accepted as a traditional teacher. Therefore, the teacher who teaches must be a *śrotriya* and a *brahmaniṣṭha*.

To know whether a teacher is a *brahmaniṣṭha* is very difficult because it takes one to know another. Hence one should not bother as much with this qualification when you meet a teacher. The knowledge of the Self being *Brahman* is subjective and private to the *mukta*. Knowledge of the Self is like a dream that is private to you alone. You will not succeed in adequately describing the dream to me because it is your private vision. A *mukta*'s understanding of the Self being *Brahman* is like that and it cannot be explained or proven to another person easily. Furthermore, there is no reason for a *mukta* to prove that he is one. What is he going to profit by proving this? The only way to know a *brahmaniṣṭha* is to become one.

Based on the above qualifications, there are three types of teachers. The first is a *śrotriya*; the second is a *brahmaniṣṭha* and the third is a *śrotriya* and *brahmaniṣṭha*. Among them, the third type is the best. Next comes the *śrotriya* and finally the *brahmaniṣṭha*. The *śrotriya* is more important for the role of a teacher than a *brahmaniṣṭha* because he is better versed in the traditional methodology of teaching and less likely to confuse the students. Unlike a *brahmaniṣṭha* who is not a *śrotriya*, where confusion can still take place if he were to teach due to the lack of the exposure to the traditional methodology. Being a *mukta* he knows the *ātman*, but may not be able to make you see it if he does not know the methodology. If you do not know of these required qualifications of a teacher, you may end up with unqualified teachers who may mislead you in the pursuit of Self-Knowledge. As the *Upaniṣad* states,

> *avidyāyāmantare vartamānāḥ svayaṃ dhīrāḥ paṇḍitaṃmanyamānāḥ*
> *dandramyamāṇāḥ pariyanti mūḍhā andhenaiva nīyamānā yathāndhāḥ*

> People who are sunk in ignorance, considering themselves wise and learned, are like blind men led by one who is blind himself. They run like fools treading crooked paths.[6]

6 Kaṭha Upaniṣad 1.2.5

12

QUALIFICATIONS OF A SEEKER: SĀDHANA CATUṢṬAYAM

Having covered the qualification of a teacher, it is also important to examine the competence or qualifications of the seeker.

Traditionally, there are four qualifications required for a seeker and these are called *sādhana catuṣṭayam*[1]. These can be found in most *Vedānta* texts, especially in the foundational manuals (*prakaraṇa grantha*). The four-fold qualifications are:

1. viveka
2. vairāgya
3. ṣaṭka sampatti
   a. śama
   b. dama
   c. uparati
   d. titikṣā
   e. śraddhā
   f. samādhāna
4. mumukṣutvam

Viveka is the ability to discriminate between the real and the unreal (*nitya anitya vastu vivekam*). This prerequisite qualification does mean that you possess the knowledge of the *ātman*, but rather the ability to discriminate. It means that your mind should be sharp enough to do discriminative enquiry. Anything that is taught gets assimilated immediately when a person has *viveka*.

Vairāgya is the lack of attachment for pleasures in this world or the hereafter. Here one is dispassionate towards securities and pleasures, because these are not the prime interests of one's life. You can either not want it completely or you can live through them in an 'as though' manner. If you really did not want it, you would have taken up *sannyāsā*. Another option is to have an objective attitude towards experiences by letting it be without you being overwhelmed by it. This attitude is an objective appreciation of securities and pleasure. You can also have a third attitude of fleeting dispassion. *Swāmi*

1 refer to Tattva Bodha by Śaṅkarācārya

Śivānanda uses the examples of dispassion born during the occurrence of death (*smaśāna vairāgyam*) or dispassion at the time of childbirth (*prasava vairāgyam*)[2]. Fleeting dispassion means a person's *vairāgya* is weak as it is influenced by situations. When we see a close person dead, we tend to lose interest in life and so does a mother during childbirth where the pain is unbearable and she promises to herself that she is not going to have another child. But when the event is over, we may resume to our usual ways. Each one of us has dispassion with respect to something that we have outgrown too like toys, games, movies, sports etc.

ṣaṭka sampatti or six-fold accomplishments are:

I. *śama* means mastery of the mind, which refers the mind being at your disposal and having the ability to say "yes" or "no" to what the mind suggests. *Śama* is not the 'control' of your mind but 'mastery'. Controlling your mind does more harm than good.

II. *dama* is the mastery over sense organs. When objects come into contact with your sense organs, desires or suggestions may emerge. For example, while being at home you may not be attracted to a candy but when you see it in front of you at shop maybe, it may create a desire to eat it. That is the difference between *śama* and *dama*. While in *śama*, the objects are not in contact with the senses but in *dama* the objects are in contact with one or more of your sense organs (sight, taste, smell, touch and sound). So, sitting here I may have *śama* towards a candy, but when it is within sight, it may not be so. Hence I need to exercise *dama*.

III. *uparati* is having completed one's duties or being ready for *sannyāsā*.

IV. *titikṣā* is endurance or forbearance. Here, one is able to endure extremes of cold/heat and pleasure/pain etc.

V. *śraddhā* is having the faith in the teacher and the scripture "*guru vedānta vākyādiṣu viśvāsaḥ śraddhā* ".[3] When what you want is not attained yet, you need to have faith until you attain it. You need lots of faith to trust what the teacher and the scriptures say. Especially so when others have attained *mokṣa*, so can you but faith is needed.

VI. *samādhāna* is having a one-pointed mind. One should be able to be focused on the goal or focus on the teaching without getting distracted. This is a one-pointed mind which can be gained

2 in the book Jnana Yoga by Swami Sivananda

3 definition from Tattva Bodha

through meditation.

Mumukṣutvam is the desire for *mokṣa*. This qualification is unique as the intensity of it is enough for all other qualifications discussed above to mature. Even if you do not have *viveka*, *vairāgyam* or *ṣaṭka sampatti*, the knowledge may work if you had *mumukṣutvam*. *Mumukṣutvam* is sometimes seen as the work of *Īśvara praṇidhāna*, or faith in or surrender to *Īśvara*. *Īśvara praṇidhāna* is referred to in the *Yoga Sūtra*.[4] You may not have other qualifications but if you have the desire for *mokṣa* knowing that *Īśvara* is the supreme reality then the other qualifications will automatically manifest in you.

Even if you do not have any qualification, you should at least pray fervently. If you were to pray sincerely, all these qualifications will come to you as a natural result. You need not even compare yourself with another person, which is the biggest problem in the pursuit of this knowledge. When you have that kind of trust on *Īśvara*, there is no need for comparison.

When you possess the four-fold qualifications, you become eligible to receive this knowledge or if you have *mumukṣutvam* alone, you are also eligible to receive it. If a person has all the four-fold qualifications in full measure, he is called an *uttama adhikāri* or the best qualified. For that person *śravaṇam* alone is enough.[5] There is no need for *mananam* and *nididhyāsanam*.

This *Śiva Samhitā* verse shows that what makes *mokṣa* possible is not your *sādhana* but knowledge itself. The primary means to it is listening to the knowledge of Self from a qualified teacher. When there are no obstacles, the knowledge works immediately. But if a person has half the measure of all these qualifications, then *śravaṇam* alone is insufficient. What he needs to do then is to work on the obstacles. The mind is like a mirror. If the mirror is dusty, it is not the fault of the light that it does not get reflected. The *papa*-s are like the dust on the mirror. You must continue to observe the *nitya karma*-s and meditation (*upasanā*) with the attitudes of *Karma Yoga* alongside *śravaṇam*, *mananam* and *nididhyāsanam*.

4 Yoga Sūtra 1.23

5 Chāndogya Upaniṣad Bhāṣya 8.9.3

13

EVERYTHING HAPPENS IN THE SELF

The text started with a grand declaration of what the Self is. It then presented the different erroneous doctrines that people teach and refuted them all. It presented *karma* and its futility in the pursuit of Self-Knowledge. It then presented *jñāna*, the knowledge of the *Upaniṣad*-s, which is the right means to know the Self. It also quoted an important *mantra* from the *Upaniṣad* which revealed the process of the primary *sādhana* for *mokṣa*. That primary *sādhana* is *śravaṇam, mananam* and *nididhyāsanam*. It is also implied that knowledge can be gained only through *śabda pramāṇa*.

Having quoted the line from the *Upaniṣad*, the text plunges straight into the subject matter of *ātmajñāna*.

दुरितेषु च पुण्येषु यो धीवृत्तिं प्रचोदयात् |
सोऽहं प्रवर्तते मत्तो जगत्सर्वं चराचरम् || ३३
सर्वं च दृश्यते मत्तः सर्वं च मयि लीयते |
न तद्भिन्नोऽहमस्मीह मद्भिन्नो न तु किञ्चन || ३४

duriteṣu ca puṇyeṣu yo dhīvṛttiṃ pracodayāt |
so'haṃ pravartate matto jagatsarvaṃ carācaram || 33
sarvaṃ ca dṛśyate mattaḥ sarvaṃ ca mayi līyate |
na tadbhinno'hamasmīha madbhinno na tu kiñcana || 34

I am that which prompts the mental functions into the paths of merit or demerit. This universe, moveable and immoveable, is from me; all things are preserved by me; all are absorbed into me; here in this universe, I am not different from it and nothing is different from me.

There are two *vāda*-s or positions in the *Vedāntic* tradition – *dṛṣṭi sṛṣṭi vāda and sṛṣṭi dṛṣṭi vāda*. The position of this verse is the *dṛṣṭi sṛṣṭi vāda*. It states that I, the Self, is the Consciousness that prompts the mental functions of merit and demerit. All the *puṇya* and *pāpa* that are being created in my life are because of me. All the movable and immovable things in the universe are also because of me. I am the creator of the universe; the universe is preserved by me and all things are resolved into me. I am the creator, preserver and the destroyer. Nothing exists but 'I', the Self or Brahman.

The gist of the verse is that there is nothing but 'I' or *ātman*. I am the source in which *puṇya* and *pāpa* rise. All transactions in the world are based on *karma* alone. When I interact with the world I have only two goals – wanting *puṇya* and avoiding *pāpa*. Unknowingly I may acquire *pāpa* but knowingly I desire to acquire only *puṇya*. All my interactions with the world are taking place in the form of *vṛtti*-s or thoughts.

Vṛtti-s take place because there is a substratum, and that substratum is *ātman*. For example, for waves to rise and fall there must be water. All thoughts depend upon the reality that is *ātman*. So, whenever my mind functions it is the *ātman* that lends its reality. It is the *ātman* that makes the experience of *pāpa* and *puṇya* possible, and whenever I avoid *pāpa* and experience only *puṇya* it is also dependent upon the *ātman*.

Then what is there to be embraced and what should I give up? Can one even ask such a question? Can one even reject or accept ātman? Or is it that every thought is invariably ātman? So, is it a question of doing something to gain the ātman? Or is it a question of knowing that I am already the ātman?

The *ātman* is in every thought; therefore, it is not a question of 'doing' something to know this. The only reason I do not know this is because of ignorance. Sometimes I do not understand even when the *śabda pramāṇa* is wielded, and it just means that the mind does not have the necessary qualifications. The problem is not in the Self-Knowledge but my mind. It is not purified enough.

The *ātman* is available in every thought regardless of the object. Every *vṛtti* proves that there is a substratum. The universe (*jagat*) is that which is known and unknown. This is important otherwise you may assume that that which is not known to you does not exist. All movable and immovable are part of *jagat*. Between the things that move and do not move, everything is included. The verse states that all things are from you, the *ātman*. It means that you, the *ātman*, are the creator, preserver and the destroyer.

The implication of this teaching is that your Self is indeed *Brahman*, Consciousness (or God). You may be shy to acknowledge that you are god but the truth is that you are indeed that.

How many 'I's are there in this universe? Every one of you has an 'I', and to you there is only one `I'. This 'I' is what is said to be the Self or *ātman*, not to be mistaken with the ego which is impermanent. So, there is only one god and that is you. This is the logic and meaning behind the word *aham* or I. The pronoun `I' can only be singular in this universe because it is my `I.' Everything else is an object in my perception. If that is the case, can there be a universe without 'I'? People can counter argue that the universe will still exist even when I die some day. How do I counter this argument?

The key question to ask to answer all the questions is, "whose universe are you talking about?" If my `I' is the body then with death, I disappear; if the `I' is the *prāṇa* then I am subject to hunger, ill-health and other physical problems. If `I' is the mind then I am perhaps angry, sad and perhaps knowledgeable. It all depends upon where the `I' is located and that creates a significant shift in the understanding of myself. The whole universe is meaningful only because I exist and value myself. The verse states that the main reason why I interact with the world is because I want *puṇya* and want to avoid *pāpa*. The whole universe rests on me; the world that I see in the waking world cannot be there if I do not exist. In the dream world, no dream can occur without me, and even in deep sleep I am there.

The universe that I create, I preserve and dissolve happens in the two states - waking and dreaming. I create the universe in both the waking state and in my dream state as well. In dream state, I create a dream world based on my past experiences. In the deep sleep state, I resolve the universe and there is no concept of even `I'. Thus, in the waking and dream stages, I am *Viṣṇu* and *Brahmā* respectively, and in deep sleep I am *Śiva*. I am the creator, preserver and dissolver of the universe.

In all my transactions, there is the `I'. If that is the case, what am I really searching for and where should the search be? It is a not a place to be reached, it is not a reality to be gained in time. If I say it is internal, it would mean that it is not external. So, where is it? Actually, it is right where I am now. The only thing I can be sure of is my reality, and there is no need for an external person to prove that to me. For that too requires my existence first before anything else. This is the second point of the *Śiva Samhitā* verse.

And finally, the verse states, there is nothing that exists other than 'I' or *aham* and I am that *ātman*. Only *ātman* exists eternally. If all the transactions, thoughts and the entire universe are dependent upon the Self (or I), then there is only one thing that exists eternally and that is myself, the *ātman*. If you were to understand this through the illustration of the wave and the ocean, then the rise of the wave is creation, wave as wave is preservation and dissolution of the wave is merger. In all the three stages, there is only water. Prior to the wave there was water, during the wave there was water and after that there is just water. Similarly, in the creation, preservation and dissolution stages there is only *ātman* and that *ātman* is I. This is the third point of the verse. While there are many waves in the ocean, there is but only 'water. Similarly, in the universe, there are many transactions and objects but *ātman* alone pervades all of it.

14

NYĀYA: ANALOGIES

जलपूर्णेष्वसङ्ख्येषु शरावेषु यथा भवेत् |
एकस्य भात्यसङ्ख्यत्वं तद्वद्भेदोऽत्र दृश्यते || ३५
उपाधिषु शरावेषु या सङ्ख्या वर्तते परा |
सा सङ्ख्या भवति यथा रवौ चात्मनि तत्तथा || ३६

jalapūrṇeṣvasaṅkhyeṣu śarāveṣu yathā bhavet |
ekasya bhātyasaṅkhyatvaṃ tadvadbhedo'tra dṛśyate || 35
upādhiṣu śarāveṣu yā saṅkhyā vartate parā |
sā saṅkhyā bhavati yathā ravau cātmani tattathā || 36

Just as the sun appears many because of the innumerable cups filled with water, similarly difference appears to be here, for owing to which there is manifold appearance of the One.

In the teaching of *ātmajñāna* there is a unique method of teaching called "*nyāya*". *Nyāya* means an 'illustration' or 'analogy'. It makes use of something that you know, to explain something you are yet to know. For example, we may call someone a buffalo, to denote a big man. You use the known buffalo to explain the built of an unknown person.

There are 20-30 *nyāya*-s available in *Vedānta*, the most famous among them being the rope-snake analogy. They are all traditional and authentic forms of teaching. The *Śiva Samhitā* is now going to introduce various *nyāya*-s for us to comprehend the teaching easily.

The current verse stated that in cups of water you see many reflected suns, but in reality there is only one sun. Similarly, there are many *jīva*-s in the world reflecting the *ātman*. If there is only one *ātman*, then why are there so many reflections?

Let us analyse the cups of water that reflect the sun. If these cups are collapsible and one cup is joined with another, the sun's reflection becomes one. It is the boundary of the individual cup that results in the several individual reflections. Likewise, what is that boundary in you that creates this individuality? It is the body-mind-sense complex. The body-mind-sense complex is like the cup that creates the boundary. If you understand that you are not the body-mind-sense complex, then you will understand that there is only *ātman* and that you are that. The whole process of the teaching is to disassociate your identification with this body-mind-sense complex.

This *nyāya* can also be used as a meditation (*upāsanā*). You can meditate that what shines in you also shines in others. You treat everyone the way you want others to treat you. As a result, you will see yourself in others.

This *nyāya* indicates an adjunct that limits (*upādhi*). In your case, the *upādhi* is the body-mind-sense complex and it seemingly limits the *ātman*.

यथैकः कल्पकः स्वप्ने नानाविधतयेष्यते |
जागरे'पि तथाप्येकस्तथैव बहुधा जगत् || ३७

yathaikaḥ kalpakaḥ svapne nānāvidhatayeṣyate |
jāgare'pi tathāpyekastathaiva bahudhā jagat || 37

Just as in a dream the dreamer appears in many different ways but is one on awakening, so the universe appears to have many forms.

The second *nyāya* is based on dreams. In a dream, there is only one dreamer but there are many individuals. There could be even a replica of oneself in the dream. Similarly, in the waking state, there is one *jīva* but many objects. This illustration is used because in the dream I create, sustain and dissolve all the things that I experience. The material I used is entirely myself. Similarly, in the waking state, I created the whole universe using myself. The whole universe I see depends upon me. I must first be there for any experience to be and I am whatever that is experienced as the universe.

The dream is not separate from myself as the material used to create the dream is myself. The same understanding is applied to the waking state. This may be logically acceptable to you but whether you see yourself as the universe is something only you would know. There can be two obstacles in assimilating this knowledge. You may not logically understand the knowledge and secondly having logically seen it but not being able to assimilate it.

Continuous *śravaṇam* and *mananam* will take care of the issues of logic. If assimilation is the issue, then the problem is mainly due to the impurity of the mind which becomes an obstacle to assimilate this knowledge. The impurities of the mind cannot be neutralised by doing more *śravaṇam*, *mananam* and *nididhyāsanam* but only by doing more *sādhana*-s. Only *karma* can remove obstacles, especially those that are driven towards the purification of the mind with *Īśvara* as the support (*adhiṣṭhāna*). This is *Karma Yoga* as discussed earlier. A *Karma Yogi* performs all actions as an offering to *Īśvara* and accepts the result of the action as a gift (*prasāda*) from him.

Observance of *yama*, *niyama*, *nitya karma*, *naimittika karma* and all role based duties are one's *svadharma* and performing them purifies the mind. There is no need to add more and more *sādhana*-s to your life. Just keeping to your *svadharma* will be adequate. Even meditation could be considered optional.

Take one *yama* and practice it for one day with total commitment. There is no need to move mountains, for it is enough to move a molehill with total commitment. We think that to be spiritual is something very difficult like performing an elaborate *pūjā* or a fire sacrifice (*homa*) that you cannot usually do. On the contrary, spirituality is all about simple observances that you can do every day with total commitment.

Make no concessions when you observe one *yama* daily. Do not give concessions to this commitment on the day you observe it. Take it as a vow (*vrata*) and do announce it in public. It is important that others know about your spiritual commitments so that they do not become obstacles in your life.

Values are hard to follow because they are internal while *nityakarma*-s are easier to follow because they are external. The *Vasiṣṭha Dharmasūtra*[1] states that the even the *Veda* cannot purify those with bad conduct. In the *Viṣnu Smṛti*[2] it is said that the value for truth (*satyam*) is greater than a thousand horse sacrifices (*aśvamedha*). *Śaṅkarācārya* stated that not only can one attain mental purification by performing *nityakarma*-s but also through the observance of *yama* and *niyama*-s with commitment.[3] This is great motivation; it is easy to remove impurities if you are committed.

सर्पबुद्धिर्यथा रज्जौ शुक्तौ वा रजतभ्रमः |
तद्वदेवमिदं विश्वं विवृतं परमात्मनि || ३८

sarpabuddhiryathā rajjau śuktau vā rajatabhramaḥ |
tadvadevamidaṃ viśvaṃ vivṛtaṃ paramātmani || 38

As through delusion a rope appears like a snake, or seashell like silver; similarly, there is the appearance of the universe in the absolute ātman.

Here comes the third and fourth *nyāya*-s. The third is the rope-snake *nyāya* and the fourth is seashell-silver *nyāya*. The verse is pointing out to two types

1 Vasiṣṭha Dharmasūtra 6.3

2 Viṣnu Smṛti 8.36

3 Taittiriya Upaniṣad Bhāṣya 1.11.2-4

of errors we commit in our lives through these very insightful *nyāya*-s.

These are two types of subjective errors you can commit at the level of the mind in taking the universe to be real, which are explained through these two *nyāya*-s. Considering the universe to be real is like taking the rope to be a snake and seashell for silver.

Let us analyse the two *nyāya*-s. You are walking in a dark alley and jump with fright when you see a snake. Someone comes along, flashes the torchlight and you realise it to be a rope, but your heart continues thumping. Your fear has not been completely allayed. Your agitation was caused by what you thought was a snake. This example shows that partial knowledge is the cause for this confusion. Similarly, you have some idea about the universe but it is not complete and that is where the problem starts. The possibility of error can take place only if you have some knowledge but not totally ignorant. If you had no knowledge there would be no errors and complete knowledge also cannot create error.

We see a snake in the rope because of the similarity. We do not see a lion in the rope. It is also implied that the snake depends upon the rope and not the rope on snake. For you to see the snake you need the rope, but not the other way.

Hence the universe that you have taken to be real is not separate from the *ātman*, just like the snake is not separate from the rope. This is known as superimposition. I am superimposing the snake on the rope and not something else. The *nyāya* highlights the lack of complete knowledge (*sampūrṇa jñāna*).

The second *nyāya* illustrates the seashell being perceived as silver. From far, a seashell will appear as though it is a piece of silver shining on a seashore but upon getting closer one will find that it is not. The distance is the inhibiting factor that does not allow you to see it as it is. This illustration aims to convey that we make a mistake because we are not looking at things with clarity.

Both the *nyāya*-s present subjective errors that we commit about the universe and the *ātman*.

रज्जुज्ञानाद्यथासर्पोमिथ्यारूपोनिवर्तते ।
आत्मज्ञानात्तथायातिमिथ्याभूतमिदंजगत् ॥ ३९

rajjujñānādyathā sarpo mithyārūpo nivartate |
ātmajñānāttathā yāti mithyābhūtamidaṃ jagat || 39

Just as the knowledge of the rope sublates the appearance of the snake, similarly because of the self-knowledge the appearance of the unreal world disappears.

The moment I see rope, the snake vanishes. Similarly, the universe vanishes the moment I know *ātman*. The universe does not vanish into space or become absent. It is just that I do not see a universe apart from the *ātman*. Just like how I do not see a wave separate from water. A universe that is not apart from me is not a universe, it is actually 'I', *ātman*. The key word in the verse is *mithyārūpa* – a false form.

The snake-rope example is presented to show that I am ignorant of the *ātman*. If I had the knowledge, I will not see the snake or the universe as separate from myself. Here the point is that when *ātmajñāna* is gained, this universe which is dependent upon me gets negated or sublated. It gets resolved into myself in terms of understanding but not so in my sensory perception. The universe will still be reported by my senses but I will not be deluded into thinking it is apart from me.

रौप्यभ्रान्तिरियंयातिशुक्तिज्ञानाद्यथाखलु ।
जगद्भ्रान्तिरियंयातिचात्मज्ञानात्सदातथा ॥४०

raupyabhrāntiriyaṃ yāti śuktijñānādyathā khalu |
jagadbhrāntiriyaṃ yāti cātmajñānāt sadā tathā ||40

Just as the delusion of the silver disappears due to the knowledge of the seashell, similarly indeed, the world appearance disappears forever because of the knowledge of the ātman.

When I know about seashell, the silver disappears, similarly when I know about *ātman*, the universe disappears. In the previous verse, *mithyā rūpa* was discussed to explain ignorance or *avidyā*. Here the word *bhrānti* is used to describe *avidyā* .

Bhrānti means misperception. For instance, the seashell is seen as silver because I am at a distance. In the rope and snake *nyāya*, the mistake was due to the absence of bright light. In the case of the seashell, it is due to the distance. The verse hence presents an opportunity to discuss about *avidyā*.

Three types of *avidyā* are mentioned by *Śaṅkarācārya* in his *Bhagavad Gītā Bhāṣya*[4]. They are absence of knowledge (*agrahaṇa*); doubts (*saṃśaya*) and false perception (*viparīta grahaṇa*).

Among the three, the primary type of ignorance is *agrahaṇa* and the rest

4 Bhagavad Gītā Bhāṣya 13.2

are secondary. One is the cause and the other two are effects. The two other types of *avidyā* are presented for greater clarity. In the context of the *Śiva Samhitā* verses, *mithyā rūpa* is the primary form of *avidyā* which causes the effect, *bhrānti*.

Śiva Samhitā is making the point that through *ātmajñāna* ignorance is removed, doubts are clarified and you do not have false ideas anymore. That is why when a person knows the Self, he will not be subject to *avidyā*. *Avidyā* is cognitive and hence the solution must also be cognitive. All you should be doing is to work towards removing *avidyā* through Self-Knowledge. Where there is light, there cannot be darkness as both cannot co-exist at the same time in the same place.

15

SUPERIMPOSITION

यथा वंशो रगभ्रान्तिर्भवेद्भेदवशाज्जनात् |
तथा जगदिदं भ्रान्तिरध्यासकल्पनाञ्जनात् | ४१

yathā vaṃśo ragabhrāntirbhavedbhedavaśājjanāt |
tathā jagadidaṃ bhrāntiradhyāsakalpanāñjanāt | 41

Just as by besmearing one's eyes with the fat of the frog one mistakes a bamboo for a snake, so, the universe appears due to superimposition.

When one puts some ointment to treat the eye, the vision gets blurred for a few mintues and even a straight bamboo appears crooked like a snake. That is not the fault of the bamboo, but the fault of the vision.

The straight bamboo appears crooked like a snake because of superimposition or erroneous vision. The *Śiva Samhitā* uses a new word for this phenomenon which is superimposition (*adhyāsa*).

Just as the ointment clouds your vision, *adhyāsa* clouds your perception of the world. The verse is trying to say that the problem of seeing the universe as real is not an objective error but a subjective one. This is a very important point.

Superimposition is all about placing one reality on another. *Śaṅkarācārya* states that superimposition takes place in two forms in our daily transactions – I am this (*aham idam*) and this is mine (*mama idam*)[1] . These two statements can teach us a lot about superimposition. In the former statement, I take myself to be something other than what I am. And in the latter I am taking ownership of something external to me as mine.

Taking the real to be unreal and the unreal to be real is *adhyāsa*. For instance, I took the snake to be real and rope to be unreal. This is the same mistake I make when I take the *ātman* to be this body. The error is that I have taken the *ātman* as unreal and the unreal body as real. This is called mutual superimposition or mutual 'reality transfer'.

Here is another example to illustrate *adhyāsa*. A king is fighting a battle with another king. Although the soldiers are the ones who are actually fighting, we still say the king fights. The soldiers are fighting while the king is not,

1 Introduction to Brahma Sūtra Bhāṣya, also known as Adhyāsa Bhāṣya

but we have superimposed the fighting soldiers onto the king. Now let us look at the same example from another perspective. For whose sake are the soldiers fighting for? If there was no king there will be no battle. A certain amount of the king's authority has been transferred to the soldiers. So, it's a two-way process – the power transfer to the soldiers and the activity transfer to the king. Whatever the soldiers do, we take that to be the king's doing; if they win, he wins and if they lose, he loses. At the same time the soldiers do not exist without the king.

The soldiers are like the body-mind-sense complex and the king is the *ātman*. Your eyes, senses, mind are all active but we attribute the activity to the *ātman*. The *ātman* does not do anything but at the same time, the consciousness of the *ātman* gets reflected onto the body-mind-sense complex and therefore it functions. This is mutual superimposition. It looks similar but it is not. The reality of the Real is transferred to the Unreal, and the Unreal is superimposed onto the Real. This misunderstanding is the problem and this is *samsāra*.

Śaṅkarācārya states that this *adhyāsa* is natural (*naisargika*) to us.[2] You do not willfully commit *adhyāsa*, or rather you are naturally disposed to this error. It is not by choice and hence natural to all of us.

Without the need of anyone telling you that you are the body, you will claim to be so. But even after telling you a hundred times that you are not this body, you will not see it because that is the nature of *adhyąsa*. This is the primary problem according to *Śaṅkarācārya* who has explained *adhyāsa* in the introduction to his *Brahma Sūtra Bhāṣya*. The main goal of *Vedānta* is to neutralise this *adhyāsa*.

For superimposition to take place there must be some similarity between the two objects. Let us look at the example of seashell and silver. I superimpose silver on seashell and vice versa. When you see a seashell you will not see a donkey but silver because of the similarity between the nature of silver and seashell.

Is there a sequence in this transfer of reality? No, both take place at the same time. *Śaṅkarācārya* illustrates this through the example of how you may get affected when your family is unwell although you are perfectly well. It takes place simultaneously just like how parenthood and the child are born at the same time. This is *adhyāsa*.

We say that "I am thin" when actually the body is thin. The body is hungry

2 Bhagavad Gītā Bhāṣya 13.2

but we say "I am hungry". This is *adhyāsa*. *Adhyāsa* can be equated to the third type of *avidyā* – false perception or *viparīta grahaṇa*. This is the type of perception where one sees the seashell as silver or rope as a snake. *Adhyāsa* is singled out because it is an important phenomenon of *samsāra*. Knowledge is gained with some effort but *adhyāsa* comes effortlessly, and I do not have a choice in this. The fact that I naturally commit *adhyāsa* is due to my sense organs which naturally report perception of the world and its objects. If I have eyes I will see and if I have ears I will hear. And this is not a problem for those in *pravṛtti mārga* as they will enjoy the world of perceptions. *Adhyāsa* is a problem only for the *mumukṣu*, because the information delivered by the sense organs does not satisfy him or her anymore.

The root cause of seeing the universe is a subjective error or *adhyāsa* and not *māyā* which is an objective. *Māyā* is an effect of *avidyā/adhyāsa*. As per this text it is *avidyā* which causes the manifestation of the universe. From your standpoint, *adhyāsa* is that which makes you see the universe as separate from the *ātman*.

16

KNOWLEDGE REMOVES SUPERIMPOSITION

आत्मज्ञानाद्यथा नास्ति रज्जुज्ञानाद्भुजङ्गमः |
यथा दोषवशाच्छुक्लः पीतो भवति नान्यथा ||
अज्ञानदोषाद् आत्मा'पि जगद्भवति दुस्त्यजम् || ४२

ātmajñānādyathā nāsti rajjujñānādbhujaṅgamaḥ |
yathā doṣavaśācchuklaḥ pīto bhavati nānyathā ||
ajñānadoṣād ātmā'pi jagadbhavati dustyajam || 42

As through knowledge of the rope, the apparent serpent disappears; similarly through the knowledge of the ātman, the universe gets resolved. As through jaundiced eyes white appears yellow; similarly through the defect of ignorance, the ātman becomes this universe, an error very difficult to be removed.

The verse states that the moment *ātman* is known, this *adhyāsa* is removed and only one reality remains – *ātman*. *Adhyāsa* is removed because there is no more second thing apart from the *ātman*. When *adhyāsa* is removed, the notional *jagat* gets resolved. Only the notion of the *jagat* is removed with the understanding that only I, the *ātman*, is the reality. You will understand that the 'I' is not centred on the body-sense-mind complex. It is like seeing only water in spite of the millions of waves in the ocean.

The key point is that the world that you see does not physically or perceptually change with the knowledge of *ātman*. It is similar to seeing the sun rise in the east and set in the west but knowing in reality that the sun neither rises nor sets. When you see it rise and set, you see it "as though". Similarly, you see the universe apart from you "as though". You see the body "as though". You see all your *prāṇa*-s, mind, intellect and all "as though". The only reality is the *ātman*. The sensory perceptions will not take away your Self-Knowledge. Otherwise the one who knows *ātman* will not be able to teach it. There will not be any *guru*-s left to teach because all of them would have merged and melted into the universe. Or they would see the student merge into oneself after the knowing oneself. The physical universe remains "as though" and hence a teacher can teach this to another person. It is a communicable knowledge. In a *mukta*'s world there is no world, there is only 'I' in which the drama of life takes place.

Another good illustration is the *Nāṭaka Dīpikā*, an illustration from the text *Pañcadaśī*[1]. Here is an adaptation of that illustration to further present the idea we are discussing, although we have briefly discussed this in an earlier chapter. You have a white screen on which you project images of different characters with different emotions. Without the screen you will not be able to see them. That blank screen is like your *ātman* on which the drama called the universe takes place. Will the white screen be affected by the drama projected on it? Will the white screen be affected by the emotions of the characters? At the same time without the white screen can there be a projection? In your case the white screen is not blank but pure Consciousness. The universe rises and falls in your Consciousness and without you there is no universe.

The fine point is that we watch this drama of the universe and we laugh, cry or get angry in different situations not knowing that the very mind that gets angry, happy etc is also not the 'I'. This is the greatest self-deception seen from the standpoint of *ātmajñāna*.

The *Śiva Samhitā* makes an important point, that it is very difficult to remove *adhyāsa* because it is natural. In *Vivekacūḍāmaṇī*[2], *Śaṅkarācārya* states that it is very rare to get a human birth because only in it can you get the desire to know yourself. It is rarer to have this desire, and even rarer to get a teacher who will be able to remove this *adhyāsa*.

That is why many *Vedānta* texts will ridicule those in the *pravṛtti mārga*, because it is a great achievement to be born a human and yet losing the opportunity to attain *mokṣa*. Missing it is like committing suicide. But if people in that *pravṛtti mārga* are blissfully ignorant, then it may be wise not to disturb them.

Adhyāsa is difficult to remove because besides being natural and it is also habitual. Because we are conditioned into thinking in a certain way, we commit further *adhyāsa*. I will give you an example; in some societies, the belief that a six-seater car is a bigger symbol of success than a four-seater. However, if you owned a two-seater car then you are even more successful. On the other hand, a bus and a truck are bigger than a six seater but are not signs of success. Such an imposed value is irrational but that is how *adhyāsa* works. This notional value is a superimposition and the rationale behind the judgment is not consistent or logical. A *mumukṣu* should question such accepted views and values of the collective.

1 Pancadaśi, chapter 10

2 Vivekacūḍāmaṇī 2

The mind is inconsistent about what it values and does not value. The point is that our subjective value is not the truth because truth is not bound by any subjective view. So, what gives one the arrogance to hold on to his views and impose them on others by insisting that he is right and others are wrong?

The *mukta* who is free from *adhyāsa* will also have his views but they are not binding. On the other hand, a person who holds on to strong views is actually being suffocated by the very views, for without them he would feel uncomfortable.

Ask yourself this question: "How many such views do I harbour?" The views that I may hold are not the absolute truth. This is kind of reflection that should be done by a *mumukṣu*. Absolute truth is not subject to contention, just as the law of gravity which is not disputable.

दोषनाशे यथा शुक्लो गृह्यते रोगिणा स्वयम् |
शुक्लज्ञानात्तथा'ज्ञाननाशाद् आत्मा तथाकृतः || ४३

doṣanāśe yathā śuklo gṛhyate rogiṇā svayam |
śuklajñānāttathā'jñānanāśād ātmā tathākṛtaḥ || 43

Just as when jaundice is removed the patient sees the colour white as it is, similarly upon the removal of ignorance the true nature of ātman is realised.

The moment ignorance is removed, the true nature of yourself is revealed. You do not create knowledge, you only remove its obstacles. For example, a dusty mirror has to be cleaned to see a clear reflection. Similarly, you remove ignorance by doing *śravaṇam*. The nature of *ātman* is that it is self-revealing (*svaprakāśa*). You need a torchlight to see in the dark, but you do not need one to see the sun because the sun is self-revealing. It is the same with *ātman* which is self-established (*svataḥ siddha*). A *mumukṣu* needs to remove only the wrong notions and nothing else. That is why *Ramaṇa Maharṣī* said that *ātmajñāna* is "*atisulabham*" or very easy. He did not say *sulabham* or easy but said *atisulabham*, very easy. It is very easy because you can be only sure about your existence. You can doubt the existence of everything else but you cannot doubt the doubter. I have to acknowledge my existence before doubting anything. I am also not different from the reality I am seeking. Do you need someone else to prove your reality, your existence? The reason you are reading this book is because you exist. You are the sun; you do not need a torch - you are the *svaprakāśa ātman*. To acknowledge and recognise this vision is the goal of *Vedānta*. This is done by removing the wrong notions and the primary tool is *śravaṇam*. You are self-established *ātman* regardless, whether you accept it or not.

The illustration in the verse is that of jaundice. When you have it, the whole universe appears coloured but when it goes, the universe appears clear. The only effort is in removing the obstacles; the rest will take care of itself.

For this knowledge to be assimilated, prayer and god's grace (*Īśvara anugraha*) help. *Īśvara anugraha* is the one that helps you to make the leap. This knowledge is generally assimilated as a growing clarity. This is not the sort of reality which can be evoked through some magic touch or some kind of initiation.

The person who has gained this Self-Knowledge with effort will eventually be a good guide to others because all the difficulties he faced will make him very experienced. He would know the pitfalls in the journey and will be very compassionate and accommodating. Conversely a person who has not undergone a rough ride to understand this knowledge will not be as empathetic and compassionate. Sometimes the rough ride helps but the only thing is that you should never give up. Your support is not the teacher or the knowledge but *Īśvara*. You can give up anything but should not give up the sole reality of the universe, *Īśvara*.

17

ĀTMAN IS WITHOUT QUALITIES

कालत्रये' पि न यथा रज्जुः सर्पो भवेदिति |
तथात्मा न भवेद्विश्वं गुणतीतो निरञ्जनः || ४४

kālatraye' pi na yathā rajjuḥ sarpo bhavediti |
tathātmā na bhavedviśvaṃ guṇatīto nirañjanaḥ || 44

Just as the rope can never become a snake in the past, present or future; so the ātman which is without any attributes, and which is pure, never becomes the universe.

The universe is now being negated. In all the three periods of time (past, present and future) the rope was never the snake. Before you saw the rope as a snake it was a rope. When you saw the snake instead of the rope, it was still a rope. After the snake was 'destroyed' you realized that it has been a rope all this while. Similarly so it is for the *ātman*. Before the universe was created it was *ātman*. While experiencing the universe, it is still the *ātman*. After the universe gets destroyed or even if my body–sense-mind complex dies, *ātman* remains. In the past, through numerous births *ātman* existed. Even now *ātman* exists and in time to come *ātman* will continue to exist, therefore eternal.

In the wake of Self-Knowledge, the universe gets resolved. All is the *ātman* because in it alone the universe rises, sustains and dissolves. The verse states that the *ātman* is without all the qualities (*guṇa*-s). The whole universe can be categorised into *sattva guṇa*– that which is balanced and intelligent; *rajas* which is active and dynamic, and *tamas* which is inert. Each of us also have all the *guṇa*-s. The one who has an innate interest in *śāstra* and knowledge is of *sattva guṇa*, people who are active have more *rajas* while someone who is lazy could be *tamas* because of the lack of interest and activity. The *ātman* does not have the three *guṇa*-s because *guṇa*-s are non-eternal. Anything which has *guṇa*-s has birth and death. They belong to the superimposed universe.

The verse states that the *ātman* is pure (*nirañjanaḥ*). Was there any contact between the snake and the rope or did the snake bite the rope? Did the snake taint the rope? No, there is no contact between the two. The snake cannot affect the rope because it is not there in the first place. The snake was born due to my misapprehension and hence a superimposition. Similarly the silver cannot stain the seashell nor the pot affect the clay. All forms and names that I have given to objects of the world are my creation and hence a subjective error. The Self is pure because it is untouched by what I have superimposed. The body-mind-sense complex is not in touch with *ātman*. The body-mind-sense complex is a superimposition and my erroneous understanding has created the belief that the *ātman* is in contact with it.

I am 100% pure and contactless. For example when one puts a rose next to a clear crystal, the latter becomes red. And when the rose is removed the crystal shines clear. Rose is like the body-mind-sense complex and the crystal, the *ātman*. You take yourself to be coloured when in reality your nature is eternal, pure, consciousness and free (*nitya*, *śuddha*, *buddha*, *mukta svabhāva*[1]). In spite of the redness, the crystal is actually clear by nature. Similarly, in spite of my body-mind-sense complex the *ātman* remains pure and untouched. It appears to be in contact with each other only because of my erroneous understanding. If there is anything worth calling pure, it is *ātman* alone. Just as at no time did the rope become the snake, also at no time did the *ātman* become this body-mind-sense complex.

There are various models to understand the universe. One model is through the five elements (*pañcabhūta*). Another model is reducing the universe into three qualities (*triguṇa*-s) – *sattva*, *rajas* and *tamas*. This reality *ātman*, is not the three *guṇa*-s. All objects and mental cognitions are made of *guṇa*-s and will have a beginning and an end. *Ātman* is not any of these three *guṇa*-s but having said that, a relationship exists between the two. The relationship is such that the *guṇa*-s depend on the *ātman*, but the *ātman* does not depend on the *guṇa*-s. The illustration to appreciate this relationship is that of water and waves. The waves depend upon the water but the water does not depend upon the wave.

The whole universe is superimposed on the *ātman* like the snake on the rope. I am the substratum of this universe like the rope is to the snake. Whether I like it or not, the universe exists in me. Whenever the universe is evident to me, I know that I am not that. Whenever any second reality or object is evident to me, I am not that because if there was a second reality, then who is witnessing it. The substratum is real, and the universe is seemingly real. We cannot say that the universe is completely non-existent because if it was, you cannot be reading this book. That is why the word *māyā* has to be understood properly and most often than not it

1 Bṛhadāraṇyaka Upaniṣad Bhāṣya 1.4.7

is misunderstood. Most teachers have misrepresented *māyā* – they see it as an illusion. Teaching does not take place in illusion. *Māyā* is not an illusion. Sometimes a question is asked – how can a 'seemingly' real *māyā* reveal something real, the *ātman*. The question is valid because the teaching is taking place in this universe. Here is an illustration to understand this. In your dream you get chased by a lion and you are running as fast as you can. And then suddenly it pounces on you. And then you wake up. Here is a case of an unreal lion that woke you up to reality. And your heartbeat still races and you are in cold sweat. An unreal lion has created all this.

Similarly, a teaching in a seemingly real world, can make you see the real. This is how the teaching works. You cannot claim the world does not exist. That is why we use a unique word – *mithyā*. The word *mithyā* means a world that is false – falsified only at the dawn of knowledge, until then it is real. *Mithyā* is also that which is dependent upon *satyam* like way the wave depends upon water, pot on clay or snake on rope. It has no independent existence.

In the pot and clay illustration, clay is *satyam* and pot is *mithyā*. Does it mean that pot does not exist? No, it just means that the pot is a dependent reality. Now look at yourself – the whole universe is dependent upon you. I am *satyam* and the universe is *mithyā*. Just because I have this knowledge does not mean that the universe disappears, it just depends upon me for its existence. I lend my reality to it, as it were. And I see that the universe is in me, non-separate for me, the *ātman*.

Śaṅkarācārya states that superimposition is so natural that it exists not just for human beings but also for other living beings[2]. The existence of living beings presupposes duality. The cow will go for the hay in front of it because it sees the hay as different from itself; otherwise it will not go for it. Duality is so natural to us that it is self-evident. It is not something theological that you have to argue over and prove. The very fact that you are talking, reading and listening indicates that you are subject to *adhyāsa*.

2 Introduction to Brahma Sūtra Bhāśya

18

ĪŚVARA AND OTHER GODS ARE NOT ETERNAL

आगमाऽपायिनोऽनित्यानाश्यत्वेनेश्वरादयः ।
आत्मबोधेनकेनापिशास्त्रादेतद्विनिश्चितम् ॥४५

āgamā'pāyino'nityā nāśyatveneśvarādayaḥ |
ātmabodhena kenāpi śāstrādetadviniścitam || 45

Īśvara and other gods, can be destroyed, come and go, and hence not eternal. Through the knowledge of the ātman, from the scriptures, this has been ascertained.

Even *Īśvara* and the gods are not eternal. The word *Īśvara* could also refer to Lord *Śiva*[1]. The gods are all subject to birth and death as they are also made up of *guṇa*-s. *Deva*-s are of *sattva guṇa*. Even *Brahmā* too has a beginning and end. There is even a possibility that a human being can reincarnate as *Brahmā* because of the *puṇya* accrued. The highest fruit of *puṇya* is the status of a *deva* and because you can attain that status you can also lose it. Birth and death hold true even for a *deva*. The verse states that you come to this conclusion because of *śāstra* which reveals what is eternal and what is not. If you do not have access to *śāstra* you will not know this truth that *deva*-s too are subject to birth and death. Even the *deva*-s are not immune to *adhyāsa*.

However, in this case the *adhyāsa* is deliberate and it is different from the natural *adhyāsa* which we discussed earlier which we cannot do anything about. Therefore, there are two types of *adhyāsa*: 1. natural and 2. deliberate. An example of deliberate *adhyāsa* is when we visualise a deity, invite him and worship him in a *pūjā*. Before you invited the deity, the object in front of you was just a plain statue made of clay or metal. Once you have invited, you see god in it. Seeing god in any form or statue is also *adhyāsa*. So, what is the value of this deliberate *adhyāsa* or superimposition?

Deliberate *adhyāsa* is a technique introduced by the *śāstra* and is very important because it enables you to do *karma* and hence purify yourself and gain *puṇya*. In any worship or *pūjā*, superimposition is assumed. The whole power of the universe is invoked in a form and is worshipped for the sake of grace (*anugraha*). The mind coupled with faith and knowledge from

1 see verse 81-82

śāstra sees *Īśvara* in that form.

We worship the *Deva*-s primarily for their grace. There is a verse[2] in the *Nirukta*[3] that states that whatever form you superimpose on a *Deva*, he will appear in that form. Because *Īśvara* is all powerful and hence he can take any form to appeal to the desire of a devotee.

The *Śiva Samhitā* verse in discussion is making a pertinent point when it states that *deva*-s are not eternal. But to assimilate this truth is not easy. It requires *vairāgya*, *viveka* and *cittaśuddhi*. If one is not qualified, this truth will not make sense to you. So, what can I do to understand this truth suppose I am not? The best advice is to continue to worship the *deva*-s or *devī*-s for mental purification. This is how the *śāstra* works - it teaches both the absolute truth and then the relative truth for our internal purification or qualification.

We should not downplay the role of worship in *Vedānta*. We pray to different deities, each playing specific roles and functions of *Īśvara*. As long as you recognise *Īśvara*, these deities exist and they have a functional value for you. The whole universe is *Īśvara* and hence you cannot ignore it.

So by what means do you arrive at this understanding that *Īśvara*'s existence is non-eternal? It is understood purely by the grace of *Īśvara*. *Īśvara* provides this knowledge and destroys himself in the process. That is the greatest sacrifice in my opinion. People sometimes claim the greatest sacrifice to be self-sacrifice. In this context, *Īśvara* sacrifices himself for my sake. That is why he is called *karuṇākara* (compassionate one), *karuṇāmūrti* (form of compassion) and *anbe sivam*[4] (love is God). He is called compassionate because at the wake of knowledge, the *Īśvara* destroys himself. You cannot destroy *Īśvara*, only he can destroy himself. This is what I call grace which is also known as *anugraha*, *krpā*, etc.

Whenever I am praying, whatever I am yearning for, whatever *sādhana*-s I am doing, it is all for the sake of knowing that I am a free Self, *ātman*. When I know that I am the only reality, then that *Īśvara* is not real any more to me. At the dawn of knowledge there is no *Īśvara* separate from me. This duality gets resolved and this understanding is indeed *mokṣa*.

It is a very interesting tradition where you cannot use your will to know *ātman* but you can use your will to pray. There is a nice verse in the *Upaniṣad*

2 Nirukta 10.17.6

3 a text on Sanskrit etymology by the author Yāska

4 a Tamil axiom from Tirumantiram

which states,

ātmā pravacanena labhyo
na medhayā na bahunā śrutena
yamevaiṣa vṛṇute tena labhyaḥ
tasyaiṣa ātmā vivṛṇute tanūṁ svām

> The *ātman* cannot be attained by the study of the *Veda*-s, not by intelligence nor by much hearing. Only by him who seeks to know the *ātman* can It be attained. To him the ātman reveals its own nature.[5]

The *mantra* above states that you cannot choose the *ātman*, the *ātman* chooses you to reveal itself. You cannot gain the *ātman* with will, the *ātman* has to shower its grace on you. That is why your whole life should be lived with a prayerful attitude. The more *karma*-s and *sādhana*-s you do, the more the chances of you obtaining the *ātman*'s grace, for *Īśvara* to sacrifice himself for you.

The moment you become a *bhakta* by recognizing *Īśvara*, the ego sense (*ahaṅkāra*) will lose its power. It is like the pride of being the head of a department that gets neutralized when you meet the chief executive officer. The moment you recognise your 'maker', your ego sense will drop. The same thing happens when you come to know the *ātman*.

To summarise, *Īśvara* is not eternal but until I realize the *ātman*, *Īśvara* is real to me. Appreciating *Īśvara* as the creator, preserver and dissolver of the universe, we do all our *sādhana*-s to purify our minds.

Īśvara is the truth till he gets falsified. Like the dream which was real till you woke up. As long as you are in a dream, it is indeed real. Once we wake up there is no reason to explain the dream's reality anymore.

The elaborate discussion about *Īśvara* is to avert a premature conclusion that *Īśvara* is *anitya*, without having the *adhikāra* to understand it. The *Śiva Samhitā* assumes that the reader is an *adhikāri* and hence its boldness.

5 Kaṭha Upaniṣad 1.2.23

19

UNIVERSE RISES IN ME

यथा वातवशात्सिन्धावुत्पन्नाः फेनबुद्बुदाः |
तथात्मनि समुद्भूतः संसारः क्षणभङ्गुरः || ४६

yathā vātavaśātsindhāvutpannāḥ phenabudbudāḥ |
tathātmani samudbhūtaḥ saṃsāraḥ kṣaṇabhaṅguraḥ || 46

Just like foam and bubbles in the sea arising through the agitation caused by the wind, this transitory world arises from the ātman.

Now we come to *nyāya* number five – foam and water. The important words in this verse are *samsāram kṣaṇabhaṅguram* - *samsāra* or the cycles of birth and death is momentary like bubbles in water. The thousands of years of human civilization are nothing compared to the age of the universe, which modern science states to be four billion years. Our lives are like bubbles in water but we make a big deal out of it. We hate others, create territories and fight over them etc. The insignificant bubble creates an upheaval. If you look at it from the stand point of this *nyāya*, we will realize that our life is insignificant. *Samsāra* is like a bubble, insignificant but at the same time contributory. Just because I am small does not mean that I do not contribute. I can continue to do what is needed to be done. If all the squirrels had thought that they were insignificant, they would not have helped *Rāma* in building the bridge to Lanka in the epic *Rāmāyana*[1].

At the same time, if you think you are a significant contributor, you will compete all your life – compete with your bosses, parents, or for your spouse's attention. The image that I am significant is also an *adhyāsa*. We have this tendency to want to be the best, and we cannot settle for second best.

It is common for us to be good in one domain, but we can be a total failure in another domain. You cannot be good at everything. For example, Hitler was a failure at basic human values but was a successful leader. If we were to recognise this truth we can become humble. This competitive nature does not help us. Competition takes place only when the degree of self-identity is very strong. And such a competitive nature cannot help a *mumukṣu*.

However, competition is fine for those in the *pravṛtti mārga* as long as it is

1 this event is recorded in only some versions of the Rāmāyana

done ethically or with *Dharma*. Progress, evolution and advancement can take place only when you are competitive, but it must be moderated with ethics. That is why in the *Upaniṣad*-s they say that there are two paths - one path that goes out into the world to enjoy and another one that goes back to the Self[2]. The former path will always exist in the world. In fact, 99.9% of the population is in this category because everyone starts with this notion that I need to be successful. Only a rare few would want to reverse this process and want to know the Self, the internal world.

So this teaching is for the rare few. Maybe one or two percent of the *Vedānta* teachings may be relevant for people in the *pravṛtti mārga*. Organisations and teachers write texts like 'Practical *Vedānta*' and stuff like that although there is nothing practical about *Vedānta*. *Vedānta* cannot be practiced liked *Karma*-s. *Vedānta* is *aparokṣa anubhūti* – a cognitive understanding that takes place immediately when knowledge is assimilated. There is no such thing as practical *Vedānta*. What is called as Practical *Vedānta* is nothing but *Sanātana Dharma* explored through *pravṛtti mārga*. The whole Hindu renaissance took place on the foundation of this 'Practical *Vedānta*'. It is high time we moved on.

Vedānta can take away the zest for life and the desire to achieve. It can make you feel lousy for wanting to achieve. If you failed in an enterprise, then it can make you accept that failure. If you are successful, it can make you go beyond that success.

If you happened to be someone wanting to go out and enjoy what the universe has to offer you in terms success and materials, then *Vedānta* is not for you. However, *Dharma* or *pravṛtti mārga* is for you. If such a person were to attend a *Vedānta* class, they will feel guilty about doing anything that is enjoyable, especially when your teacher is around. In *Vedānta* you need to clarify, it is like sculpting; it is intricate. The teacher must encourage questioning and must listen to all questions to understand the inclination and disposition of the seekers. In a big group this is very difficult because the teacher cannot give individual attention to everyone. This is what happens when one teaches *Vedānta* in a group setting. The teacher may be unconsciously indoctrinating the learners who are unprepared and in the process perhaps even destroy their aspirations.

So in summary this verse states that the *samsāra* or universe rises and falls in me like bubbles in water. I experience this every day. When I am awake, the universe is there and when I am asleep it gets resolved in me.

2 see Kaṭha Upaniṣad 1.2.1

20

DIVERSITY IS IMPERMANENT

अभेदो भासते नित्यं वस्तुभेदो न भासते |
द्वित्वत्रित्वादिभेदस्तु भ्रमत्वे पर्यवस्यति || ४७

abhedo bhāsate nityaṃ vastubhedo na bhāsate |
dvitvatritvādibhedastu bhramatve paryavasyati || 47

The non-difference is eternal; there is no difference amongst things. This division into two, three and more is nothing but an error.

Abheda means non-difference or unity and that is the nature of *ātman*. *Bheda* means difference or diversity and is impermanent. It is impermanent because it is subject to change, has a beginning and end, and gets falsified at the dawn of knowledge. I see differences because of *avidyā*.

Traditionally the *bheda*-s are grouped into three. The first *bheda* is called *sajātiya bheda* i.e., the difference between two objects of the same species (*jāti*) like two apples; the second one is *vijātiya bheda* i.e., the difference between two objects of two different species like a chair and a pot. And the third is *svagata bheda* i.e., the difference within one object, for example, the eyes, hand and legs of a human being. All objects of the universe will have at least one of these three *bhedas*. There cannot be a fourth type of *bheda*.

One of the definitions of *Brahman* or *ātman* is that it is the reality which does not have these *bheda*-s or differences, in particular the *svagata bheda*. It is easy to demolish the first two *bheda*-s to understand *Brahman*. *Brahman* being One, there is no room for *sajātiya* and *vijātiya bheda*-s. But in *svagata bheda* I can make an error. I may think that *Brahman* is one reality but there could be movement within *Brahman*. I may think it is one mass with a head or a hand. I can think like that because knowing *Brahman* is entirely an understanding and cognitively you can commit an error.

Even when I say that "I am *Brahman*", I may mistake that this body is *Brahman* or the mind is *Brahman*. The third *bheda* will help one negate such errors. That is why *svagata bheda* is very important. So, when these three differences are not there, there are only few words you can use to understand *Brahman*, such as 'without modifications' (*nirvikāratvam*) and an anvil or immovable (*kūṭastha*).

The first two types of *bheda*-s seem easier to understand. The third one, *svagata bheda*, is not obvious. We may think there is one *Brahman* and within it there are differences or changes. From the standpoint of *Brahman* there is not even the slightest change. How much you understand this depends upon your *mananam*. It is not something that you can know like an object in your hand. It is purely an understanding. You need to see this reality as absolutely untouched by anything. That is why we the word pure (*śuddha*) is used. Or else we cannot use the word *śuddha* on *Brahman*.

However, *Īśvara* enjoys *svagata bheda* and is hence subject to change. It is like this; *Īśvara* is the total sum of the universe's energy. As the universe is in a state of flux, *Īśvara* is the sum of all the changes. On the other hand, *Brahman* is to be understood as one without modification and therefore without the three types of *bheda*-s.

What is the relationship between the changing and the changeless? The changing depends upon the changeless. Where there is the changing pot, there is the changeless clay. Where there is the changing wave, there is the changeless water. What does the wave need to do to realise that it is water? What does the pot need to do, to know that it is clay? It needs to just 'know' that it is already that which it is seeking to be. Similarly, I am already *ātman* and all I need is the knowledge that I am the *ātman*. How does this knowledge take place? It takes place through *śravaṇam*, *mananam* and *nididhyāsanam*.

One may think that *śravaṇam mananam* and *nididhyāsanam* also brings about a change. Yes, while they bring about a change in my thinking, they do not bring about a change in *Brahman* or *ātman*. That is the key point. Moreover *śravaṇam*, *mananam* etc are *jñāna sādhana*-s and not *karma*-s. While all other actions bring about a change in the object or the subject, here the very mind that is doing the *śravaṇam* is not separate from the *ātman* that it is trying to know. Therefore, there is no change.

Ātmajñāna is like a beggar discovering that he was the prince all along or like the tenth man. The tenth man was not created but came to 'know' that he was already the tenth man. It is accomplishing the already accomplished. In the same manner, *śravaṇam*, *mananam* and *nididhyāsanam* do not create the *ātman*. They only reveal an ever-present *ātman*. To know it, you do not have to gain anything but remove ignorance.

If you teach that you need to do something to gain that knowledge, then you are implying the need for some kind of mental activity to know

Brahman or *ātman*. Some *Yoga* schools claim that you have to forcefully change the nature of the mind to gain *mokṣa* because only in a still mind lies *Brahman*. They usually quote the popular verse from *Yoga Sūtra*, '*Yogaḥ citta vṛttinirodhaḥ*'[1] (Yoga is the cessation of thoughts). The implication of such a teaching is that you were X before you did *Yoga* and now you are Y after doing *Yoga*. So a change is needed for you to succeed in *Yoga*. However, no amount of change can produce the changeless and no amount of activity can create that which has no activity in it. A reality that is devoid of the three *bheda*-s is always available, and therefore no action which produces change is going to make you know *Brahman*. Hence, the third *bheda*, *svagata bheda*, is very important, to correct the wrong teachings of some modern *Vedānta* schools who teach *Yoga* and meditation as a means to *mokṣa*.

How does one understand that the nature of *Brahman* is without change? The deep sleep state (*suṣupti*) is the best example because in deep sleep there is no modification or change. The *suṣupti* state indicates the homogeneous nature of my Self. Two *Upaniṣad*-s talk about this,

uddālako hāruṇiḥ śvetaketuṃ putramuvāca svapnāntaṃ me somya
vijānīhīti yatraitatpuruṣaḥ svapiti nāma satā somya tadā
sampanno bhavati svamapīto bhavati tasmādenaṁ
svapitītyācakṣate svaṁhyapīto bhavati

Once *Uddālaka Āruṇi* said to his son *Śvetaketu*,
'Dear boy, know from me the true nature of sleep. When a man
is said to be sleeping, then, dear boy, he has become united with
Being and has attained his own nature. Hence people speak of
him as sleeping, for them he has attained his own nature.[2]

tad vā asyaitad aticchando 'pahatapāpmābhayaṃ rūpam
tad yathā priyayā striyā saṃpariṣvakto na bāhyaṃ kiṃ cana vedanāntaram
evam evāyaṃ puruṣaḥ prājñenātmanā saṃpariṣvakto na bāhyaṃ kiṃ cana vedanāntaram
tad vā asyaitad āptakāmam ātmakāmam akāmaṃ rūpam śokāntaram

That is his form – beyond desires, free from evils and fearless.
As a man, fully embraced by his beloved wife, does not know
anything at all, either external or internal, so does this infinite
being (*ātman*), fully embraced by the *ātman* (in deep sleep), not
know anything at all, either external or internal. That is his form

1 Yoga Sūtra 1.2
2 Chāndogya Upaniṣad 6.8.1

– in which all objects of desire have been attained and are but the *ātman*, and which is free from desire and devoid of grief.[3]

Chāndogya Upaniṣad takes the view that deep sleep itself can be equated with *ātman*. This equation is made so that we can understand the changeless nature of *ātman* through an experience known to us very well. But we should not treat this equation literally as the *ātman* is not the state of deep sleep too. Deep sleep is just a tool to convey the idea.

So, while deep sleep state is not the *ātman*, it gives us an idea of the nature of the *ātman*. It is like a double-edged sword. If suppose the deep sleep state was to be the *ātman*, then when I wake up I cease to be the *ātman*. So, to understand myself do I need to be constantly asleep? But what is needed is the knowledge that even while in waking and dream states I am not separate from the *ātman*.

Self-Knowledge is a matter of cognitive understanding. Sometimes we are tricked into thinking that deep sleep state alone is the *ātman*. This is particularly true for *Yoga* schools. They take *samādhi* or a state without any thought modifications to be like the deep sleep state. The *Yogic Samādhi* is excellent to understand the homogeneous nature of *ātman* but it will not generate *ātmajñāna*. If you subscribe to this view then every human being would have become liberated after coming out of deep sleep.

The philosophy of the *Yoga Sūtra*, a very popular text, particularly faces this problem. Philosophically its position is untenable but we should not throw the baby out with the bathwater. *Yoga Sūtra* has many other valuable teachings. It is perhaps the most ancient text on psychology. There is no other text that dwells on the mind as much as the *Yoga Sūtra* does. The *asamprajñāta samādhiit*[4] teaches is perhaps the greatest accomplishment a human mind can achieve. The *Yoga Sūtra* helps us investigate and analyze the mind by recognising its obstacles and appreciating the positive attributes that help in strengthening the mind. In that sense, you cannot relegate the value of *Yoga Sūtra*. But the *Yoga Sūtra* is not a *Vedānta* text and hence not as useful in the topic of *mokṣa*.

Sometimes *Vedānta* teachers downplay the supportive role of meditation in *jñāna sādhana*. Meditative disciplines help in developing *adhikāra*. I wished more traditional *Vedānta* teachers taught meditation without dismissing its merits. Many contemporary *Vedānta* teachers request that you abandon all

3 Bṛhadāraṇyaka Upaniṣad 4.3.21

4 Yoga Sūtra 1.18

traditional practices such as *Yoga*, chanting, etc. *Vedānta* is all good but you need a mind prepared to assimilate this knowledge. Hence *Yoga* is a very good practice to purify the mind.

Sureśvara, a disciple of *Śaṅkarācārya*, in his *Naiṣkarmyasiddhi* places *Yoga* as an important practice prior to *jñāna*,

nityakarmānuṣṭhānāddharmotpattirdharmotpatteḥ
pāpchānistataścittaśuddhistataḥ

saṃsārayāthātmyāvabodhastato vairāgyaṃ tato
mumukśutvaṃ tatastadupāyaparyeṣaṇaṃ tataḥ
sarvakarmatatsādhanasaṃnyāsastato yogābhyāsastataścittasya
pratyakpravaṇatā tatastattvamasyādivākyārthaparijñānaṃ
tato'vidyocchedastataśca svātmanyevāvasthānaṃ "brahmaiva
san brahmāpyeti " "vimuktaśca vimucyate " iti

From performance of the daily rituals comes *puṇya* (*Dharma*), from *puṇya* comes the removal of *pāpa* (sins), from this comes purity of mind, from this comes an evaluation of the life of births and deaths, from this comes dispassion, from this comes a desire for *mokṣa*, from this comes a search for the means to it (*mokṣa*), from this comes the renunciation of all actions and duties, from this comes the practice of Yoga, from this the inward looking mind, from this knowledge of meaning of statement like "That You Are"[5], from this removal of ignorance, from this establishment in the Self alone, according to the statements "Verily, being the *Brahman*, he attains *Brahman*"[6] and "Liberated, he is liberated".[7] [8]

The above verse shows the value of *Yoga* in *Vedānta* and in the pursuit of *mokṣā*. I would also like to stress one more point. In the modern context, some schools think that meditation alone is enough for *cittaśuddhi*. But *Patanjali*, the author of *Yoga Sūtra*, does not support this view. He presupposes that a seeker would have observed the *yama*-s and *niyama*-s before starting on meditation. Only a mind that has observed the *yama*-s and *niyama*-s will be able to meditate well and hence be very conducive to *jñāna sādhana*.

5 Chāndogya Upaniṣad 6.8.7
6 Bṛhadāraṇyaka Upaniṣad 4.4.6
7 Kaṭha Upaniṣad 2.2.1
8 Naiṣkarmyasiddhi 1.51

21

UNIVERSE IS TIMELESS ĀTMAN

यद्भूतंयच्चभाव्यंवैमूर्तामूर्तंतथैवच ।
सर्वमेवजगदिदंविवृतंपरमात्मनि ॥४८

yadbhūtaṃ yacca bhāvyaṃ vai mūrtāmūrtaṃ tathaiva ca |
sarvameva jagadidaṃ vivṛtaṃ paramātmani || 48

The entire universe which was, which is and which will be, both having form and formless, manifested and unmanifested is nothing but the appearance in absolute ātman.

Whatever 'was', 'is' and 'will be' are superimpositions on the *ātman*. The beginning of creation is when the un-manifest starts to manifest itself. Prior to creation, the universe was not manifest but it existed like the way a tree exists in a seed.[1] Time implies change while un-manifest implies no change. So, without change there is no time. Our time measurements are based on the rotation of the earth on its axis. If we shifted time backwards to the changeless, time cannot be measured per se.

Do not forget that our concept of time starts with creation. The verse mentions *mūrtāmūrta* because the universe is a combination of form (*mūrta*) and formless (*amūrta*). The universe encompasses everything which has a form and which does not have a form. This *sarvam jagat* or universe is a manifestation or appearance of the *paramātma* (*vivrtam paramātmani*). The universe exists because of *paramātma* and hence a dependant reality. Even as you live in the universe, the *ātman* is in spite of this time. Time exists in *ātman* only. This verse is not meant just for study but is meant for *mananam*. The author is repeating the same point from different perspectives.

---

1 see Chāndogya Upaniṣad 6.12.1-2

22

IGNORANCE IS IMAGINED

कल्पकैःकल्पिताविद्यामिथ्याजातामृषात्मिका।
एतन्मूलंजगदिदंकथंसत्यंभविष्यति॥४९

kalpakaiḥ kalpitāvidyā mithyā jātā mṛṣātmikā|
etanmūlaṃ jagadidaṃ kathaṃ satyaṃ bhaviṣyati|| 49

This imaginary ignorance is born of falsity and hence by nature unreal. How can the world based on such a root be real?

This verse questions and ridicules our false notions and perception of reality. The first point to understand is that this universe, made of forms and formless, and which is an endless cycle of past and future, is seated on an imagined ignorance (*kalpita avidyā*). The root of the universe is based on something that is set up by ignorance. A question can be asked at this juncture, which is whether your nature of *ātman* differs in the state of ignorance and knowledge. The answer is No, and there is no room for *avidyā* in the *ātman*. As a result, the very concept of *avidyā* is also *mithyā*, hence the verse states *kalpitāvidyā*. It was as if a brown pot became a golden pot at the dawn of knowledge, but the clay still remains the same. This leap in understanding takes place in your *nididhyāsanam*.

I see a universe because of the assumption that I am subject to ignorance. If I attained knowledge, then the universe ceases to be. This whole notion of a universe seen by me is actually set up by an *avidyā* that I have assumed. Just like the ignorance that is imagined, the false creation also has no reality.

This *avidyā* is seated in my mind and there are three types of *avidyā* [1]according to *Śaṅkarācārya*:

1. absence of knowledge,
2. doubt and
3. false knowledge

Absence of knowledge is the same for all people. However, doubt and false knowledge are subjective and different for each one of us. And the universe is seated on this subjective *avidyā* and therefore it is considered imagined.

Of what use is a universe based on your imagination? What truth can there

1 see Bṛhadāraṇyaka Upaniṣad Bhaṣya 3.3.1 and Bhagavad Gītā Bhaṣya 13.2

be in this universe? We concluded the universe to be *mithyā* or a dependent reality because I am ignorant. The *śāstra* takes it further and raises the bar. It states, everything including *avidyā* is a false creation.

That is why you do not have to waste your time analysing *avidyā*. Many traditions have been misled because of that. Your only purpose should be in gaining Self-Knowledge. It is like looking for the light switch upon walking into a dark room and not analysing the darkness.

People who analyse and try to understand *avidyā* get into problems. The *śāstra* is telling you that *avidyā* is *mithyā* and that you must spend more time analysing the *śāstra jñāna*. This is very important for a *sādhaka*. The *Śiva Samhitā* is taking a very bold stand on *avidyā*. This is because you may attribute value to this discussion about the universe and *avidyā*. However, the text states that it is not so and calls the universe useless (*mṛṣātmikā*).

In fact, this instruction is more valid for the teacher than to the student. It is entirely up to the teacher what he shares by way of *śravaṇam* and which will become the subject for *mananam* for the student.

If the teacher keeps on talking about the *mithyā jagat*, it will not help the student. That is why we can keep talking about methodology, pedagogy etc., but it will not help you. In *śravaṇam*, the direct teaching of the *ātman* is more important. The teaching must be done in a small group for the teacher to wield the *pramāṇa* and control it.

23

RENOUNCE AND TAKE REFUGE IN ĀTMAN

चैतन्यात्सर्वमुत्पन्नं जगदेतच्चराचरं ।
तस्मात्सर्वं परित्यज्य चैतन्यं तु समाश्रयेत् ।। ५०

caitanyātsarvamutpannaṃ jagadetaccarācaraṃ |
tasmātsarvaṃ parityajya caitanyaṃ tu samāśrayet || 50

All this universe, moveable or immoveable, has arisen from Consciousness, so one should renounce it completely and take refuge in Consciousness.

This verse is very similar to the opening verse of the *Īśāvāsya Upaniṣad.*

īśā vāsyamidaṁ sarvaṃ yatkiñca jagatyāṃ jagat

All this should be covered by the Lord,
whatsoever moves on the earth.[1]

Another way to understand this universe is through the use of the concept of *carācaram*. *Cara* means movable and *acara* means immovable. In this *jagat*, whatever you see as movable and immovable is indeed from Consciousness or *ātman*. *Śiva Samhitā* asks one to renounce everything and take refuge in *caitanya* (*caitanyam tam samāśraye*). On the other hand, Buddhism asks one to give up everything (*sarvam parityajya*) and thereafter take refuge in the Buddha, *Dharma* (the teachings) and *Sangha* (the spiritual community)[2]. This is another crucial difference between *Sanātana Dharma* and Buddhism.

Early Buddhism was taught on the premise of monasticism viz. abandonment and the teaching of emptiness, void, momentariness etc... However, modern Buddhism has lots of similarities with *Vedānta*, especially in Consciousness and happiness studies which do appear to be quite at variance with early Buddhism.

1 Isavasya Upanisad 1

2 buddhaṃ śaraṇaṃ gacchāmi
dharmaṃ śaraṇaṃ gacchāmi
saṅghaṃ śaraṇaṃ gacchāmi

It is easy to say renounce everything. But after renouncing what do you depend upon? The question is why are you renouncing? Are you renouncing because someone told you to? And why renounce, if there was nothing worth seeking?

Vedānta appears to make inroads where Buddhism stops. It does that by asking one to renounce everything with a dependence on *caitanyam*, Consciousness. In contrast, this is a positive approach as opposed to the abandonment of early Buddhism.

The discussions and dispassionate analysis of Buddhism conducted thus far may present a negative picture of the religion and Buddha. It is worth to know that the *Purāṇa*-s have presented both favourable and unfavourable depictions of the Buddha. Several *Purāṇa*-s have also presented Buddha as an incarnation of *Viṣṇu*. Our attitude towards Buddha should be disassociated from the dispassionate analysis of Buddhism's philosophical conclusions. In no way should the analyses lead to disrespect towards a peaceful teacher and exemplar like Buddha and the religion Buddhism.

The renunciation referred to in this verse does not mean *sannyāsā*, but rather the appreciation that all pursuits are not as important as the pursuit to know Consciousness. Consciousness is worth pursuing because from it, the whole universe emerged and depends on for its existence.

The same teaching appears in *Sādhana Pañcakam*, a text written by *Śaṅkarācārya* and which has forty prescriptions for a *mumukṣu*.

dṛḍhataraṃ karmāśu santyajyatām

Give up all *karma*s firmly.

The desire for the *ātman* leads you to renounce the importance for everything else. This renunciation is not physical renunciation. Honestly you cannot renounce anything. Renunciation is not the displacement of an object, but a displacement in understanding. Renunciation does not mean that you remove the objects of experience in your life, but rather to know the intrinsic value of an object and not the superimposed value. For example, a car is a car, not a status symbol.

You should objectively appreciate the realities in the world. You use any object for what it delivers and not for anything more; this objectivity can also be viewed as *sannyāsā*. There is no point in taking up *sannyāsā* if you still have value for things. You can even get attached to the *paramparā* or to the ochre robes. The tradition keeps the knowledge alive but it should not become more important than the knowledge. This superimposition of values can happen in the very environment in which this teaching takes place. So, one has to be careful or you will have attributed values such as, "I am a *mumukṣu* not a *karmaṭha*." "I do not study your kind of *Vedānta*, I am studying traditional *Vedānta*," "I have got the best teacher". All these statements are outcomes of the very superimpositions that you are trying to remove.

When these superimpositions are renounced, knowledge takes place automatically. This is the reason *Ramaṇa Mahārṣi* stated that the real *jñāni* is not a *sannyāsin* but an *atī- āśramī*[3]. He is beyond the *āśrama*-s (the four traditional stages of life) as well as *varṇa* (caste or vocation). A *jñāni* can be wearing ochre robes but does not depend upon the ochre robes. What *Ramaṇa Mahārṣi* stated is also supported by the *Upaniṣad*.[4]

Learning has to be judgment free. Judgment is not always negative, it can be also positive. Looking at oneself with great esteem is also a problem. One should have a functional self-esteem but not low self-esteem. This is especially hard in modern life. Sometimes we give a donation thinking we want *puṇya* or with the notion that I am a giver. Sometimes we donate thinking we are fortunate and that we are doing someone a favour. Instead try to give as a duty – do it and forget about it. There is no need to justify it or analyse it. That is why doing all actions in a spirit of *Karma Yoga* is very meritorious.

We make many such judgements at the subconscious level and are not even aware of them. Renunciation does not always have to be the taking up of *sannyāsā*, which is reserved for those with strong *vairāgya*. As a common man, you can also renounce your superimposed values. There should be no room for judgements for a *mumukṣu*. The only person to be judged is the person in the mirror.

These judgements could not be evident to us because they are in the subconscious and come naturally to us. In modern psychology, it is called a 'belief system'. We naturally get agitated when anyone shakes our belief system. The belief system could be judgements about one's educational qualifications, work, social status and caste affiliations. I cannot accept another person's view because I think I am always right.

There is another kind of *adhyāsa* which is looking for self-worth; we fulfill

---

3 see Talk 291 in the Talks with Sri Ramana Maharshi

4 Śvetāśvatara Upaniṣad 6.21

this by getting a religion, an occupation or an education. Sometimes, I have a value for something that cannot fulfill and so I create a proxy. For example, I have a value for religiosity but I may not be religious. As a result, I will want to marry someone religious or have a close friend who is religious so that those desires of mine are fulfilled through that proxy. We identify through association and we want to rub shoulders with those who are prominent. Question this attitude!

For the sake of transactions and relationships, I accept and respect some values that others have. I do not step on others' toes but that does not mean I follow their footsteps in attributing those values. The need to find self-worth is fine for a person who is in *pravṛtti mārga*, but the need has to be examined and neutralised by the one in *nivṛtti mārga*.

24

BRAHMAN AS SPACE

घटस्याभ्यन्तरे बाह्ये यथाकाशं प्रवर्तते |
तथात्माभ्यन्तरे बाह्ये ब्रह्माण्डस्य प्रवर्तते || ५१

ghaṭasyābhyantare bāhye yathākāśaṃ pravartate |
tathātmābhyantare bāhye brahmāṇḍasya pravartate || 51

Just as space exists inside and outside a pot, so the ātman exists inside and outside the universe. Here comes the sixth nyāya – ghaṭākāśa nyāya. I am going to share a bit about space before explaining the nyāya.

The five elements (*pañcabhūta*) – space, air, fire, water and earth, have a gradation. It starts from the subtlest (space) and becomes grosser progressively. That is why another word for creation is grossification (*pancīkaraṇam*). You have to understand why this model is given. This model is not to prove that the five elements led to the creation of the universe because the modern periodic table will demolish this belief. The periodic table is the tabular display of all the chemical elements known to man, which is 118 in total thus far. The *pañcabhūta* system falls flat in front of 118, but why are we still accepting this five-elemental model for creation?

The *pañcabhūta* model states that the world we see and feel can be understood through five types of elements from subtle to gross. When we analyse the *pañcabhūta*, we understand that from space comes air, from air fire, from fire water and from water earth. And if you looked at it closely, water can remove earth, fire will make water evaporate, absence of air will extinguish fire and the lack of space will make air unsupportable. One depends upon the other – that is why the process is called grossification.

The grossest is earth and the subtlest is space because you cannot objectify space. In fact, the Buddhists do not accept five, but only four elements. They do not accept space because you cannot objectify it. If space cannot be proven, it means it has to be known not as an object but as a concept. The *Upaniṣad*-s use space as a tool to understand *Brahman*[1].

Let us take an empty room and fill it up with people till there is no more space left. By rule, if something is not there, that means it has been

1 see Bṛhadāraṇyaka Upaniṣad2.1.5 , 5.1.1, Chāndogya Upaniṣad 1.9.1-2, 4.10.5, 8.14.1

displaced. So, in this case, where did the space go? The space has not been displaced even with all the people in the room because the space we see is neither an object nor entirely a concept. It stands somewhere between. Space accommodates everything without losing itself. It is there but cannot be proved by perception alone. Hence it is seen to be the subtlest.

However, some traditions view space as a material called ether. There are traditions that contend that this universe came from space alone, but that space is itself an element which is a product of creation. The justification for such a view is that sound depends upon space. If there was no space, there will be no sound. That is why the *Rg Veda*[2] states, that whatever was revealed as *śruti*, was in space (*vyoman*).

The *Veda*-s were revealed to *ṛṣīs* who were called *mantradṛṣṭā* (seers of mantra). That means that at one point in time, they started to 'see' the *mantra*-s. The *Rg Veda* states that before the revelation of the *mantra*-s to the *ṛṣī*-s, the *mantra*-s were in space and eventually the revelation took place through the space of the *ṛṣī*-s' hearts (*hṛdaya ākāśa*).

The verse states that space pervades a pot (*ghaṭa*) both inside and outside. All of us know that in any empty pot, there is space within it and of course outside it too. Now if you broke the pot what happens to the pot space? The pot space now has merged with the outside space. The question is whether it merged or were 'both' spaces only one?

See that pot as yourself. We think there is something within us and something outside us. We think that this individual is like a pot space which will merge with the all-pervading *Brahman* space outside. This separation is in the mind with respect to the body and the *ātman*. This limitation is called an *upādhī*, which seemingly limits. The pot space and the outside space are seemingly different. If they were actually different, the pot space will be there even after breaking the pot. Before the pot there was space, during the pot there was space and after the pot also there is space. *Brahman* was there before the *jīva*; during the *jīva*'s life and after the *jīva* dies, *Brahman* is also there. So, *Brahman* is always there regardless of the forms you take.

The reason I see the two different spaces is because I lend reality to the pot. The mistake I made with respect to the pot is the same mistake I make with respect to this body. This is called *adhyāsa*. I see myself as the limited being starting from the *ahaṅkāra* (the ego sense) onwards and lend it reality. I lend reality to the body or the pot space, only because of my *avidyā*. Although

2 Rg Veda 1.164.39

there is only space, I assume there are two spaces.

The verse concludes that in the ever-changing universe, there is only one *ātman*. Here the *Yoga* and *Sāṅkhya* schools are dismissed because they believe that there are many *ātman*-s.

The word *ātman* can be used to mean several things. For example, upon death people say that the *ātman* has left the body. This means that the corpse has no *ātman*. This view has a big defect because the *Upaniṣad*-s teach that the whole universe is *Brahman* or *ātman*. So can we say that the corpse is not in the universe? So, what leaves the body? It is the subtle body (*sūkṣmaśarīra*) that has left, not the *ātman*. Then why do we say that the *ātman* has left the body? This error is due to ignorance, and hence we identify the *ātman* with the subtle body.

The word '*ātman*' just means 'Self' and it can be used to mean anything pertaining to our being. Here is an illustration to better understand this. A coconut with husk falls from the tree, and you remove the husk. After the husk has been removed, what remains is also called a coconut. And then you break the coconut, and what is left is the kernel. And you now call the kernel that is left a coconut too. And then you grate the kernel and the gratings are also called coconut.

Similarly, you take each layer off the *ātman* and what remains can also be called the *ātman*. You remove the body, what remains is the *ātman*, you remove the subtle body *ātman* remains and if you remove the causal body, only the *ātman* remains.

Hence, we ignorantly mistake the subtle body that leaves at death to be the *ātman* but in fact we should use the word *ātman* only to that Self which is the core of your being which is not subject to change or displaced in space. I am not saying that you should change your jargon when you talk to others but you should understand that the *ātman* never leaves nor dies. That is why sometimes they use the word 'real self' to distinguish it from the 'unreal self', which is the body-mind-sense complex. The real self pervades everything and yet untouched by it. That is why *Śaṅkarācārya* uses the term '*antarātman*' and '*pratyagātman*' to indicate the real self, *paramātman*, to distinguish it from the *jivātman*, the individual self.

The coconut illustration is a good way to show how we can use one word to describe different things. Similarly, the word *ātman* can be used to describe different realities.

असंलग्नं यथाकाशं मिथ्याभूतेषु वस्तुषु |
असंलग्नस्तथात्मा तु कार्यवर्गेषु नान्यथा || ५२

asaṃlagnaṃ yathākāśaṃ mithyābhūteṣu vastuṣu |
asaṃlagnastathātmā tu kāryavargeṣu nānyathā || 52

As the space pervading everything is untouched by them, so the ātman in spite of pervading all forms of effects is untouched by them.

The verse states that space pervades the four unreal elements because in space alone the other four elements exist. Like the space that is unattached to the four elements, the *ātman* is unattached to the five elements that constitute the universe. The elements are an effect and hence *mithyā* or dependent reality. *Brahman* or *ātman* is the cause and hence *satyam*. Space and the four elements are the best illustration for showing that the cause is untouched by the effect. *Pancabhūta*-s have birth and destruction and if they are in contact with *ātman* then *ātman* too is subject to change. But there is no contact between the two. Hence the verse uses the words *asamlagna ātman* (unattached *ātman*).

Space is a good indicator to understand *ātman* because it is the first thing to emerge from *Brahman*. It is the most proximate element to *Brahman* by virtue of its subtlety. The *Bhagavad Gītā* states the same point:

yathā sarvagataṃ saukṣmyādākāśaṃ nopalipyate
sarvatrāvasthito dehe tathātmā nopalipyate

As the all-pervading space is not tainted because of its subtlety,
so the *ātman* seated everywhere in the body is not tainted.[3]

Space helps you to understand that *Brahman* is all pervasive, accommodating and untouched. You can occupy a room but space will still be there. You leave the room, space will still be there unaffected. It has not been displaced and is the closest indicator to *Brahman* and hence a great tool to understand *Brahman*.

3 Bhagavad Gītā 13.33

SACCIDĀNANDA ĀTMAN

ईश्वरादि जगत् सर्वम् आत्मव्याप्तं समन्ततः ।
एकोऽस्ति सच्चिदानन्दः पूर्णो द्वैतविवर्जितः ॥ ५३

īśvarādi jagat sarvam ātmavyāptaṃ samantataḥ |
eko'sti saccidānandaḥ pūrṇo dvaitavivarjjitaḥ || 53

From Īśvara down to everything else in the entire universe is pervaded by the Self. It is one, it is saccidānanda . It is whole and free from duality.

From *Īśvara* to the smallest thing in the universe is pervaded by *ātman*. The moment you say something pervades the other, the second reality gets dependent. This reality that pervades everything is called *saccidānanda*, a new word introduced by the text. *Saccidānanda* is another definitive word for *ātman*. *Sat* means 'truth' and that which exists in all three periods of time. *Cit* means 'Consciousness' or that which enables all knowledge to take place and lends reality to all. The word *ānanda* means 'happiness' or what is popularly referred to as bliss.

Bliss is a very misleading word. It makes it seem as if there is something greater than happiness! If I were to ask you whether you were happy, you would say 'yes' or 'no'. That is sufficient to describe the emotional state you are in and hence the word 'bliss' is quite unnecessary, especially in our discussions about the *ātman*!

There is something unique about the word *saccidānanda* which can be broken up into *sat* + *cit* + *ānanda*. These three descriptive words are not to be mistaken as three attributes of *Brahman*. If *Brahman* had attributes then it should not be *nirguṇa* and therefore not *Brahman* any more. Attributes are like *nāma* and *rūpa* and therefore *mithyā*. We cannot use three separate words to describe *Brahman* either. If we used three separate words then *Brahman* would be seen to possess three different aspects and hence becomes subject to change. In Sanskrit, there are two ways to describe an object – *viśeṣaṇam* and *lakṣaṇaṃ*.

Viśeṣaṇam is an attribute. For example, let us look at this chair – it is grey in colour, round in shape and one feet long. We have talked about its volume, colour and shape and these three qualities are independent of each other. We can create different permutations with them. For example, the chair can be round and a foot long but in red. Or it can be red, one feet long but square. This is *viśeṣaṇam*, three distinctive attributes, each of them independent.

The word *saccidānanda* does not refer to this type of definition. Rather it refers to *lakṣaṇaṃ* which means that the very word itself, points to the referred object. Let us take sugar as an example. Sugar is sweet or rather sugar = sweet. Do you say "sweet sugar"? Sweetness is the nature of sugar, so what is sweet is sugar. You cannot say sweet sugar but you can say grey chair. The grey colour and the chair are two different things. But sugar and sweetness cannot be distinguished because they mean the same thing. *Saccidānanda* is like that, a *lakṣaṇaṃ*. It defines the *svarūpa* or the nature of *ātman*.

Why then does the author use *saccidānanda* and not any other word to describe *ātman*? We saw the model of the *ātman* pervading the entire, body-mind-sense complex. The mind is the subtlest thing in the body which constitutes of gross and subtle elements. To understand *Brahman*, I must analyse the mind first because it is subtler than the body and *prāṇa*.

If I were to analyze the way the mind works, I can reduce its behaviour into three fundamental 'wants'. They appear like 'wants' but are almost like 'needs', because you seem to have no choice in the matter. The first thing is that the mind dislikes death. If that is not true there would be no hospitals.

Yudhiṣṭhira states in the *Mahābhārata*[1] that although so many people die, one never thinks that "I will die". Even animals do not want to die; they will run when you try to catch them. This instinct to survive is in people too. Everything I do, from gathering food to building shelters is to survive another day. It shows that instinctively I do not want to die. When I dye or colour my hair, it means that I do not want to die too, when I put on cosmetic to hide those wrinkles, it means that I do not want to die. In fact, everything I do is driven towards not wanting to die or perpetuating my life by looking youthful too.

The second thing I want is not to be called stupid. No one feels good when called stupid because you know instinctively that you have the capacity to 'know'. Our inquisitive nature shows the desire for knowledge. That is why infants will put everything into their mouth and grasp everything they can because the senses are programmed to 'know'. The sense organs give perceptive knowledge or *pratyakṣa jñāna*.

1 Yakṣa Praśna in Aranya Parva, 311–12

Lastly, everyone wants happiness and no one likes sorrow. If I were to have written about the saddest things in life chapter after chapter, would you continue reading this book? Somehow sadness does not sit well with us. Some people like to be sad but that is because they find happiness in being sad. Also, sometimes you can be happy even in pain, for instance while observing a fast or performing any form of physical austerity. But innately you do not want sorrow. You will never pursue anything that creates sadness for yourself. So, the nature the Self is *sat*, *cit* and *ānanda* and these are reflected through the mind's wants.

Fundamentally, the first two we share with animals. No animal wants to die; and every animal is curious and will try to explore. Animals also enjoy what comes to them but do not have an evolved form of enjoyment like humans. The next question is why does the mind behave the way it does? Why does it not want to die, be ignorant and sorrowful.

The *śāstra* states that the mind is the subtlest thing and hence like a mirror reflects the nature of *ātman*. Like the crystal that takes on the colour of the proximate rose, the mind reflects the nature of *ātman*. If mind does not want to die, it means that the *ātman* is immortal; if the mind does not want to be ignorant, it means the *ātman* is all-knowing and if the mind wants to be happy it means the *ātman* is happiness. By understanding the nature of the mind, you understand *ātman*. Not knowing that I am immortal, all-knowledgeable and already happy, I keep searching for all of this in the external world. I make this mistake because the body-sense-mind complex is structured like that. It only knows how to go out but not inwards. No education teaches you to go inside except *Vedic* education. Everything else only teaches you to graze the outside world.

The moment you understand your nature to be *saccidānanda*, you are complete. You do not look for immortality anymore, you do not look for knowledge anymore and you do not look for happiness anymore because all of these you are.

The verse adds that the *ātman* is without a second (*dvaita vivarjitaḥ*). Only when there is a second reality, can you seek something. You cannot seek that which is not apart from you. If I say seek yourself, you cannot because you are already what you are seeking. The verse states the *ātman* is one or *ekosti*. This *ekosti* is the same as the *ekam jñāna* of the first verse. The *śāstra* quotes the same word to indicate it is speaking about the same reality. There cannot be two *ekam*-s.

26

SELF-ILLUMINATING ĀTMAN

यस्मात् प्रकाशको नास्ति स्वप्रकाशो भवेत्ततः ।
स्वप्रकशो यतस्तस्माद् आत्मा ज्योतिः स्वरूपकः ।। ५४

yasmāt prakāśako nāsti svaprakāśo bhavettataḥ |
svaprakaśo yatastasmād ātmā jyotiḥ svarūpakaḥ || 54

The self-illuminating is one for which there is no other illuminator. Because it illumines itself, the ātman is the form of light.

Ātman is *svaprakāśa* or self-illuminating and does not need a separate energy source, like the torchlight which needs batteries to illumine and the lamp which needs the oil and wick. You can use light to find something that is not lit up but if it is already lit, you do not need the light to see it. *Svaprakāśa* hence means, that which is self-evident and obvious. The implication of this verse is that if you are already illumined, can you look elsewhere for yourself? It also means that you could be knocking at the wrong *āśrama*-s, the wrong philosophies, and practices, to look for the Self, when actually you are the self-evident *ātman*.

If I do not need anything to see myself, what is then really obstructing me? It is ignorance.

When something is *svaprakāśa*, it is that which lights up everything else. The whole universe that I experience is lit up by the *ātman*. It is *jyotiḥ jyoti* – light of lights.

Na tatra sūryo bhāti na candratārakaṃ,
nemā vidyuto bhānti kuto yamagniḥ
tamevabhāntam anubhāti sarvaṃ
tasya bhāsā sarvamidam vibhāti

> There the sun does not shine, nor the moon or the stars; nor do these flashes of lightning shine there. How can this fire do so? Everything shines according as He does so; by His light all this shines diversely.[1]

The fact that you are reading this book and thinking about it means that you are the *svaprakāśa ātman*. You are conscious of all these because you make it evident. And that takes place because the Self is self-evident. The

1 Muṇḍaka Upaniṣad, 2.2.10; Kaṭha Upaniṣad, 2.2.15

ātman does not need anything to reveal itself. The *Upaniṣad* states that a *vṛtti* or a thought is enough to show that you are the *ātman* because all thoughts are not separate from it.

pratibodhaviditaṃ matamamṛtatvaṃ hi vindate
ātmanā vindate vīryaṃ vidyayā vindate'mṛtam

> When *Brahman* is known in every state of cognition, It is known in reality, because one thus attains immortality. Through *ātman* is attained strength and through knowledge is attained immortality.[2]

There is a popular axiom by Descarte, "I think, therefore I am"[3]. The *Vedāntic* version is "I am, therefore I think". I do not need a thought to reveal myself. For example, in sleep I have no thoughts but when I wake up I know I had slept. In fact, the absence of thoughts in deep sleep does not mean that I do not exist in that state.

Some people mistake the *ātman* for physical light and meditate upon that light. Sometimes people imagine a light in the heart and meditate upon it. Such meditation will not lead to *mokṣa* because the meditation is not on knowledge but a superimposition.

The traditional meditation using light is more metaphorical than visual. Light is a metaphor to understand the nature of the Self. When the *śāstra* refers to *ātman* as light, it is not the physical light. The light is an indirect indicator (*upalakṣanaṃ*) to understand the self-luminous nature of the Self. Even the physical sun will one day burn out but the *śāstra* states that the Self outlives all these because it is eternal (*sat*). In fact, it is the *ātman*, that lends reality to everything.

However, visualisation meditation techniques are useful as *upāsanā*-s because they help to strengthen the mind. One particular result of such meditation is a one-pointed mind (*citta ekāgrata*). From the standpoint of *ātman*jñāna, such techniques may not be the direct means to knowledge but we cannot completely disregard them too. These are very important techniques to strengthen the mind, without which we cannot assimilate this knowledge.

As discussed earlier, most *Vedānta* schools including the traditional schools place less importance on these *upāsanā*-s. They do not practice meditation and instead give more emphasis to knowledge - *śravaṇam*. Although *śravaṇam* is the key, if the mind is not prepared, assimilation will

2 Kena Upaniṣad 2.4

3 In latin "Cogito ergo sum", appears in his work "Discourse on the Method"

not take place. Even to pay attention during *śravaṇam*, meditation helps. The ability to pay attention is *citta ekāgrata*. A one-pointed mind is essential for *śravaṇam* because while doing *śravaṇam*, you can be thinking about your dinner or a forthcoming appointment. You could possibly miss an important teaching during *śravaṇam* if your mind was distracted.

Although *citta ekāgrata* can be developed through many means, meditation is one such means. This does not refer to the *dhyāna* that is revealed in the *Upaniṣad*-s, in the form of *śravaṇam, mananam* and *nididhyāsanam*. I am referring to simple *upāsanā*-s. Even taking the name of a deity, or focusing on the image of a deity can help in making the mind one-pointed.

This one-pointed mind is an important pre-requisite in *Vedānta* or *ātmavicāra* (self-enquiry). As presented in a previous chapter, this qualification is called *samādhāna*. You could use any technique that you have been taught to calm the mind. But do not mistake it to be the means to know the Self. *Japa* as a *mānasa karma* (mental action) is equally effective. If you do it verbally, it may not be so. But before you do mental *japa*, you have to master the verbal *japa* or else after the tenth repetition your mind could get distracted. You can also choose what you like to meditate on. One of the principles of *Tantra* is that we should always meditate upon the things that we like. If you follow a meditation technique that you do not like, you will easily give up.

In the case of *kāyika karma* or physical action, it is fine if you do not feel connected to the deity you are offering worship to. You can be a *Śiva bhakta* yet you could be offering prayers to *Viṣṇu* because while offering prayers your mind could be with *Śiva*. But in meditation, this disconnect in not possible because the very thing that is doing the activity is the mind and the mind cannot be anywhere else.

So, in summary, you must meditate on something that you enjoy. One of the meditation techniques recommended by a *Tantra śāstra*[4] is to recollect an experience that brought you joy. Every day at a stipulated time, you could be silent and with your eyes closed recollect all the joyful experiences of the day.

4 see Vijñānabhairava Tantra, 71

27

ĀTMAN NOT LIMITED BY TIME AND SPACE

अवच्छिन्नो यतो नास्ति देशकालस्वरूपकः |
आत्मनः सर्वथा तस्माद् आत्मा पूर्णो भवेत्खलु || ५५

avacchinno yato nāsti deśakālasvarūpakaḥ |
ātmanaḥ sarvathā tasmād ātmā pūrṇo bhavetkhalu || 55

Because the ātman is in no way limited by place, time or shape, therefore it is indeed whole and complete.

This verse follows on from the previous verse which stated that *ātman* is *jyoti svarūpa* and does not need anything else to light it up. This verse states that *ātman* is not bound by time and space. *Deśa* means space; previously we discussed space as an element, and here space is used in the conventional sense. *Kāla* is time. Time and space cannot bind *ātman*. In fact time and space depend on *ātman* for its existence.

The body-mind-sense complex and the external world are bound by time and space. One limitation of space is that you cannot be in two places at the same time; when you are here you cannot be elsewhere. You can only be in one place at a time.

One limitation of time is that everything other than the *ātman* has a beginning and an end in time. We know *ātman* to be not created and eternal. And hence time cannot limit *ātman*.

The *ātman* is all-pervasive and is not bound by space. In fact, time and space exist because of *ātman*. Very simply, the concepts of time and space exist in only two states - waking and dream states. In the deep sleep state there is no notion of time and space. Without a mind, there is neither space nor time. And you are not the mind too.

Everything depends on *ātman* but the latter depends upon nothing. Therefore, the verse states *ātman* is *purṇa* or complete. It is certainly complete because there is not place where it does not exist and there is no time that the *ātman* did not exist. The *ātman* that the *śāstra* reveals is complete and this *ātman* is you. You are complete.

28

ĀTMAN NOT LIMITED BY FIVE ELEMENTS

यस्मान्न विद्यते नाशः पञ्चभुतैर् वृथात्मकैः |
तस्मादात्मा भवेन्नित्यस्तन्नाशो न भवेत्खलु || ५६

yasmānna vidyate nāśaḥ pañcabhutair vṛthātmakaiḥ |
tasmādātmā bhavennityastannāśo na bhavetkhalu || 56

Since it is not destroyed along with the five elements, the ātman is eternal. In fact it is beyond destruction.

The *pañcabhūta* cannot destroy the *ātman*, just as time and space cannot limit the *ātman*. *Pañcabhūta* is introduced now because it exists in time and space. *Pañcabhūta* and their products including the body-mind-sense complex cannot limit the *ātman*. The gross aspect of the *pañcabhūta* constitutes the gross body and its subtle aspect, *tanmātrā*-s, constitute the mind. The point is that if the body gets destroyed, you are not destroyed; if the mind gets destroyed, you are not destroyed. That is why in deep sleep, the body and mind get 'as though' destroyed to illustrate that you can exist without the awareness of the body and mind. I use the words 'as though' to indicate that they do not get destroyed literally. Every day there is an opportunity when the mind and body appear to get destroyed but that does not mean you ceased not exist. You still got up from sleep into the waking state. This is a good experience to show that even without the body consciousness and mind consciousness you can exist.

When the pot is destroyed, the clay is still there. Similarly, when body and mind get destroyed, the *ātman* remains; not that you were not the *ātman* when the body and mind were alive.

na tvevāhaṃ jātu nāsaṃ na tvaṃ neme janādhipāḥ
na caiva na bhaviṣyāmaḥ sarve vayamataḥ param
dehino'sminyathā dehe kaumāraṃ yauvanaṃ jarā
tathā dehāntaraprāptirdhīrastatra na muhyati

> There was never a time when these monarchs, you, or I did not exist; nor shall we ever cease to exist in the future. Just as the soul acquires a childhood body, a youth body, and an old age body during this life; similarly, the soul acquires another

body after death. This should not delude the wise.[1]

Even when you were alive you were the *ātman*. The point that is being made here is that *pañcabhūta* cannot destroy you because even if they are destroyed, the *ātman* remains. I, the *ātman*, witness the destruction of the *pañcabhūta*. When the wave merges into the water, the water witnesses it and does not get destroyed. Similarly, when the body-mind-sense complex gets destroyed, the *ātman* does not get destroyed, it is untouched. That is why it is called *śuddha caitanya*. Another way to understand is when the snake gets destroyed, the rope remains. Therefore, *ātman* is eternal, without a beginning or end. You are eternal without a beginning or end.

All that we call destruction takes place in space and time. Destruction takes place every second when an old cell dies and a new one is born. The moment you are born, you are dying. The meaning of the word *śarīram* (body) is *śīryate iti śarīra* - that which will be cremated one day. When you know your Self, it does not mean that the mind disappears or the body disappears. Instead they get resolved because *ātman* pervades all these, like water in waves.

यस्मात्तदन्यो नास्तीह तस्मादेकोऽस्ति सर्वदा |
यस्मात्तदन्यो मिथ्या स्यादात्मा सत्यो भवेत् खलु || ५७

yasmāttadanyo nāstīha tasmādeko'sti sarvadā |
yasmāttadanyo mithyā syādātmā satyo bhavet khalu || 57

Because there is nothing in the world other than It, it is the one eternal. Because that which is other than it, is false; the ātman alone is true.

This verse is another summary statement. When you look at these verses, they appear as though repetitive but this repetition is very important. Repetition is helpful in *mananam* to clarify the subject from different angles, so that you are not fixated to any one perspective. Repetition is also required because we have different obstacles in understanding this knowledge. This is the same reason why we have so many *Upaniṣad*-s. Our mind is like a diamond or a crystal with many cuts in which light gets reflected from different directions. Likewise, the obstacles in our mind are from different directions. As a result, the *śāstra* handles the obstacles from different perspectives.

Sometimes the teaching tradition uses a single word to denote different ideas, and sometimes one idea can be presented using different words. This is done so that the listener is not bored or fixated. If *Vedānta* bores you,

1 Bhagavad Gītā 2.12-13

it means that you could be possibly looking for something interesting or entertaining. It is like you not wanting to watch a movie twice because you are looking for entertainment and it bores you the second time. The mind behaves like that even while learning *Vedānta*. The *śāstra* will repeat the teaching from different perspectives to sublate the notion that you need to look for something interesting.

The repetition helps because each time you hear, you are a different person and the impact may be different. Remember that over time, you would have changed and the teaching that did not work before, may work now. That has happened to me in my life and I have observed that phenomenon taking place with the learners in my classes many times as well. This is how we mature and evolve in our understanding.

This verse states that nothing other than the *ātman* exists. That shows that anything that I see as apart from myself, is only a part of Self. Verses like this one may appear insignificant but if you sit back and think, they will give you great insights. The verse states that everything that you see other than the *ātman* exists in you and is not separate from you. Everything that depends upon you comes and goes but *ātman* does not come and go.

Ātman exists forever and anything else that you see other than the *ātman* is *mithyā*. *Mithyā* is also defined as something that gets falsified at the dawn of knowledge. Whenever you use the word 'my', such as – my house, my bed, my body, my *prāna* etc., there is a sense of ownership; or rather you have given ownership. What comes after 'my' is the object that you own. Whatever that gets objectified is *mithyā*. *Ātman* alone is *satyam*, the rest is *mithyā*. The *Vedānta Diṇḍima* states,

brahma satyam, jagat mithyā; jīvo brahmaiva na aparaḥ

Brahman (or *ātman*) is eternal; the universe is false. *Jīva* is certainly *Brahman* and not separate from it.[2]

2 Vedānta Diṇḍima 67

REMOVAL OF AVIDYĀ LEADS TO HAPPINESS

अविद्याभूतसंसारे दुःखनाशे सुखं यतः |
ज्ञानादाद्यन्तशून्यं स्यात्तस्मादात्मा भवेत्सुखम् || ५८

avidyābhūtasaṃsāre duḥkhanāśe sukhaṃ yataḥ |
jñānādādyantaśūnyaṃ syāttasmādātmā bhavetsukham || 58

Happiness is gained by the destruction of sorrow and Saṃsāra arises from ignorance. The ātman which is consciousness without beginning or end is indeed (the real) Happiness.

This verse restates the phrase from the first verse of the text - *jñānādādyantaśūnyaṃ*, to remind that we are still talking about the same *ātman*. *Avidyā bhūta samsāra* – *samsāra* is born from ignorance. A mumukśu will find *samsāra* to be a world without an essence. He does not have a taste for it. *Samsāra* exists only because I do not know myself. Sorrow or *duḥkha* is one of the attributes of *samsāra* and you are trying to remove it because you are *saccidānanda*. You naturally seek *ānanda* and whenever there is *duḥkha*, you do not accept it because it does not sit well with your true nature.

The verse states that in the pursuit of Self-Knowledge, the destruction of *duḥkha* takes place and sukham is attained. They are not two different things but are two sides of the same coin. The destruction of sorrow is accompanied by the attainment of happiness. Also, when *duḥkha* is removed, *samsāra* is removed.

How is *duḥkha* removed? Let us first analyse the *duḥkha* which is called *samsāra*. If one were to look at oneself, what is it that makes us want to accomplish something? It is desire. Desires are caused by inadequacy. You cannot desire what you already have. That is why you will never desire another nose but you may desire a change in the structure of your nose. Therefore, desire presupposes a sense of inadequacy and this inadequacy drives all of us crazy. Instead of living your life, you are always trying to become someone or something else. We are programmed from young to be like that. It is not a problem for the one who is enjoying life in *pravṛtti mārga*. It is only a problem for the one who sees a defect in this *pravṛtti mārga*. So, do not ever tell others who are enjoying their life that they are inadequate!

This 'life of becoming' is indeed *samsāra*. And you do it by changing the things around you and yourself. We have feelings like "I want to be more beautiful" or "I want to be more educated". This life of becoming has no end and it can be very tormenting. Every minute you want a new experience, a feather in your cap, to be successful and to prove to the world. This proving instinct is very interesting. You do not want to prove everything to everyone. You only want to prove to the one who has value for what you want to prove. Suppose your lover values money, then you will try to be rich to prove your worth and so on. Think about what a torture it is. Your existence is valued and validated by someone other than you!

Someone's idea of success will buy you in. And it is easy to buy because of one's sense of inadequacy. For example, someone knocks on your door to sell a vacuum cleaner. You say you already have one but suppose he says, "Wait wait wait! Look at this one, it is 1,500 watts." You did not know the power of your cleaner because you did not know such a thing existed and the current vacuum cleaner was doing its job. Still you continue the conversation and remark that your cleaner's power is 600 watts. Then the salesman shows a picture of microbes in carpets that look very scary. And tells you the ill-effects of these microbes on your young children. The sale is done.

This happened because a sense of inadequacy was created during the conversation. It is easy to sell anything as long as you create a sense of inadequacy in the potential buyer. That is what expert salesmen do. It is like an insurance policy. If I painted a bleak future, there is a higher chance that you will buy it. You would have bought it if you needed it, but now you would certainly buy it because the adversity gets magnified and it only points out that you are a limited being.

This life of becoming is *duḥkha* and it is sorrowful because not even for one minute are you happy with yourself. Even if you were to be happy, someone will point out your deficiency. For example, suddenly one day the husband tells the wife, "You have put on weight," and there goes the wife on a spree to slimming centres. He would hardly said, "You have been a nice person to me all this while". All you need is someone to destabilize you and make you feel inadequate. But if you were really adequate, nobody's words can disturb you because a complete being cannot be improved further. You flip over the pages of a newspaper, and inside it almost all advertisements tell you that you are incomplete, directly or indirectly. Only the *śāstra* states you are complete and it is the total opposite of what you read in the tabloids and newspapers. You flip open the newspaper and you get *duḥkha*, instead if you explored the *Upaniṣad*-s, you would understand your nature to be *saccidānanda* and you will find the way out of this self-inadequacy.

On one side, you are completely overwhelmed with the idea that without this or that you are a total failure, but if you take a few steps backwards and ask yourself "Have I achieved enough?" and the answer could be that you are already living in excess. The poorest fellow also wants to 'become', and the richest fellow also wants to 'become'. The drive is common to both. One guy is comfortably uncomfortable and the other is uncomfortably uncomfortable. Internally both are uncomfortable. And this is what leads you to spirituality most of the time - the inner throbbing feeling that "I am small", "I am no good" or "no one likes me". You are always conforming to someone else's standards. A complete person will seldom point out someone else's inadequacies. Mostly it is the inadequate people who are out to get at each other. People who compete are adequate. Both the winner and loser are indeed inadequate. On the other hand, a *mukta* is one who is complete and hence does not have self-inadequacy because there is nothing more to gain. That is why most of the *mukta*-s or *svāmi*-s will not live in societies because they being what they are, they will not fit well in society. By being with us they will be alright but we get unhappy with them because they do not respond the way we expect them to respond. I am already becoming and I want others to become too. Poor *svāmi*-s who have to endure this nonsense from us.

That is why the first step in this path to *mokṣa* is not going out but in. You have to cultivate an inward-looking mind. If you start comparing yourself with others all the time it will not help you because all comparisons pertain to the body-sense-mind complex only. You cannot compare yourself with the *ātman*.

To summarise, this life of becoming is *duḥkha* and the branches of this tree of *duḥkha* reach out and touch others. When you are sad you make others unhappy and want to agitate others. It is like the boss who gets a bad appraisal and gives an even worse appraisal to his subordinates. Such behaviour comes from the notion that you are inadequate. The goal of *śāstra* is to help you make the transition from "I am inadequate" to "I am complete" (*aham alpa to aham pūrṇam*). The transition can be made by investigating inadequacy and desire.

Avidyā leads to inadequacy, inadequacy causes desire and desire gives rise to numerous *karma*-s. So, this whole chain rests on *avidyā* and the effort required is to remove *avidyā* through *vidyā*. When *avidyā* is removed, *duḥkha* is removed and in the process you gain *sukham*. This *sukham* is also called *ānanda*.

This *ānanda* must be understood properly. A popular mistake people make is to think that if you are a *mukta*, you are in a perennial state of happiness, even if you happen to be at a tsunami stricken area or at a funeral. This popular mistake must be investigated.

Based on the teachings of *Pañcadaśī*[1], there are two types of *ānanda*:

1. *svarupānanda* or *brahmānanda* - happiness due to Self-Knowledge
2. *vṛttimayānanda* or *viṣayānanda* - happiness based on thoughts or objects.

All happy experiences fall under the second category. Happiness rests on the mind while pleasure rests on the sense organs. There is really no physical happiness; happiness takes place in the mind. *Manolaya* is another term used for happiness, which means that the mind is in an undifferentiated state.

This happiness can be further divided into *priya*, *moda* and *pramoda* as per the *Upaniṣad*[2] which analyses *ānanda*. All conventional happiness we know can be divided into these three. *Priya* refers to the happiness the thought of an object gives. For example, the thought of someone you love will give you happiness. That person may not be in front of you but the thought of the person is sufficient to make you happy.

Now let us assume that the person you love is in front of you, the eyes report this data and you would feel happier. This happiness is called *moda* which happens when the object of desire is within the range of your sense organs. When you give that person a lovely hug, the happiness is even better and it is called *pramoda*, when the object of desire is experienced in you.

Hence, happiness ranges from *priya*, a thought; *moda*, within contact and *pramoda* becoming one with it. We go through all these three types of happiness daily. The good thing is that this was analysed and graded many thousands of years ago by the *Vedic ṛśis*. All happiness experiences take place in the form of thought. That is why some *vṛtti*-s sit well with you and

1 verse 11.87 states 3 types of happiness. The third type of happiness is called vāsanānanda which is not relevant to our discussion.

2 Taittīrīya Upaniṣad 2.5

some do not sit well with you. However, happiness always sits well with you.

If you take the position that a *mukta* is always happy, you are implying that he is always having happy thoughts and in a sense paralysed by happiness as he has no other *vṛtti*-s. Even if he encounters a sad situation, the mind is filled only with happiness *vṛtti*-s. Can he relate to anything then? I want you to see the implication of this type of impractical teachings that is being circulated in spiritual circles. The *Upaniṣad* corrects these mistakes; as it states that these three types of happiness are not the happiness that is presented as *ānanda* in the word *saccidānanda*.

Is *mokṣa* then dependent on *vṛtti*-s? If you are looking for a *vṛtti*, then it means that you could be looking for an object-centred happiness. Maybe the lack of object-centred happiness in your life creates the need to look for those objects that will give you *priya*, *moda* and *pramoda vṛtti*-s. If you happen to be seeking the three happiness *vṛtti*-s through *Vedānta*, then you are definitely at the wrong address because *Vedānta* will not give you *vṛttimayānanda* i.e., happiness based on thoughts or objects. A *mumukṣu* will not be looking for *vṛtti*-based happiness; instead he is seeking the removal of the very need to have this *vṛtti*. *Vṛttimayānanda* is entirely object driven. All the three types of happiness will come through your sensory organs. If *mokṣa* is going to give you another form of *vṛtti*, then it is limiting you because it means that without that *vṛtti* you are not free. Knowledge of *ātman* is therefore not another object-centred *vṛtti* like any other.

The *ānanda* in *saccidānanda* refers to *svarupānanda*. It is the *ānanda* of one's own nature, not a happiness *vṛtti*, but in knowing yourself as *pūrṇam*, complete.[3] *Svarupānanda* cannot come and go like *vṛttimayānanda*. It is not *ānanda* anymore but it is knowing yourself to be *ananta* or limitless. *Ānanda* in *Vedānta* is also not bliss because bliss implies a state. All states have a beginning and an end but *svarupānanda* has no beginning or end.

Let us analyse the word *ananta* (limitless). When you say, you are limitless, it means that the boundary of your body-mind-sense complex has to be now expanded to include everything, the whole universe. If everything is engulfed, is there a second thing outside your Consciousness? When you know that you are the universe, is there a second thing that can be desired? You cannot desire a second thing if you have become everything. There is no separation between the *ātman* and the universe. Hence you are

3 Sureśvara defines ānanda to be knowledge of Brahman in Taittirīya Upaniṣad Bhāṣya Vārtikam 2.720

complete. This is not another state of experience but it is the understanding that you are already that limitless *ātman*. This is *svarupānanda*; it is knowing that I 'am' complete, not that I 'became' complete.

Assuming that you know that you are limitless *ātman*, does that mean that you will not go after an object? No. It is not that you will not go after an object. But even if you did, it is not a problem. Even if you did not attain it, it is not a problem; even if you attained it is not a problem. Even if you are a failure or success it does not matter. Whatever be the situation you remain as the limitless *ātman*. It does not matter anymore. This is real freedom.

There are three types of freedom,

1. freedom <u>of</u> *vṛtti*,
2. freedom <u>from</u> *vṛtti*
3. freedom <u>with</u> *vṛtti*?

Freedom of *vṛtti* means you can do whatever you want with the *vṛtti*-s. Freedom from *vṛtti* means you are only free when you have no *vṛtti*-s and then there is freedom with *vṛtti*. Real freedom is with (or without) the *vṛtti*-s. Real freedom is 'in spite of' not 'despite of' the *vṛtti*-s. 'Despite of' means you are trying to remove something while 'in spite of' means irrespective of what you have, you are free.

In spite of this universe, I am complete and this is by knowing myself to be the limitless *ātman*. That is why in the thirteen *Mukhya Upaniṣad*-s[4] the word *saccidānanda* cannot be found; there is only *satyam, jñānam anantam.* [5]Instead of *ānanda* you have *ananta. Satyam* is the same as *sat*, *jñānam* is *cit* and *anantam* is *ānanda*. The real meaning of *ānanda* is indeed *ananta*.

Hence *saccidānanda* is a derivation of *satyam, jñānam, anantam*. Different *Upaniṣad*-s have explored different aspects of *saccidānanda*. The *Upaniṣad* explores the concept of *ātman* being *ānanda*.

ānandam brahmano vidvan na bhibheti kadācana

The person who knows *Brahman* as *ānanda* has no fear.[6]

Fear is a *samsāra lakṣanam*, a definition of *samsāra*. Many *Upaniṣad*-s do teach about *satyam* and *caitanyam*. The tradition combined these ideas and created the word *saccidānanda*.

---

4 the Mukhya Upaniṣad-s are the most important and ancient of all the recorded Upaniṣad-s. Almost all of them have been commented by Śaṅkarācārya

5 Taittirīya Upaniṣad 2.1.1

6 Taittirīya Upaniṣad 2.4.1

So *svarupānanda* is not a state that I am looking for. It is an understanding that I am complete and that I have nothing more to achieve. There is this contentment (*tṛpti*) when the life of becoming comes to an end. There is no need to become anything because I am already that.

When you gain this knowledge, perhaps you will get a *vṛtti* that makes you happy for a while but after which you do not look for more *vṛtti*-s to make you happier. This is it. The becoming process is over.

This also means that you should not look for behavioural changes in a *mukta* or *jñāni*. You also do not need to have a behavioural change. That is why different *mukta*-s behave differently. There is no standard behaviour. What I am trying to explain is that you should not expect any absolute behavioural changes in yourself with respect to *ātmajñāna*. All changes will only take place cognitively. Behaviour may change or may not change. It does not matter; rather you should allow all changes at the level of behavior to take place spontaneously and naturally.

Proceeding further, the verse states that the knowledge of the reality which has no beginning or end is *ananta*. This *ananta*, when known gives us *ānanda*. This is the *sukham* it is referring to; the *sukham* of *svarupānanda*.

That *ātman* which is *sukhaṃ*, is nothing but the knowledge of knowing myself to be without a beginning nor end. That is the teaching of this verse. We have also demolished the misunderstanding that *mokṣa* is a state of happiness. That is why the people who look for states become eternally lost. If your freedom was confined to a particular state then once you are out of it you are a *samsāri*. The typical solution prescribed for this problem by modern *Yoga* schools is to keep meditating, all the time. This makes the issue more complicated. All these prescriptions come from a foolish understanding that you 'need to do' something to be free. If you were to be free, then you are free at all times – freedom with *vṛtti*-s. "*Yatra yatra mano yāti tatra tatra samādhayāḥ*"[7] – wherever the mind goes, there you are free. The meaning of the verse is that you are free in every state of your mind.

Expecting happiness is a big mistake people make while pursuing *Vedānta*. It is important that we address this issue or else, you will think that you are not free when you are in a sorrowful moment. Happiness and sorrow are all *vṛtti*-s. Do not look for happiness in *Vedānta*. Instead you should be looking for the resolution of the need to be happy. The person who is really happy is the person who does not find a need to be happy! That is why

7 Dṛg Dṛśya Viveka 30, and a similar verse in Vijñāna Bhairava Tantra 116

that it is called *svarupānanda*, my real nature. I do not need to be happy. Whatever state I am in, I am okay. I am always eternal (*ādyantaśūnyaṃ*) and *amātrā*[8] – stateless or partless.

This real happiness is not having the need to be happy.[9] That is why it is also called *paramānanda*, which means the greatest happiness. The *Pañcadaśī* also calls it *Brahmānanda.*[10] The *mukta* has the attitude of acceptance regardless of experiences. He seeks what he wants to seek and does not go after things that he does not want. He enjoys that freedom without any of his experiences binding him because he knows nothing can bind the *ātman*. It is quite different for a *mumukśu* who should entertain discretion over his thoughts, words and deeds.

However, the tradition uses the word *ānanda* for a reason. It could be an incentive to initially desire the Self, because if it was shared that *mokṣa* has got nothing to do with happiness that you know of, then it would not have sustained your interest as much. So it is good to initially look at *Vedānta* as a pursuit of happiness. It is like a provisional belief until you understand it properly.

We shall now examine the behavior of the *mukta*. Each *mukta* is different in the way they would live their lives. One may love going to the temples to offer worship; another may say "Ah it's only a form that is in the temple" and choose not to offer worship. Likewise the behaviours between two *mukta*-s can be contradictory. So, we cannot use behaviour as a yardstick to judge a *mukta*. There is a popular Tamil proverb that says that *siddha*-s (*mukta*-s) behave like *pitta*-s (mad or eccentric). Here madness is not schizophrenic behaviour but implies that we cannot expect any standard behaviour from them. Essentially *mukta*-s do not have any notion that there is a standard behaviour. In fact *śāstra* states that they really do not care and neither will your judgment have any impact on them.

You may ask what prompts the happy and sad *vṛtti*-s in a *mukta*. The sadness *vṛtti*-s and the happiness *vṛtti*-s take place in the mind of the *mukta* as *prārabdha*. The ensuing discussion is only valid from the standpoint of an onlooker analysing a *mukta*. From the standpoint of a *mukta* such issues do not exist or are even important.

---

8 Māṇḍūkya Upaniṣad 12

9 see Sureśvara's Taittirīya Upaniṣad Bhāṣya Vārtikam 2.543

10 Pancadaśī11.87

The experiences of life remain etched in the minds of the *mukta*. He would know his name and also where he lives. The memories of his happiness, sorrows and his value system will also be there in his mind. The sadness *vṛtti*-s and the happiness *vṛtti*-s will manifest in the mind of the *mukta* in conducive situations. The only difference between the *mukta* and the common man is that such *vṛtti*-s will not destabilize the understanding of oneself for the *mukta*, not so for the common man.

Many *mukta*-s also do *sevā* because they have value for the welfare of all beings. They will not do *sevā* if these *vṛtti*-s were not there in their minds. These are prompted by their memory, and they do not oppose *Dharma* and also conducive to *Karma Yoga*. Hence the innate value system will continue to produce such *vṛtti*-s for a *mukta*.

In fact *mukta*-s at times can become the most active of people. Look at *Swāmi Cinmayānanda* as an example. It is said that before *Swāmi Cinmayānanda* attained *Mahāsamādhi* (death of a *mukta*) only 20% to 40% of his heart was supposedly functioning but he would still tirelessly stay up late into the night and wake up early in the morning. His tirelessly work was for the welfare of the people (*lokasangraha*). This is the reason why behavior may not be an important indicator of *mokṣa* or a *mukta*.

There is this story about a famous *swāmi*. He was ill and was admitted to a hospital. It was told that another famous saint came to see him to enquire about his health. The saint had miraculous powers and hence asked the *swāmi* if he could cure his illness as he looked very unwell. The *swāmi* responded to him that it was not necessary since it was his *prārabdha* and he had better go through it. So *jñāna* can work in many ways. Another *mukta* could have possibly said, "Yes, please cure it so that I can continue teaching others." There is no right or wrong behavior for a *mukta*. It only proves that *mukta*-s have residual and fuctional memories but it is just that in spite of them they are free. This is what is meant by 'freedom with *vṛtti*-s'. There could be countless *vṛtti*-s rushing into a *mukta*, but it is up to the *mukta* whether he wants to entertain them or not. In fact he is completely undisturbed by it. And even if he entertains them, the *mukta* has no notion that he is entertaining the *vṛtti* because there is no egocentric notion. The notion that "I am doing action" is not there although the mind responds spontaneously to various situations.

āpūryamāṇamacalapratiṣṭhaṅ samudramāpaḥ praviśanti yadvat.
tadvatkāmā yaṅ praviśanti sarvē sa śāntimāpnōti na kāmakāmī

> He attains peace into whom all desires enter as waters enter the ocean which, filled from all sides, remains undisturbed; but not the man who is full of desires.[11]

The common man is bound by thoughts while the *mukta* is free from thoughts while having them all. Here is a short story: I saw a moving bus in which my friend Kevin was in. I called Kevin on his cellphone and asked, "Where are you going?", he responded, "I am not doing anything. The bus is traveling, I am not." Similarly, as an onlooker I am seeing all the work that a *mukta* does but from the standpoint of the *mukta* he is doing nothing. That is the freedom that a *mukta* enjoys.

We also think that a *mukta* should behave only in a *dhārmic* way although he naturally would. That notion should also be destroyed. To neutralise such notions, in the *Tantric* tradition, the guru will subject the student to do things that are *adharmic* in a controlled environment to neutralise this sort of expectation that one should do only *dharmic* acts. Even *Rāmakṛṣṇa Paramahamsa* had to undergo this in the hands of his guru, *Brahmani Bhairavi*. This is for the removal of the '*śobhana adhyāsa*' which is a superimposition where I think that only good is acceptable and not that which is contrary.

Sureśvara, a disciple of *Śaṅkarācārya* (his other disciples are *Toṭaka*, *Padmapāda* and *Hastāmalaka*, makes an important point that although a *mukta* has no value for *Dharma*, he will somehow be inclined to do only *Dharma*[12]. This is due to the prior performance of *dharmic* acts that preceded *jñāna*. These *dharmic* acts form the texture and memories of the *mukta*'s mind. Therefore, when he attains this knowledge, he spontaneously responds with *Dharma*. How could we then account for the '*adharmic*' acts of the *mukta*? *Mukta*-s do get angry, or may smoke, overeat etc. The reason for these is *prārabdha*. In spite of having done *Dharma* and attained *jñāna*, there seems to be this *prārabdha*. From the *jñāni*'s standpoint there is no *prārabdha*, because *prārabdha* belongs to the body-mind-sense complex and that *mukta* has negated it. The *prārabdha* is only valid from the onlooker's point of view.

---

11 Bhagavad Gītā 2.70

12 Naiṣkarmyasiddhi 4.62-63

tattvajñānodayādūrdhvaṃ prārabdhaṃ naiva vidyate
dehādīnāmasatyatvāt yathā svapnaḥ prabodhataḥ

After the origination of the knowledge of the Self, *prārabdha* verily ceases to exist, inasmuch as the body and the like become non-existent; just as a dream does not exist on waking.[13]

13 Aparokṣānubhūti 91

30

TIME IS IMAGINED

यस्मान्नाशितमज्ञानं ज्ञानेन विश्वकारणं |
तस्मादात्मा भवेज्ज्ञानं ज्ञानं तस्मात् सनातनम् || ५९

yasmānnāśitamajñānaṃ jñānena viśvakāraṇaṃ |
tasmādātmā bhavejjñānaṃ jñānaṃ tasmāt sanātanam || 59

Because ignorance, the cause of the world, is destroyed by knowledge, therefore the ātman is knowledge (Consciousness) and therefore that knowledge (Consciousness) is eternal.

The moment I attain *jñāna*, *ajñāna* gets destroyed. Where there is light, darkness cannot be there. Through this knowledge, the *viśvakāraṇam* – cause of everything i.e., ignorance (the whole universe is born out of ignorance) is destroyed. It is not literally destroyed. It gets destroyed "as it were." That means the universe remains but there is a difference between the *jñāni*'s universe and the *ajñāni*'s universe. An *ajñāni* sees the universe whereas the *jñāni* sees himself as the universe or rather the universe as not separate from him. Because the universe is no more a second reality, it is as good as not seeing a universe at all. The *jñāni* sees *Brahman* or *ātman* alone.

This *jñāna* is nothing but the *ātman*. Here *jñāna* is not the knowledge as we know it, something to be gained, but Consciousness or the same *ekam jñāna*m *nityam* referred to in the opening verse of the text. It is interesting that in the same verse, *jñāna* can mean two different things. One used to mean something to be gained as knowledge, and the other is *svarūpajñānam* – Consciousness or *caitanyam*.

That *jñānam* or *cit* is *sanātanam*, which is another name for *nityam* or eternal. The author is repeating the same idea in different words, so that our mental obstacles are removed. The *śāstra* is compassionate and the authors of *śāstra*-s are never tired of repeating.

कालतो विविधं विश्वं यदा चैव भवेदिदं |
तदेकोऽस्ति स एवात्मा कल्पनापथवर्जितः || ६०

kālato vividhaṃ viśvaṃ yadā caiva bhavedidaṃ |
tadeko'sti sa evātmā kalpanāpathavarjitaḥ || 60

Since in time this manifold universe takes its origin, therefore there is One who is verily the ātman, unchanging through all times, who is one and unthinkable.

This is a loaded verse which states that in time alone, the universe is born because birth presupposes time. What I call universe is seated on time because time is nothing other than measuring change. When you state that the universe is seated in time, it means that the universe is always changing.

Time, *kāla*, is equated to another term *kalpanā* which means imagination. The *śāstra* states *kāla* is *kalpanā*, i.e imagined. Time is not an object. Change is objective but time is subjective. The western calendar system presents 60 seconds as being a minute but the Indian system considers 48 seconds to be a minute. The 24-hour day is very popular but the *śāstra* talks about a 30-hour day. In another country, it could be a 40-hour day. So, while time scales can change, 'change' is always constant. The earth will still rotate on its axis in the same way but how you measure it can be different. That is why the verse states that time is *kalpanā*. Time is in your head. Time is subject to you and not vice versa. You have created your own misery by thinking that you are subject to time. It is like creating a cage and locking yourself in it.

If *kāla* is the basis for the universe and *kāla* is your imagination then this universe of names and forms is as good as your imagination. The *śāstra* goes further and states that the *ātman* is "*ekosti*" or one. The word *eka* comes again. The *ātman* which is *ekam*, *ādyantaśūnyaṃ* is not subject to imagination. This *ātman* is not dependent upon your thought but is the content of your thought. The very substratum and content of your thought is *ātman*. The very presence of a thought indicates its content, *ātman*. Where there is pot, there is clay; where there is wave, there is water; where there is thought, there is *ātman*. The *upādhī*-s become the means to know its content. By the effect we understand the cause. We do not need any other proof.

Ātman is not subject to any imagination. It is *svaprakāśa*. It does not need any other light to illuminate it. Therefore, there is no room for imagination in this *ātman*. In other words, there is no room for disputation.

बाह्यानि सर्वभूतानि विनाशं यान्ति कालतः |
यतो वाचो निवर्तन्ते आत्मा द्वैतविवर्जितः || ६१

bāhyāni sarvabhūtāni vināśaṃ yānti kālataḥ |
yato vāco nivartante ātmā dvaitavivarjitaḥ || 61

All these external things will perish in the course of time but the ātman which is non-dual in nature and is beyond verbal expression will continue to exist.

All external objects are subject to the destruction by time because all objects are created in time. The moment *kāla* is not there, the external objects are also destroyed because they are seated in time. Therefore, when our ignorance is removed, it is as good as the universe being resolved – the whole universe is resolved into *ātman*. To look at it from another standpoint, every object undergoes change. For example, from the time I was born, every millisecond, I am changing. Creation and destruction are figments of your imagination. The moment you create something; the earlier form is destroyed. When once destroyed, it is created again and it is all taking place in your thoughts.

The verse states *ātman* is *yato vāco nivartante ātman dvaitavivarjitaḥ*. A similar verse appears in the *Upaniṣad*,

yato vāco nivartante aprāpya manaso saḥ

failing to reach which, words turn back along with the mind[1]

This *ātman* cannot be adequately described by words because every word that you use is *mithyā*, the very thing that you want to resolve and negate. I use the very thing that is not the Self to understand the Self. It is like using one thorn to remove another thorn.

1 Taittirīya Upaniṣad 2.9.1

31

SAMĀDHI

न खं वायुर्न चाग्निश्च न जलं पृथिवी न च |
नैतत्कार्यं नेश्वरादि पूर्णैकात्मा भवेत्खलु || ६२

na khaṃ vāyurna cāgniśca na jalaṃ pṛthivī na ca |
naitatkāryaṃ neśvarādi pūrṇaikātmā bhavetkhalu || 62

Neither space, air, fire, water, earth nor their combinations, not even Īśvara is complete. Indeed the ātman alone is complete.

This verse presents the *dṛṣṭi sṛṣṭi vāda*. So, the author dismisses the five elements and their products – the entire universe. *Kham* is another name for space in Vedic Sanskrit. Even *Īśvara* is dismissed in this verse as he is not *pūrṇa*. This view is acceptable only if you have assimilated Self-Knowledge well. Until then *Īśvara* is *pūrṇa* and I am *alpa* (limited). It is through *Īśvara*'s grace alone that this knowledge is possible.

The *Upaniṣad* states that you cannot choose this knowledge. As stated earlier, you have to let the *ātman*, which is not separate from *Īśvara*, choose you. Self-Knowledge indeed takes place in *mithyā* or duality. The grace of *Īśvara* takes place in duality and is conferred by the very same *Īśvara*. Therefore, you need *Īśvara* until you know the Self clearly. The whole pursuit takes place in *mithyā*. The seeker, the *śravaṇam mananam nididhyāsanam* are all in *mithyā*. *Cittaśuddhi* also is in *mithyā*. To be very honest, *mokṣa* too takes place in *mithyā*[1]. It is *anugraha* that allows you to enjoy the fruit of knowledge, *mokṣa*. Until then whether you like it or not, *Īśvara* is *pūrṇa* and *satyam*. You have to see it that way because without it there can be no worship and no possibility of *cittaśuddhi*.

The verse states that *ātman* alone is *pūrṇam* or complete. It is as good as saying *Brahman* is *pūrṇam* because *ātman* is *Brahman*. Sometimes people view the *ātman* and *Brahman* relationship as an equation. The word equation is not valid here because equation implies two different things being the same. *Ātman* and *Brahman* is not an equation but one and the same. They are two different names for the same reality. The equation is used only for the sake of teaching.

आत्मानमात्मना योगी पश्यत्यात्मनि निश्चितं |

1 see Gauḍapāda's Māṇḍūkya Kārikā, verse 2.32

सर्वसङ्कल्पसङ्न्यासि त्यक्तमिथ्याभवग्रहः || ६३

ātmānamātmanā yogī paśyatyātmani niścitaṃ |
sarvasaṅkalpasaṅnyāsi tyaktamithyābhavagrahaḥ || 63

The one who has renounced all desires and given up attachment to false existence is sure to see the ātman in the ātman by means of the ātman.

The first line has three *ātman*-s: *ātmānam*, *ātmano*, *ātmani*. The verse refers to a *sarva saṅkalpa sannyasin*, person who has renounced all intentions. Intentions are but desires to be accomplished. *Sarva saṅkalpa sannyāsin* is someone who has given up the dependency on both desires and *karma*-s[2]. He has no more desires to be accomplished.

This *sarva saṅkalpa sannyāsin* sees the *ātman* through the *ātman* in oneself. The first *ātman* refers to *saccidānanda ātman*, the second *ātman* is the *ātman* that I falsely understood as *jīvātman*. The last *ātman* is to indicate that I should not externalise the *ātman* but see it in myself. So, the third *ātman* indicates the location of the *ātman* so as to show the absence of external dependence. It also means that the *ātman* is not separate from myself and I do not have to change a thing to know the Self. Similar verses appear in the *Bhagavad Gītā*,

prajahāti yadā kāmānsarvānpārtha manogatān
ātmanyevātmanā tuṣṭaḥ sthitaprajñastadocyate

When one is completely free from all desires of the
mind and is satisfied with the *ātman* by the joy of *ātman*,
then one is called a man of wisdom, *O Arjuna*.[3]

yastvātmaratireva syādātmatṛptaśca mānavaḥ
ātmanyeva ca santuṣṭastasya kāryaṃ na vidyate

The one who rejoices the *ātman*, who is delighted with
the *ātman*, and who is content with the *ātman* alone, for
such a Self-realized person there is no duty.[4]

The word '*sthitaprajña*' used in the *Bhagavad Gītā* refers to a *mukta*.

The meaning of the verse is that a *mukta* is one who finds delight in oneself. The reason why the third *ātman* is mentioned is because in modern and medieval *Yoga* schools, you see the *ātman* inside but not outside. These

2 the term sarva saṅkalpa sannyāsi also appears in Bhagavad Gītā 6.4

3 Bhagavad Gītā 2.55

4 Bhagavad Gītā 3.17

schools teach some form of superconsciousness experience as the ultimate goal. So that is why the third *ātman* is introduced to resolve this problem by stating that the Self is seen not through meditation but by knowing the Self.

The *sarvasaṅkalpa sannyāsin* understands the three '*ātman*-s'. He sees himself as a free person and renounces the *mithyābhavagraha*, i.e., the universe of names and forms. The renunciation is like the way you realize yourself to be that missing tenth man. When you know the Self, the wrong notions are as though renounced. Similarly, the universe does not physically vanish but vanishes in one's understanding that there is no separate universe apart from the *ātman*.

आत्मनात्मनि चात्मानं दृष्टानन्तं सुखात्मकं |
विस्मृत्य विश्वं रमते समाधेस्तीव्रततस्तथा || ६४

ātmanātmani cātmānaṃ dṛṣṭvānantaṃ sukhātmakaṃ |
vismṛtya viśvaṃ ramate samādhestīvratatastathā || 64

Having seen the eternal ātman which is of the nature of happiness in the ātman by means of the ātman, he does not see the world as before and delights in intense samādhi.

For the first time, the word *samādhi* appears and gives us an opportunity for discussion because we must understand the word *samādhi* properly.

The verse states that seeing the *ātman* as myself, one gains limitless happiness i.e., *svarūpānanda*. The biggest mistake we make is to confuse *vṛttimayānanda* with *mokṣa*. How do we justify that this verse refers to *svarūpānanda*? We can infer that by the presence of the word *ananta* (limitless) in the verse. The word *ananta* and *ādyantaśūnyaṃ* referred to in the first verse mean the same. It tells us that *mokṣa* is not another state of mind with a beginning and end. We should look at the Self as the very essence of happiness, as the limitless reality. It is seeing myself as the *satyam, jñānam, anantam brahma*[5]. Hence the word *ananta* indicates that the verse is not talking about *vṛttimayānanda* but *svarūpānanda*.

Let us examine the line *ramate tīvratata samādhi*. *Ramate* literally means enjoying or revelling. The word *Rāma* is also derived from *ramate*. *Tīvra* means very intense. Hence we can infer that this *samādhi* does not refer to the conventional definitions of *samādhi*. Hence, we must dissect the word *samādhi*. The verse is not talking about an ordinary *samādhi* but a *Vedāntic samādhi* or the *Upaniṣad samādhi*. We need to recognise that the ancient *samādhi* as taught in the *Upaniṣad*-s was not called only *samādhi*.

5 Taittirīya Upaniṣad 2.1.1

The most misleading and popular term today in spiritual circles is *samādhi* because many teachers today use it to promise an experience of it through some means.

If you were to paraphrase the verse, it means that the person, who sees the *ātman* as oneself, attains limitless happiness in this profound state of *samādhi*. And in the process, the universe gets resolved.

The subject of *samādhi* is a very complex one. Different schools emphasized different aspects when defining *samādhi*. *Samādhi* can be used as both a verb and a noun. Some schools use it as a state of mind and the others as a practice.

Definition of Samādhi

Let us first dissect the word *samādhi* and see its etymological derivation. *Samādhi* is *samā* + *dhī*. *Samā* means *samatvam* which is tranquility or equanimity; *dhī* means mind and is another word for *buddhi*. In this derivation *samādhi* means an equanimous mind. It is a state of mind and not a practice.

The second way to break up the word is *sam* + *ā* + *dhī*. '*Sam*' means 'together', '*ā*' means 'towards' and '*dhī*' means 'to reflect'. It means the mind reflecting with clear direction or intention. This refers to a practice. When I say 'practice *samādhi*', then this is the derivation. When I say, "you are in a state of *samādhi*", then the first definition is relevant. In summary, the first *samādhi* is a state and the second *samādhi* is an action or practice.

But sometimes we can use the words "you are in *samādhi*" to describe someone meditating. Therefore, the words can be confusing if you do not know the context in which they are used. The word *samādhi* is used by two popular *sampradāya*-s, *Yoga* and *Vedānta*.

Samādhi in Yoga Tradition

In the *Yoga* tradition, the earliest reference to *samādhi* is found in the second verse of the *Yoga Sūtra*, '*Yoga cittavṛtti nirodha*'. The meaning of the verse is that *Yoga* is the suppression of thought modifications. It is a state where all thoughts have been negated and suppressed. In *Yoga* you get into *samādhi* through the practices of *pratyāhāra* (withdrawal of senses) and *dhyāna*. In the *Yoga Sūtra*, there are two types of *samādhi* - *samprajñāta samādhi* and *asamprajñāta samādhi*.

Samprajñāta samādhi means *samādhi* with cognitions or cognitive *samādhi*. *Sam* means 'to gather' and *prajña* is 'cognition'. Another name for it in the

Yoga Sūtra is *sabīja* (with seed). *Asamprajñāta samādhi* is non-cognitive *samādhi* and another name for it is *nirbīja* (without seed).

Asamprajñāta or *nirbīja* means it is not dependent upon anything. It is without any support.

Sabīja means that you use all the thought forms and mental tendencies (*vāsana*-s) to support the meditation. One leads to the other. *Sabīja* leads to *nirbīja*. To go to *asamprajñāta samādhi* one needs to go through *samprajñāta samādhi*. In popular culture, they call *asamprajñāta samādhi* as the superconscious state, transcendental meditation, stillness, void and bliss. Some claim to have experienced happiness in the state of *samādhi*, but this is one of the most difficult presentations of *samādhi* because happiness presupposes a *vṛtti*. So *samādhi*, which is supposed to be a thought-free state cannot be happiness. It refutes the very definition of *samādhi* and hence an oxymoron.

In summary, the *Yoga* tradition's conception of *samādhi* is something to be done, with more emphasis given to practice. And when you attain *samādhi*, it is a state.

Samādhi in Vedānta Tradition

Now let us look at how the traditional *Vedānta sampradāya* looks at *samādhi*. In the early *Vedānta sampradāya*, during times of *Śaṅkarācārya* and his disciples, *samādhi* was not a term popularly used in teaching. During those times, *samādhi* was either seen as a state similar to deep sleep[6] or the practice of *śravaṇam, mananam, nididhyāsanam*[7]. In *Vedānta sampradāya*, *samādhi* is understood as two types: *savikalpa samādhi* and *nirvikalpa samādhi*.

The word *vikalpa* in both *nirvikalpa* and *savikalpa* means 'doubt'. So *savikalpa samādhi* means a state with doubt and *nirvikalpa samādhi* is a state without doubt. The latter is a state of understanding or knowledge. So, in the context of traditional *Vedānta*, *savikalpa samādhi* and *nirvikalpa samādhi*-s are states of mind and knowledge.

Nirvikalpa samādhi refers to a tranquil state of mind having no doubts about the Self. That is a definition of a person who is a *mukta*, *jivanmukta*, *jñāni*, *Brahmaniṣṭha*, *siddha* etc. He is always in this state because he has no doubts about the Self and is calm. In fact the *ātman* is of the nature of tranquility (*śānta ātman*)[8]. The *mukta* is always in *nirvikalpa samādhi* and hence the

6 Brahma Sūtra Bhāṣya 2.1.9

7 Brahma Sūtra Bhāṣya 2.3.39

8 Kaṭha Upaniṣad 1.3.13

phrase '*tīvra samādhi*' is used in *Śiva Samhitā*. And the word '*ramate*' means always delighting in himself. These words are similar to the *Bhagavad Gītā*'s '*ātmanyeva ca santuṣṭaḥ*'[9] .

Savikalpa samādhi is the state of a person who has done *śravaṇam* and *mananam* but is yet to accomplish the goal of *nididhyāsanam*. His vision is, "I know the knowledge of *Brahman* but I am yet to see myself as that *Brahman*". Only the last bit of the establishment of Self-Knowledge is left. Such people are in *savikalpa samādhi*.

In the text *SarvaVedānta Siddhāntasāra Sangraha*, there is a beautiful illustration of a clay elephant for these two types of *samādhi*[10]. It is implied that when you look at a clay elephant and see it as a clay elephant, you are in *savikalpa samādhi*; but if you saw it as clay <u>only</u> then you are in *nirvikalpa samādhi*. The ignorant only see the elephant; they do not see the clay. They are like a child that sees a big clay elephant in the room and says, "Mother there is an elephant." The child will not say "clay elephant." Similarly, the ignorant will take the universe as real. For the person who has done *śravaṇam* and *mananam*, it will be a clay elephant; in other words, this universe that I see is nothing but *Brahman*. But the *mukta* will see only clay in that elephant. He will not see a universe but just *ātman*.

Challenges Posed by the Yoga-Vedanta Tradition

A different challenge emerged when a few teachers attempted to build a bridge between the two schools - *Vedānta* and *Yoga*. And due to this a new school of *Vedānta* called '*Yoga Vedānta*' was born. And as a result, in the *Vedānta sampradāya* there are two schools today - *Yoga Vedānta* and traditional *Vedānta*.

Yoga Vedānta is a *Vedānta* school that assimilated *Yoga* into it. The *Aṣtānga Yoga* and *Haṭha Yoga* were both fused with *Vedānta*. *Yoga Vedānta* then equated the *savikalpa samādhi* to *samprajñāta samādhi* and *nirvikalpa samādhi* to *asamprajñāta samādhi*. Traditional *Vedānta* did not create such equations but when *Yoga Vedānta* school emerged around 1200 CE these new ideas slowly started to become popular. Let us examine the words once again to understand this better.

'*Sa*' (in *savikalpa*) means 'with' and '*nir*' (in *nirvikalpa*) means 'without'. However, in *Yoga Vedānta*, they defined *vikalpa* as 'thought', which is another valid definition.

---

9 Bhagavad Gītā 3.17

10 Sarvavedānta Siddhāntasāra Saṅgraha 821

So *savikalpa samādhi* is *samādhi* with cognitions and *nirvikalpa samādhi* means *samādhi* without cognitions. Hence, the definitions became the same as *samprajñāta samādhi* and *asamprajñāta samādhi* defined in the *Yoga Sūtra.*

Swāmi Vivekānanda too equated the two in modern times. You can find this in the published works bearing his authorship where he describes *nirvikalpa samādhi* as *asamprajñāta samādhi.* But he was not the first person to do this. It was done as early as eight hundred years ago. The *ācārya*-s who wrote *Vivekacūdamaṇī*, *Dṛg Dṛśya Viveka*, *Vedāntasāra*, *Jīvanmuktiviveka* and *Pañcadaśī* may have also contributed to the development of the *Yoga Vedānta* school although it was perhaps *Swāmi Vivekānanda* who restated it in the last one hundred years or so. Although more research needs to be done on the different types of *samādhi* taught in specific *Vedānta śāstra*-s.

Yoga Vedānta has become the biggest and single most popular *Vedānta* school in the world today as it has crept into even new age philosophies, along with the massive proliferation of postural *Yoga* in the West. Unfortunately, there is an inconsistency in this school of thought. The *Yoga Sūtra*'s definition of *samādhi* has a beginning and end in time because you can go into the *samādhi* state and come out of it. If you subscribed to this definition, then you will be unable reconcile it with the words *ādyantaśūṇyam* and *ananta* in *Śiva Samhitā* which qualified *mokṣa.*

The issue is that we have equated all *samādhi*-s to be the *yogic samādhi*, where you enter a state and eventually come out of it after some time. And also where both 'practice' and 'states' are termed as *samādhi* without any distinction.

In traditional *Vedānta* both the *samādhi*-s are only states of mind, with the difference in the degree of assimilation of knowledge.

In the context of this verse, the *samādhi* that is being referred to has to be interpreted as *nirvikalpa samādhi*, a state where there are no doubts. The two words *tīvratā* and *ramate* are very important because they help us to qualify this state to be so. The verses prior to this verse stated the *ātman* to be *ekam*, *nityam*, *ādyantaśūnyaṃ* and hence it is justified to interpret the verse in this way.

We are constantly facing so many types of *samādhi*-s in many spiritual books and discourses these days. By now you should be able discern its validity in the pursuit of *mokṣa*.

The important point to note is that the word *samādhi* does not appear in any of the thirteen *Mukhya Upaniṣad*-s.[11] *Samādhi* is a relatively unimportant word in the *Vedānta* tradition used to denote something quite different from how it has been portrayed today due to the influence of the *Yoga Sūtra*.

Reference to Samādhi in Vedānta and Yoga Vedānta Texts

In many modern *Vedāntic* texts, most of which having been influenced by *Yoga*, there are references to *samādhi*. In fact, the text *Vedāntasāra*[12] adapts the practice *Patanjali Yoga* or *Aśṭānga Yoga* for *niddhidhyāsanam* after *śravaṇam* and *mananam*. This view is quite different from the view of *Sureśvara* who states that the *Yoga* should precede *śravaṇam* etc.[13]

The text *Dṛg Dṛśya Viveka* states,

yatra yatra mano yāti tatra tatra samādhayaḥ

Wherever the mind goes, there is *samādhi*.[14]

The above verse means that you are always in *samādhi*. This is another description of *nirvikalpa samādhi*. The text *Vijñānabhairava Tantra* states the same point with a slight variation,

yatra yatra mano yāti tatra tatra śivāvasthā

Wherever the mind goes, there is state of *Śiva*.[15]

The word *samādhi* also appears in the *Bhagavad Gītā* and the *Brahma Sūtra*. Here are the verses,

bhogaiśvaryaprasaktānāṃ tayāpahṛtacetasām
vyavasāyātmikā buddhiḥ samādhau na vidhīyate

One-pointed conviction does not become established in the minds of those who delight in enjoyment and affluence, and whose intellects are carried away by that (speech).[16]

The word *samādhi* in the above verse is used to mean concentration. Another verse states,

śrutivipratipannā te yadā sthāsyati niścalā

11 with the sole exception of Maitrāyaṇīya Upaniṣad, 8.18, which presents a six-limbed yoga (ṣaḍanga yoga) quite diferent from the aśṭānga yoga of Patanjali

12 Vedāntasāra 200-208

13 in his Naiṣkarmyasiddhi (the verse has been quoted in the commentary on verse 47)

14 Dṛg Dṛśya Viveka 30

15 Vijñānabhairava Tantra 116

16 Bhagavad Gītā 2.44

samādhāvacalā buddhistadā yogamavāpsyasi

When your mind that has become bewildered by hearing will become unshakable and steadfast in the Self (*samādhi*), then you will attain *Yoga* that arises from discrimination.[17]

In the verse above it is used to refer to the quality of knowledge and as steadfastness in the *ātman*. Again *samādhi* as steady knowledge or *sthitaprajña lakṣaṇam* appears in the next verse,

sthitaprajñasya kā bhāṣā samādhisthasya keśava
sthitadhīḥ kiṃ prabhāṣeta kimāsīta vrajeta kim

What is the description of a man of steady wisdom who is in *samādhi* (Self-absorbed)?
How does the man of steady wisdom speak? How does he sit? How does he move about?[18]

In the *Brahma Sūtra*, the word *samādhi* appears in the following *sūtra*,

samādhyabhāvācha

And (the *jīva* must be an agent) because (a contrary supposition will) lead to a negation of *samādhi* (on *Brahman*).[19]

Śaṅkarācārya in his commentary on the above *sutra* states *samādhi* was taught in the *Upaniṣad* as something to be done, referring to *śravaṇam*, *mananam* and *nididhyāsanam*. And he quotes a few *Upaniṣad* verses to support this view.

In the *Brahma Sūtra* commentary[20], *Śaṅkarācārya* comments on the futility of *samādhi* as a *yogic* state (where you go into the state of thoughtlessness and return) and equates it to being similar to deep sleep. Both the states are similar because you go in ignorant and come out ignorant. You do not generate any new knowledge about the Self in *samādhi*. The process of Self-Knowledge is cognitive and takes place only through teaching. Hence it is not a state where there are no thoughts. You are free with or without thoughts. The only difference between sleep and *samādhi* is that you do not go into *samādhi* because of fatigue unlike sleep. You wilfully go into the state through meditation.

---

17 Bhagavad Gītā 2.53
18 ibid 2.54
19 Brahma Sūtra 2.3.39
20 Brahma Sūtra Bhāṣya 2.1.9

In his *Māṇḍūkya Kārika* commentary[21] *Śaṅkarācārya* has given another definition of *samādhi* in which he suggests that to be similar to *nididhyāsanam*.

Summary of Discussion on Samādhi

In summary, the word *samādhi* can be interpreted differently. Hence, we can conclude that it is not a technical term. It can be used as a 'means', 'a practice' or 'a state' depending on the context. It all depends upon how you want to present the purpose of the verse. You do not find the word *samādhi* as a technical jargon in the commentaries of *Śaṅkarācārya*.

However, the *Śiva Samhitā*'s reference to *samādhi* is qualified by three words – *ananta*, *ramate* and *tīvra*. Hence we can interpret that this does not refer to the *samādhi* used in the *Yoga* schools as a mind free from thoughts. The word *samādhi* was also not used elsewhere in this chapter, and so its meaning cannot oppose what was previously taught in terms of the Self being *ananta* and *ādyantaśūṇyaṃ* in the first verse. Hence, we can interpret the word *samādhi* to be a state of complete knowledge, *mokṣa*.

At the same time, we cannot totally dismiss the practice of keeping the mind free of thoughts. There is no greater purifier of the mind than this *samādhi* meditation as taught by the *Yoga* tradition. Anyone who practices and mastered *yogic samādhi* is an *uttama adhikāri* if he happens to be a *Vaidika* (one who follows the *Vedic* tradition). It means that the mind is ripe for the assimilation of the knowledge when *śravaṇam*, *mananam* and *nididhyāsanam* take place.

21 Māṇḍūkya Kārika Bhāṣya 3.37

32

MĀYĀ

मायैव विश्वजननी नान्यातत्त्वधियापरा |
यदा नाशं समायाति विश्वम् नास्ति तदा खलु || ६५

māyaiva viśvajananī nānyātattvadhiyāparā |
yadā nāśaṃ samāyāti viśvam nāsti tadā khalu || 65

Māyā is the mother of the universe. Not from any other principle has the universe been created. When this māyā is destroyed, the universe no longer exists.

Henceforth we are going to look at another famous and misconceived doctrine in *Vedānta* - *māyā*. The interesting thing is that the word *māyā* did not appear so far in the past 64 verses. Thus far we have been doing fine in knowing the *ātman* without any idea of *māyā* because there were other ways to present the universe. We saw that the universe was a product of *avidyā*[1] and we had no challenges accepting that position. Now it appears as if the text has created a new issue because the current verse states *māyā* is *viśva janani* i.e., creator of the universe. In *Sanātana Dharma*, it is common to present *Brahman* in the masculine form and *māyā* or *prakṛti* as feminine.

The main points of the verse are:

1. the whole universe is created from *māyā*;
2. there is no other reality other than *māyā* from which the universe came
3. when *māyā* is destroyed, the universe ceases to exist.
4. and that knowledge destroys *māyā*.

The above points also equally apply to *avidyā* and so people assume that *māyā* is equal to *avidyā*. But they are not the same.

More often than not, *Vedāntin*-s take this view that *māyā* is *avidyā*. While it is not a big problem if you were to equate the two but I do think there is value in distinguishing the two. Let us now examine why *māyā* is discussed at this stage of the text. In fact, there could be a reason why the *Śiva Samhitā* chose to introduce *māyā* at this juncture.

हेयं सर्वमिदं विश्वं मायाविलसितं यतः |

1 see verse 49

ततो न प्रीति विषयस्तनुवित्त सुखात्मकः || ६६

heyaṃ sarvamidaṃ viśvaṃ māyāvilasitaṃ yataḥ |
tato na prīti viṣayastanuvitta sukhātmakaḥ || 66

All this is Māyā and is to be rejected; the body, riches and pleasure are, by their own nature, not worthy of delight.

A negative perspective is given to *māyā* in this verse. It states that because the universe is *māyā*, it cannot be enjoyed. It is neither pleasurable nor delightful. It is not pleasurable because whatever I take as pleasurable has a beginning and end so I cannot say it is infinitely pleasant. Anything that is not infinitely pleasant is indeed sorrow because in its absence I pine for it. And every time I go after it, my life becomes miserable struggling to attain it. If you looked at your life at present and prepare a mental list of the things that you are seeking, a wall will not be sufficient. Some of the things that you want to achieve would also have multiple dependencies. You would have to do a series of actions to achieve your goals.

The verse states that if the universe and *māyā* were to give you happiness then you would not be seeking happiness in your life. Another way of looking at it is in seeing the objects and experiences you are seeking as being made of *pañcabhūta* and your body is also *pañcabhūta*. So, if there was happiness in the *pañcabhūta*, there should also be happiness in this body too. This supposition implies that happiness comes guaranteed the moment you have this body. But the fact is that no object can give me eternal happiness. Every object will give me pleasure at a point and misery at another point. It is like your best friend turned worst enemy. The person did not change; neither did your sensory organs but in your mind, pain arises when you perceive that person who has become an enemy.

Likes and dislikes are caused by my values and knowledge. That is why there are certain people you dislike and people you like. For example, you dislike a certain individual but if you were to ask his wife about him, she will probably say that he is the best person she knows. Even Hitler had a lover, Eva Braun. It means that the person you hate may be liked by someone else. Think about it; my conclusion that something is good or bad, pleasurable or painful is basically a notion caused by my values and my beliefs. Hence there is really no permanent or intrinsic joy in this world.

Does that mean that we should renounce the world? No, we cannot. And all those people who think they are renouncing the world because it is *māyā* are also part of the *māyā*. You cannot renounce the world thinking it is *māyā*. The word *māyā* is a term that has to be understood properly. The first thing you should do is to dissect the word *māyā*. *Māyā* is defined as '*yā mā sā*'. *Sā* is 'she', *yā* means 'that' and *mā* means is 'not'. *Māyā* literally means 'that which is not'. It is defined this way because at one moment 'it was not', at another 'it is' and again 'it is not'. Whatever does not have an absolute reality and does not exist in the three periods of time is *māyā*. Based on this understanding *māyā* is essentially a name and form or *nāmarūpa* of the universe.

What is the relationship between *māyā* and *avidyā*? From the previous verse, it seemed as if the universe was born out of *māyā* and you also know that the universe is born out of *avidyā* so there is a possibility that we can equate the two. Now it is time for us to fine-tune our understanding.

Māyā is better appreciated if seen as a product of *avidyā*[2]. The whole universe or *māyā* that I see separate from my *ātman* is because of *avidyā*. While *māyā* is a product of *avidyā*, you cannot measure the distance between *avidyā* and *māyā*. You cannot say at this point, *avidyā* happened and after some seconds *māyā* came about. You cannot give a chronological sequence to it. Although it all happens simultaneously we say the root cause is *avidyā*. This is a point that you must always understand. The root cause is *avidyā*, and because of that alone I see *māyā*.

Māyā has many synonyms. One word for *māyā* is *prakṛti* which also means the universe.

Another word for *māyā* is *mithyā* - something that does not have an independent and eternal existence. *Māyā* like *mithyā*, is *jaḍam* (inert). *Ātman* is the one lending reality to it. *Māyā* is a noun and *mithyā* is an ontological term, a term that explains the nature of an object.

Māyā is popularly defined as illusion today. Illusion means a trick or something that is non-existent. This is a wrong definition of *māyā*. *Māyā* is the universe. When *śāstra*-s state that *māyā* is not satisfying, it means that the universe is not satisfying me not that it is an illusion. Imagine if someone said that you reading this book is an illusion? If you take the universe to be an illusion then any teaching to dispel illusion is equally an illusion. The word 'illusion' is itself misleading, and is therefore not the best translation for *māyā*.

Suppose you define illusion as something that is provisionally real then there is no problem. If someone takes the view that illusion is something

2 Śaṅkarācārya frequently uses the word avidyākṛta (caused by ignorance) in his commentaries

real but not real always, then also we have no issues. It is a matter of defining the word properly; it is the understanding of the word that causes the confusion. The statement that the world is an illusion is self-contradictory because the statement too is an illusion.

The erroneous view that *māyā* is illusion must be corrected. *Māyā* should be seen as a dependent reality or *mithyā*. Furthermore, *māyā* is dependent on *avidyā*.

Swāmi Vidyāraṇya attempted to organise the definitions of *māyā* by presenting it from three perspectives,

tucchānirvacanīyā ca vāstavī cetyasau tridhā
jñeyā māyā tribhirbodhaiḥ śrautayauktikalaukikaiḥ

> *Māyā* is looked upon in three ways. From the point of view of *śruti*, it is negligible (or non-existent); upon reasoning it is neither real nor unreal and for the ordinary people it is real (or existent)[3].

Māyā as *tuccham*: *Tuccham* means unreal or non-existent. This view is based on *śruti*. *Śruti* means *śāstra* and includes both *śruti* and *smṛti*. The *śruti* teaches that there is no *māyā*. That is why in ten of the eleven *Upaniṣad*-s that *Śaṅkarācārya* commented upon, there is not much discussion about *māyā*.[4] Only in two of the eleven *Upaniṣad*-s , is there a direct reference to *māyā*.[5]

From the *śruti*'s point of view, *māyā* is non-existent. That shows that the aim of the *śruti* is not to teach *māyā* but *Brahman* because once *Brahman* is taught, *māyā* is resolved. This could be the reason why the *Śiva Samhitā* had introduced the discussion on *māyā* much later into the chapter. *Avidyā* is pre-supposed because the very fact that you have a desire to know *Brahman* indicates that you are ignorant. *Śāstra* does not need to prove your ignorance. It should only reveal the absolute reality, *Brahman*. The *mukta* too takes this view. There is no *māyā* for a *mukta* because he does not see the universe as separate from him. The moment you do not see anything separate from yourself there is no room for *māyā*. In fact the universe depends on you but you do not depend it.

The second perspective is that *māyā* is *anirvacanīya* (neither real nor unreal). It is so for the one who has analysed the nature of the universe.

3 Pancadaśī 6.30

4 except for two occasions in his commentaries on Kaṭha Upaniṣad 1.3.12 and Kena Upaniṣad 3.2

5 Śvetāśvatara Upaniṣad 4.9-10; Bṛhadāraṇyaka Upaniṣad 2.5.19

This view is based on *yukti* which means inference, reasoning and logic. The universe cannot be considered unreal because it is evident to you. But neither can you say it is real because it appears to be real only in one state of existence, the waking state. In the dream state, you see another type of universe in subtle forms and in the deep sleep you see nothing. As a result, we take the middle path in defining the universe to be neither unreal nor real i.e., *anirvacanīya.*

To arrive at this view you do not need the *śāstra*; rational thinking is enough. You only need the *śāstra* to completely resolve this issue, not to tell you that the universe is neither real nor unreal. The discriminative or discerning enquirer (*jijñāsu*) sees the universe as *anirvacanīya.*

The the third perspective is that *māyā* is *vāstava* or real for the common man. The *śāstra* did not use the word *satyam* but instead used the word *vāstava* because *satyam* may cause confusion about the world being absolutely real. This third view is based on common sense (*laukikam*). This is the view of the person who is not interested in rationalising about life or the world. This person does not analyse, or question reality. He takes life as it comes. That is why *Vedānta* should not be taught to everyone, especially to this type of people. These are the people in *pravṛtti*, probably the 99.9% of the world population. You should not trivialize their existence because we have trains, air conditioners, smart phones and super highways because of them, who take the world to be real. These people are the *karmin*-s.

To sum up, for the *jñāni* there is no *māyā*; for the *jijñāsu* it is *anirvacanīya* and for the karmin it is *vāstava.*

The *ācārya, Swāmi Vidyāraṇya,* is teaching us how to understand this *māyā* in a systematic and organised manner. Therefore, we should never say the world is a product of *māyā* to everyone because many take the world to be real. The *jijñāsu* would look at the universe as *anirvacanīya* for the sake of *cittaśuddhi.*

You would have observed that the people who talk the most about *māyā* are the very people who are subject to it. That means the people who do not talk about *māyā* are the people for whom there is no *māyā* or *mithyā* for them.

We can understand these three definitions of *māyā* by using the clay-elephant illustration.[6] For those who consider *māyā* as *vāstava* it is an elephant; for those who consider *māyā* as *anirvacanīya*, it is a clay elephant

6 see commentary on verse 64

and for those who consider *māyā* as non-existent, it is clay. For the *karmin* the world is real like an elephant. For the *jijñāsu*, it is a clay elephant, neither real nor unreal and for the *mukta*, in his vision there is only clay. There is no *māyā* or universe apart from him. The clay elephant illustration will help you to understand the three perspectives of *māyā*. So whenever *śāstra* talks about *māyā*, you know which view it takes.

Whenever the *śāstra* states the whole universe to be like a castle in the sky, then it is taking the view of the universe being *tuccham*. Even the concept of the rope and the snake to a certain extent is only this perspective. The snake never existed. The snake vanishes with the dawn of knowledge, i.e., when you see the rope the snake disappears. The snake is indeed *tuccham*. Only when you are seeking the knowledge do you consider the world as provisionally real. The moment it is gained, there is no universe to reckon with. It does not mean that the universe vanishes. It just means that you do not see the universe as separate from you.

So, what should you be working on in your *sādhana*? Teachers tend to say, "work on *māyā*." That is impossible because *māyā* is not yours. But what you can do is to work on *avidyā*, which is yours. When *avidyā* is resolved, everything else is resolved. When cause is resolved, the effect too is resolved. To refine it further, your work on *avidyā*, is nothing but gaining Self-Knowledge. It is like removing darkness in a room. You do not take a pail to remove the darkness. You just need to switch on the light and the darkness is gone. That is why *śruti* alone teaches that which is *satyam* and *nityam*. The *śāstra* is not there to teach you *māyā* or *avidyā*; it only teaches, *Brahman*. On closer examination, you would have realised that you do not need to discuss *māyā* at all.

But while the discussion on *māyā* is not that useful, the discussion about the nature of *māyā* being *mithyā* is more purposeful, because that will help you to resolve the universe that you see into the *ātman*. What I mean is that in the word *mithyā* there is room for analysis whereas *māyā* is just a word. It is as good as saying 'universe' for the word *māyā*. But when I say *mithyā* there is an additional value in the word. You use the word *mithyā* to define the world as a dependent reality. You need to see a cause and effect relationship – one depending upon the other (*mithyā* depending upon *satyam*). So, there is value at looking at it as *mithyā*.

It is a good thing that the *Śiva Samhitā* introduced *māyā* later. If you noticed, this text takes the *dṛṣṭi sṛṣṭi vāda*. If you discussed *māyā* first, then it is *sṛṣṭi dṛṣṭi vāda*. If *māyā* was introduced earlier, you would have taken the universe to be an objective reality, including you, who are a part of it. By introducing *avidyā* before *māyā* you can resolve everything that is set up by *avidyā*.

Suppose the text had not dealt with *māyā*, then you could come back to the question about *māyā* talked about in other texts. So the text introduces *māyā* in anticipation of such difficulties and then resolves it as well. Now that we have understood *māyā*, it is easy to resolve it by saying that it is seated on *avidyā*. If you had not known what *avidyā* was, you would have had a big problem with *māyā*. *Māyā* would be left hanging in the air with no resolution.

The text *Tattva Bodha* gives another twist to the discussion by connecting *māyā* to *Īśvara* and *avidyā* to the *jīva*.

avidyā upādhiḥ san ātmā jīva ityucyatē,
māyā upādhiḥ san īśvara ityucyatē

The *ātman* conditioned by *avidyā* is the individual
(*jīva*), the *ātman* conditioned by *Māyā* is *Īśvara*

This approach of *sṛṣṭi dṛṣṭi vāda*, takes the whole universe as a product of *Īśvara*'s *māyā śakti*; and I, the *jīva* possessing *avidyā*. This approach has its own merits.

There is another perspective found which states that even after *avidyā* is removed, *māyā* remains[7] because it is an objective reality compared to *avidyā* which is subjective. This should be understood properly or else you may assume that *māyā* remains even after the rise of knowledge.

If you are serious about assimilating this knowledge, then you must anchor yourself to the view that *māyā* is an effect of *avidyā*. At the same time, we do not equate the two because it would imply that the subjective *avidyā* that you have, is the universe that you see and that they are of the same material.

We are creating that gap between *avidyā* and *māyā* because you may think that working on *avidyā* is the same as working on *māyā*. I hope you can appreciate this subtle difference. People assume that they can attain *mokṣa* by working on *māyā*. It is not going to happen. It will only happen when I take the view that *māyā* itself is an effect of *avidyā* and work on removing *avidyā*.

---

7 Pañcadaśī 4.17

Also with *avidyā* being subjective and *māyā* being objective, the nature of ignorance in each one of us can be different. Our doubts and false knowledge can vary but the perception of the objective world may not vary. In that sense, we see the universe as the same but the interpretations and superimpositions are different.

The purpose of the *śāstra* is not to prove *māyā* or *avidyā*. The *śāstra* only wants us to tackle *avidyā* and for that a cause and effect premise is presented. It is not a subject to be elaborately discussed. If you understand it this way, you will find *Vedānta* to be a very pleasant ride. If you understand it as any other way i.e., *māyā* etc., it will be a torture because you will be simultaneously enlightened while seeing *māyā*, which is absurd.

You must be clear about *Vedānta siddhānta*. Only then can you refute the other *siddhānta*-s and for that to happen you must keep exposing yourself to this knowledge over a length of time.

33

NEGATION OF SUPERIMPOSITION: ADHYĀROPA APAVĀDA

अरिर्मित्रमुदासीनस्त्रिविधंस्यादिदंजगत् ।
व्यवहारेषुनियतंदृश्यतेनान्यथापुनः ॥
प्रियाप्रियादिभेदस्तुवस्तुषुनियतःस्फुटम् ॥ ६७

arirmitramudāsīnastrividhaṃ syādidaṃ jagat |
vyavahāreṣu niyataṃ dṛśyate nānyathā punaḥ ||
priyāpriyādibhedastu vastuṣu niyataḥ sphuṭam || 67

This world appears in three different aspects - inimical, friendly or indifferent. This is consistently seen to be thus in one's everyday dealings and it is not otherwise. Distinctions such as agreeable or disagreeable are clearly not inherent in objects.

The world we experience can also be categorised into pleasant (*priyam*) and unpleasant (*apriyam*) and indifferent (*udāsīnam*). In all our transactions, we make one of these judgements. The world appears as an enemy, for example when there is a tsunami or earthquake; the world is friendly when there is clear rainbow in the sky and we are indifferent towards the world, for perhaps when using the road or walking on the pavement. The *jagat* is categorised based on the feelings we have towards its objects. Even in our transactions or relationships, we create superimpositions based on the above three categories.

Many of our judgments are multi-stepped. The complex nature of the mind is such that a lot of decisions are made by the mind without it being conscious. A lot of judgments and conclusions that we make are from the sub-conscious. Before your sensory organs encounter the objects or without you even having a choice, your mind had already made conclusions.

Our knowledge very much influences our conclusions. Most of our transactional judgments take place without our choice. Sometimes our conclusions can be wrong too, and this is known through some new knowledge.

This is important because the feelings of enmity, friendship and indifference are my own transactional conclusions. For example, a tsunami may be a problem for me but it may mean more food for fishes. Think about it; what is adversity to you may be a blessing to another being. The more and more we realize this, the less judgmental we become. This judgment is itself an *adhyāsa*, a superimposition that I make and sometimes it is something that I do unconsciously. We are going to discuss about this *adhyāsa* from the *śāstra*'s point of view.

Even *Dharma* is a superimposition. If it was universal then every animal will have *Dharma*. Both *Dharma* and *adharma* are based on my judgements. So what is the value of *Dharma* if both are superimpositions? The answer is that *Dharma* alone can purify your mind, not *adharma*. Although *adharma* is as good as *Dharma* in its nature, *Dharma* has a value because it is required to assimilate this truth. It neutralises mental impurities.

yajñadānatapaḥkarma na tyājyaṃ kāryameva tat
yajño dānaṃ tapaścaiva pāvanāni manīṣiṇām

The *karma* of sacrifice, charity and austerity is not to be abandoned; it is surely to be undertaken. Sacrifice, charity and austerity are purifiers of the wise.[1]

But in the process of observing this *Dharma*, one must understand that I adhere to this *Dharma* only for the sake of *cittaśuddhi*. Other than that, I have no other value for *Dharma*. This is primarily so for the *mumukṣu*-s. If you were to develop excessive value for *Dharma*, then it may bind you too.

आत्मोपाधिवशादेवं भवेत्पुत्रादि नान्यथा |
मायाविलसितं विश्वं ज्ञात्वैव श्रुतियुक्तितः ||
अध्यारोप अपवादाभ्यां लयं कुर्वन्ति योगिनः || ६८

ātmopādhivaśādevaṃ bhavetputrādi nānyathā |
māyāvilasitaṃ viśvaṃ jñātvaiva śrutiyuktitaḥ ||
adhyāropa apavādābhyāṃ layaṃ kurvanti yoginaḥ || 68

The Self appears as son etc. because of the limited adjunct (upādhi). With the help of the Veda and reasoning, yogi-s understand that the whole universe is a play of māyā and they resolve it through adhyāropa apavāda.

It is interesting to note that not many texts make a mention of the methodology of *adhyāropa apavāda*. *Śiva Samhitā* is one of those rare texts that makes a reference to this term. It does not appear explicitly in the *Bhagavad Gītā*, *Brahma Sūtra* or in the early *Upaniṣad*-s. *Adhyāropa apavāda* is a traditional methodology to teach *ātmajñāna*. It is not one method but

1 Bhagavad Gītā 18.5

it is the name given for many *prakriyā*-s or methodologies under the same category.

I would like to explain more about *adhyāropa apavāda*. The earliest reference to this word appears in *Śaṅkarācārya*'s commentaries[2]. The *Śiva Samhitā* verse states that all the relations that we have are an *upādhi* of the *ātman*. As discussed previously, *upādhi* means limiting adjuncts. In the pot-clay illustration, pot is the limiting adjunct for clay. Similarly, wave is the *upādhi* of water. *Upādhi* as a limiting adjunct, is something that 'seemingly' limits something else.

The verse states that all relations – son, father etc. are *upādhi* of the *ātman*. The first *upādhi* is the body-sense-mind complex. The body-sense-mind complex has other *upādhi*-s such as brother, father and grandfather. So, from the *ātman*'s point of view even māyā is an *upādhi*.

The verse is very complete. It states that through the *adhyāropa apavāda*, this universe that I have taken to be *anirvacanīya* (neither real nor unreal) can be resolved. The universe of names and forms gets resolved through the understanding that the *ātman* is non-separate like the way clay is not separate from the pot.

When you gain this knowledge, the universe does not suddenly vanish. If it were to vanish, even the *brahmaniṣṭha* will not be able to teach this knowledge because he would not see a second person in front of him. When you are teaching someone, you are indeed seeing a universe. This is another problem with some new age teachers. They claim, "this whole universe does not exist." Their statement does not make any sense. As stated earlier, if I were to say that everything in this universe is an illusion then even my statement that it is an illusion is equally illusory. The resolution of the universe does not make the universe disappear but rather resolved into its content which is the *ātman*. It is like the wave resolving into water and the pot into clay purely through knowledge without having to destroy the *upādhi*.

Adhyāropa is another name for *adhyāsa* (superimposition). *Adhyāropa apavāda* is the teaching method of the *Veda*. As stated in previous chapters, *adhyāsa* is taking one thing to be another; for example, taking the rope to be the snake; seashell as silver, clay as pot, water as wave, crystal as red, gold as ornaments etc.

Apavāda means 'negation' of the *nāma* and *rūpa* which are attributes of

2 Bhagavad Gītā 13.13, Bṛhadāraṇyaka Upaniṣad 4.4.25

māyā. This can also mean the negation of that which presents duality. All teachings of the *Upaniṣad*-s follow this method. The *Upaniṣad* negates what has been assumed to be something other than what it truly is. The *Upaniṣad*-s' task is *apavāda*.

The *apavāda* is done purely through the words of the *śruti* and *yukti* as the verse states; *srutiyuktitah*. The *apavāda* cannot be done without the *śruti* as it is the only valid means of knowledge to know the Self. And its process is *śravaṇam, mananam* and *nididhyāsanam*. The *yukti* is the logic employed in *śravaṇam, mananam* and *nididhyāsanam* (or in *mananam*) and it should not be contrary to the *śruti*'s teachings. Because logic cannot lead you to the Self independently. It should be used along with the purport of the śruti or the *Upaniṣad*-s.

dustarkātsuviramyatāṃ śrutimatastarko'nusandhīyatām

May you avoid the fallacious reasoning. May you reason along with the śruti.[3]

The other key point in this verse is that one should not accept the teachings of the *śruti* or the *Veda* blindly. The teachings of the *Veda* or the *Upaniṣad*-s must be consistent with logic, *yukti*. Hence the reason for *Śaṅkarācārya* to claim that we would not accept the statement that "fire is cold and non-luminous" even if a thousand statements from the *Veda*-s claim it to be so.[4] Because it is not valid, as it contradicts our logic and experience.

However, there are two types of *adhyāropa*:

1. Natural (*Naisargika*): I am born with this assumption that I am this body-sense-mind complex. *Śaṅkarācārya* states that the wonder of this *māyā* is such that even after telling you that you are the *ātman*, you will not see it. But without anyone telling you, will consider the body-mind-sense complex as yourself[5]. That is why it is called natural *adhyāsa*.
2. Deliberate: This one refers to the teaching model of the *Veda*. The *karmakāṇḍa* as taught by the *Samhitā*, *Brāhmaṇa* and *Āraṇyaka* do the *adhyāropa*. The *apavāda* is done by the *Upaniṣad*. This is because in the first three sections, the rituals and practices are prescribed assuming that you are the doer and an enjoyer with a body-mind-sense complex. The *śāstra* consciously makes you do this *adhyāropa* for *cittaśuddhi*.

3 sādhanapañcakaṃ 3
4 see Bhagavad Gītā Bhāṣya 18.66
5 Kaṭha Upaniṣad Bhāṣya 1.4.3

First I assume myself to be this body-mind-sense complex although I am the *ātman*, the *Brahman*, the *satcidānanda svarūpa.*

The knowledge that does the *apavāda* appears in the last section of the *Veda*, viz the *Upaniṣad*-s. Prior to that comes the deliberate *adhyāsa* for the sake of realising this end. The *Veda* does this by prescribing *karma* and then *upāsanā*, and finally negates everything through *jñāna*. This *adhyāropa apavāda* is prescribed by the *Veda* itself. First it states you must do *karma* and *upāsanā* and by doing that you qualify yourself for the *apavāda* to be effective. If you do not do the *adhyāropa*, the *apavāda* will not be effective. It will be just another academic exercise.

The key takeaway is that *Dharma* in the form of *karma* and *upāsanā* are the only means to purify myself so that the *apavāda* can be effective. This is the broad definition of this *Vedic prakriyā – adhyāropa apavāda.*

Adhyāropa is purposeful teaching, not purposeless. If it was purposeless, there is no need for the *Veda* to talk about *adhyāropa*; *apavāda* alone would have been sufficient. It is like going through elementary school to graduate to high school. This shows a link and a gradual progress; without the elementary education, you cannot get into higher education. This elementary school is like *adhyāropa* and high school is the *apavāda*. This is how the *mumukṣu* sees the value of *karma*, *yoga* and *upāsanā*.

Adhyāropa also means that the *nirguṇa Brahman* or *ātman* is given qualities. I take myself to be the body and a doer. I need to, or otherwise how can I do a *pūjā*? In *adhyāropa*, the attribute-less *Brahman* is given attributes for a purpose. I perform my *Dharma* for *artha* and *kāma* and if I am a *mumukṣu*, I do it with the right intention so that my mind gets purified. *Adhyāropa* is a strategy to pursue *artha* and *kāma* to purify myself.

This method cannot be found explicitly stated in any early *śāstra*-s. However, it is found in the *sampradāya* or the teaching tradition. This methodology is passed down in a *paramparā*, which is a tradition handed down from one person to another. As a traditional teacher one must know how to handle the teaching methodology. It is not a matter of knowing the word or memorizing the *śāstra*, but having the ability to wield the word such that it achieves what it aims to achieve i.e., *mokṣa*. The word remains a technical jargon if you have not assimilated it. Using this methodology, *Śaṅkarācārya*, through his written works has established how to interpret the words such that one sees oneself as *ātman* with clarity.

निखिलोपाधिहीनोवैयदाभवतिपुरुषः ।

तदाविवक्षतेऽखंडज्ञानरूपीनिरञ्जनः ॥ ६९

nikhilopādhihīno vai yadā bhavati pūruṣaḥ |
tadā vivakṣate'khaṇḍajñānarūpī nirañjanaḥ || 69

Only when Puruṣa (or a person) is free from all limiting adjuncts can it be said that he is part-less Consciousness and Pure.

The word '*puruṣa*' does not refer to the *puruṣa* as defined by the *Sāṅkhya* school. Here it means both 'person' and '*Brahman*'. It can refer to both meanings depending on the way you see the purport of the verse. The *Upaniṣad* states,

puruṣa evedaṃ viśvaṃ karma tapo brahma parāmṛtam
etadyo veda nihitaṃ guhāyāṃ so'vidyāgranthiṃ vikiratīha somya

The *puruṣa* alone is all this universe - *Karma* and *Tapas*. All this is *Brahman*, the highest and the immortal who knows this as seated in the cavity of the heart, unties the knot of ignorance even here, Oh good looking youth.[6]

When all the *upādhi*-s or *nāmarūpa* are absent in your vision, then you 'become' *puruṣa*. The word 'become' here does not mean a change of state but just a figure of speech similar to the words of the *Upaniṣad*,

brahmavid brahmaiva bhavati

The knower of *Brahman* becomes *Brahman*.[7]

The *ātman* has been always pure (*nirañjanaḥ*) and partless or indivisible consciousness (*akhaṇḍajñāna*). The *ātman* is pure and untouched by the *guṇa*-s. At no time is the *ātman* in touch with the body just as the clay is not in touch with the pot, the water with the wave, the crystal with the red rose and the rope with the snake. *Ātman* is thoughtless even while having all cognitions. *Ātman* is not born when the body-mind-sense complex is born; it does not die when the body-sense-mind complex dies; it is not happy when you are happy, and not sad when you are sad. All these identifications take place only if you take yourself to be the body-sense-mind complex. When a person completely disassociates or resolves the limiting adjuncts, then he 'becomes' that Pure and part-less Consciousness.

With this verse, the *Śiva Samhitā* has completed the direct teaching of *ātmajñāna*. The rest of the verses will present other related topics.

---

6 Muṇḍaka Upaniṣad 2.1.10

7 Muṇḍaka Upaniṣad 3.2.9

34

CREATION

A student went to teacher A and requested him to teach algebra; the teacher turned him away when he found out that the student had no elementary knowledge of algebra. The student then went to teacher B who realised that the student did not know anything about algebra but knew basic arithmetic, so offered to teach him that first before teaching algebra. *Śāstra* is like that compassionate teacher B who did not turn away the student but took the effort to prepare him for further study.

If a student did not understand the (highest) knowledge taught by a teacher, then it is the responsibility of the teacher to prepare the student such that he is ready for the journey to the highest truth. In the case of creation, the *śāstra* like a compassionate teacher presents the universe as *anirvacanīya* (neither real nor unreal) so that the seeker can understand it with minimal effort. To better understand the universe as *anirvacanīya*, the *śāstra* should present how the universe is created and explain creation. The *Śiva Saṃhitā* therefore presents creation and shifts from its earlier *dṛṣṭi sṛṣṭi vāda* position to *sṛṣṭi dṛṣṭi vāda*.

From verses 70 to 94, it presents about the various aspects of creation. The *śāstra* is providing a safety net for the seeker for whom the *dṛṣṭi sṛṣṭi vāda* is not effective. The safety net of creation provides the seeker something to fall back on and continue his sādhana. The text also contributes a few unique ideas while explaining creation.

स हि कामयते पुरुषः सृजते च प्रजाः स्वयं |
अविद्या भासते यस्मात् तस्मान्मिथ्या स्वभावतः || ७०

sa hi kāmayate puruṣaḥ sṛjate ca prajāḥ svayaṃ |
avidyā bhāsate yasmāt tasmānmithyā svabhāvataḥ || 70

The Puruṣa itself desires and procreates. From its will came out ignorance, which is by nature false.

The whole universe is a manifestation of *puruṣa* or *Brahman* or *Īśvara*. The key point is that the source of this creation is *Īśvara*. The verse also makes an important point that *avidyā* or ignorance was the first object of creation. This has been stated earlier where *avidyā* was seen to be the cause of the universe[1]. And when it comes to the creation of the universe, *avidyā* is often viewed as *māyā*. This view too is supported by the text which stated that *māyā* is the mother of the universe.[2]

The reason why *avidyā* is equated with *māyā* is because creation cannot take place with knowledge. It has been stated that knowledge will make the universe disappear[3] and hence the opposite of knowledge (i.e., ignorance) alone can create the universe. Hence, the *Śiva Samhitā* states that *avidyā* was the first object of creation which is indeed *māyā*. The current verse further states that this *māyā* is *mithyā* i.e., false or a dependent reality.

शुद्धे ब्रह्मणि संबद्धो विद्यया सहितो भवेत् |
ब्रह्मा तेजोंशतो याति यत आभासते नभः || ७१

śuddhe brahmani saṃbaddho vidyayā sahito bhavet |
brahmā tejoṁśato yāti yata ābhāsate nabhaḥ || 71

Upon the relation of attribute-less Brahman and ignorance results in Brahman becoming Brahmā, and from him space appears.

This whole creation proceeds from *māyā* as the causative principle. From this *Brahman* which has associated itself with *māyā* comes out *Brahmā* or *avyakta*[4]; from that *Brahmā*'s *tejas* comes space or *ākāśa*, the first element of the *pancabhūta*-s. *Tejas* means the ability to shine and indicates that the reality we call *avyakta* is not an unconscious being or inert. Only a conscious being can create.

तस्मात्प्रकाशतेवायुर्वायोरग्निस्ततोजलं ।
प्रकाशतेततःपृथ्वीकल्पनेयंस्थितासति ॥७२

tasmātprakāśate vāyurvāyoragnistato jalaṃ |
prakāśate tataḥ pṛthvī kalpaneyaṃ sthitā sati || 72

From space emanated air, from air came fire, from fire water and from water earth. This is how creation happened.

Having created space, the other four elements are now created through the process called *pancīkaraṇam*. From space comes air; from air comes fire; from fire, water; from water, earth. This is the order in which creation was established with the *pancabhūta*-s.

---

1 see verse 59

2 see verse 65

3 see verse 40

4 this model of creation is consistent with the Puruṣa Sūkta of the Rg Veda.

आकाशद्वायुराकाशपवनादग्निसंभवः ।
खवाताग्नेर्जलंव्योमवाताग्निवारितोमही ॥७३

ākāśadvāyur ākāśapavanād agnisaṃbhavaḥ |
khavātāgner jalaṃ vyomavātāgnivārito mahī || 73

From the space air; from air and space combined came fire; from the triple compound of space, air, and fire came water; and from the combination of space, air, fire and water was produced the gross earth.

From space came air, from the combination of space and air, fire came; from the combination of space, air and fire, water came and from the combination of space, air, fire and water came earth. This shows that the elements are interconnected and hence evolutionary.

खं शब्दलक्षणं वायुश् चञ्चलं स्पर्शलक्षणः |
स्याद्रूपलक्षणं तेजः सलिलं रसलक्षणम् ||
गन्धलक्षणिका पृथ्वी नान्यथा भवति ध्रुवम् || ७४

khaṃ śabdalakṣaṇaṃ vāyuś cañcalaṃ sparśalakṣaṇaḥ |
syādrūpalakṣaṇaṃ tejaḥ salilaṃ rasalakṣaṇam ||
gandhalakṣaṇikā pṛthvī nānyathā bhavati dhruvam || 74

The quality of space is sound; of air motion and touch; form is the quality of fire and taste of water. And smell is the quality of the earth. There is no doubt about this.

This is a very interesting verse because it explains the quality of each element. The quality of space is sound. If there was no space there is no sound. Next is air whose quality is touch; the quality of fire is form; the quality of water is taste and the quality of earth is smell. Sound travels in space; air can be felt and air can produce sound because air includes space. You can see fire; feel it and when it burns you can hear it. You can taste water, see it, touch it and hear it when water moves. You can smell earth, taste it, see its form, touch it and during an earthquake, hear its sound.

The *pancabhūta*-s have subtle to gross elements. And the grosser it gets, it includes the qualities of prior elements. Therefore, our gross body also includes the subtle elements. From the food we eat, the gross parts go to the gross body and the subtle parts to the subtle body. It is for this reason that the *śāstra* urges you to consume *sāttvika* food if *sattva guna* is what you would like to develop.[5]

5 see Bhagavad Gītā 17.8

The subtle portion of eaten *sāttvika food* goes to the mind.[6]

स्यादेकगुणमाकाशंद्विगुणोवायुरुच्यते।
तथैवत्रिगुणंतेजोभवन्त्यापश्चतुर्गुणाः॥
शब्दःस्पर्शश्चरूपंचरसोगन्धस्तथैवच।
एतत्पञ्चगुणापृथ्वीकल्पकैःकल्प्यतेऽधुना॥७५

syādekaguṇamākāśaṃ dviguṇo vāyurucyate |
tathaiva triguṇaṃ tejo bhavantyāpaś caturguṇāḥ ||
śabdaḥ sparśaśca rūpaṃ ca raso gandhas tathaiva ca |
etatpañcaguṇā pṛthvī kalpakaiḥ kalpyate'dhunā || 75

Space has one quality; air two, fire three, water four and earth five qualities, viz, - sound, touch, taste, form and smell. Thus has been declared by the wise.

This verse further reiterates what was discussed in the previous verse. Space has just one quality; air has two, fire has three, water has four and earth, five. In the next few verses, the *Śiva Samhitā* will present the creation of the individual or *jīva*.

6 see Chāndogya Upaniṣad 6.6.2

35

CREATION AND THE INDIVIDUAL

चक्षुषा गृह्यते रूपं गन्धो घ्राणेन गृह्यते |
रसो रसनया स्पर्शस्त्वचा सङ्गृह्यते परम् ||
श्रोत्रेण गृह्यते शब्दो नियतं भाति नान्यथा || ७६

cakṣuṣā gṛhyate rūpaṃ gandho ghrāṇena gṛhyate |
raso rasanayā sparśastvacā saṅgṛhyate param ||
śrotreṇa gṛhyate śabdo niyataṃ bhāti nānyathā || 76

Form is perceived through the eyes, smell through the nose, taste through the tongue, touch through the skin and sound through the ear. This is definitely how it is. It is not otherwise.

The individual is made up of the same elements as anything else in this universe. The *jñānendriya*-s or organs of perception correspond to the *pañcabhūta*-s. Eyes are from fire and hence see form; nose is equivalent to earth and therefore picks up smell; tongue corresponds to water and picks up taste; skin corresponds to air and picks up touch and ear corresponds to space and picks up sound.

The make-up of this body-mind-sense complex is not different from the other objects with only the degree of sentience being different. The implication of this is that knowing yourself is as good as knowing the universe; "knowing that by which you know everything".[1] To ensure that a pot of rice is sufficiently cooked, all you need to do is to check one grain. It is as good as checking every grain in the pot.

Our understanding of the world is like a mathematical fraction. The numerator changes but the denominator remains the same. In all actions where "I see, I work, I eat, I watch, I dance", it is always the 'I' who is experiencing everything. The 'I' is the denominator while the various different actions are the numerators. The numerator keeps changing but the denominator remains changeless. Given a choice, which one would you examine between the two? The denominator, isn't it? But it is the numerator that people are spending their time on. Only a rare few are interested in the denominator.

Similarly, we are so obsessed with solving the various problems in our

1 verse 18; Muṇḍaka Upaniṣad 1.1.3

lives that we forget that the problem is with ourselves. One forgets that one should fix oneself if not, the problem becomes bigger. If someone tells you that by studying *Vedānta* all your problems will be gone, that guy is creating another problem by giving you the expectation that all your problems will be solved. The correct attitude is to 'let the problems be' when you undertake *Vedānta* study.

The connection of the *jīva* with the universe is to indicate that the external universe is not different from the internal universe. In fact, there is no internal or external universe. There is only one universe which is seen by one person and that is the 'I'.

चैतन्यात्सर्वमुत्पन्नंजगदेतच्चराचरं ।
अस्तिचेत्कल्पनेयंस्यान्नास्तिचेदस्तिचिन्मयम् ॥७७

caitanyātsarvamutpannaṃ jagadetaccarācaraṃ |
asti cetkalpaneyaṃ syānnāsti cedasti cinmayam || 77

All this universe, animate and inanimate, has arisen from Consciousness; whether or not its existence can be proven, Consciousness does exist.

After explaining creation, the current verse states that from *caitanyam* everything came. There are two ways to look at its purport. If *caitanyam* is *Brahman* then creation came from *Brahman*. If you look at Consciousness as yourself then the entire creation came from yourself. Both the *dṛṣṭi sṛṣṭi vāda* and the *sṛṣṭi dṛṣṭi vāda* are permissible here. From Consciousness came the movable and immovable things.

Regardless of whether you want to prove that creation exists or not, *caitanyam* exists. Because in the presence of Consciousness alone can any discussion take place. The implication is that in *ātman* alone does the negation or acceptance take place.

This is the reason why there cannot be any disputant for a *Vedāntin*. The proponent and the disputant are one. *Śaṅkarācārya* stated that *Advaita* (non-duality) cannot be disproven and that any disputant can be won over through the knowledge of the Self.[2] It also shows that *Vedānta* is not subject to disputation. If you knew yourself clearly, no one could unsettle your understanding because the roots of your understanding would be deeply entrenched in the vision of *Advaita*.

Regarding creation, *mukta*-s may appear to be contradicting themselves when it comes to defining its reality. In fact, there is no real contradiction

2 Taittirīya Upaniṣad Bhāṣya 2.8.5

per se. Understanding the way *mukta*-s look at creation will help you in resolving this seeming contradiction.

Mukta-s look at creation from two perspectives: 1. I do not see the universe as separate from me and 2. from my standpoint there is no universe. This is also stated in the *Bhagavad Gītā*,

mayā tatamidaṃ sarvaṃ jagadavyaktamūrtinā |
matsthāni sarvabhūtāni na cāhaṃ teṣvavasthitaḥ ||
na ca matsthāni bhūtāni paśya me yogamaiśvaram
bhūtabhṛnna ca bhūtastho mamātmā bhūtabhāvanaḥ ||

This entire universe is pervaded by Me, in an unmanifest form. All beings abide in Me, but I do not abide in them. And yet beings do not abide in Me. Behold my divine *Yoga*. I am the upholder of all beings and yet I am not in them. I alone cause their existence.[3]

Both may appear as contradictory statements. That is why *mukta*-s are sometimes confusing because they can come from two standpoints. From one standpoint, I can say that I am nothing because I am none of this and from another point of view, I can say that nothing is separate from me. Therefore, the statements may appear contradictory. But the *mukta* has the ability to talk like this in riddles because they can take both standpoints with comfort. Statements such as '*prajñānam brahma*'[4] (Consciousness is *Brahman*) and '*sarvam khalvidam brahma*'[5] (Everything is *Brahman*) may appear contradictory. Yet such statements can be resolved when you know the traditional methodology well. That is why when we find contradictions in the statements of a *mukta*, understand that the problem is not theirs but ours. If I knew the traditional methodology I can resolve them easily. You can find this issue in many of the teachings of *Ramaṇa Mahāṛṣi*, *Nisargadatta Mahārāj* and *Rāmakṛṣṇa Paramahamsa*. *Vedānta* is such that when contradictory positions are presented, resolution can take place and knowledge is gained.

पृथ्वीशीर्णाजलेमग्नाजलंमग्नञ्चतेजसि ।
लीनंवायौतथातेजोव्योम्निवातोलयंययौ ॥
अविद्यायांमहाकाशोलीयतेपरमेपदे ॥७८

pṛthvī śīrṇā jale magnā jalaṃ magnañca tejasi |
līnaṃ vāyau tathā tejo vyomni vāto layaṃ yayau ||

3 Bhagavad Gītā 9.4-5

4 Aitareya Upaniṣad3.3

5 Chāndogya Upaniṣad3.14.1

avidyāyām mahākāśo līyate parame pade || 78

Earth withers and is dissolved in water; water is resolved into fire; fire similarly merges in air, air is absorbed in space and space is resolved in avidyā which merges into the Absolute (Brahman).

The word *paramapadam* in the verse is another word for *Brahman* that appears in the *Upaniṣad*-s.[6] The verse now shows how to resolve this universe into *Brahman*. It also tries to establish one element's hold over the other. You remove earth by pouring water and you remove water by evaporating it. When you have fire, you extinguish it by depriving it of air and if you remove space, air cannot exist.

The whole creation is a product of *māyā*. The first act in creation is the manifestation of space which is the beginning of names and forms. *Māyā* is not a separate power standing apart from the *pañcabhūta*-s. It is not that *māyā* created the *pañcabhūta*-s, but rather *māyā* is the very *pañcabhūta* or *triguṇa*. This is a fine point that we need to recognize.

6 see Kaṭha Upaniṣad 1.3.9

36

MĀYĀ : THE POWERS OF PROJECTION AND CONCEALMENT

विक्षेपावरणाशक्तिर्दुरन्तादुःखरूपिणी ।
जडरूपामहामायारजःसत्त्वतमोगुणा ॥७९

vikṣepāvaraṇā śaktir durantāduḥkharūpiṇī |
jaḍarūpā mahāmāyā rajaḥ sattvatamoguṇā || 79

Māyā has the power of projection and concealment and endless nature of sorrow. She is inert; has the three attributes of sattva, rajas and tamas.

Having resolved the universe into *māyā* and knowing that its substratum is *paramapadam* (*Brahman*), the text further elaborates on *māyā*. This *mahāmāyā* is inert and has no real existence because it depends upon something else, *Brahman*. It is made of three *guṇa*-s and it has two *śakti*-s – one is called *vikśepa* and other is *āvaraṇa*.[1]

Some editions of *Śiva Saṁhitā* use the word *sukharūpiṇi* instead of *duhkharūpiṇi*. The usage of *sukharūpiṇi* would mean that *māyā* creates the instinct in all beings to seek pleasure.

सामायावरणाशक्त्यावृताविज्ञानरूपिणी ।
दर्शयेज्जगदाकारंतंविक्षेपस्वभावतः ॥८०

sā māyāvaraṇā śaktyāvṛtāvijñānarūpiṇī|
darśayejjagadākāraṃ taṃ vikṣepasvabhāvataḥ|| 80

Veiled by the power of concealment, māyā has the form of varied forms. She makes the universe appear through her innate power of projection.

The *vikṣepa śakti* and *āvaraṇa śakti*, the two powers that act simultaneously and are not two separate powers. Let us look at the pot and clay example. The pot is both the projector and the concealer – the pot is projected from the clay, and the pot conceals the clay. The universe is projected from Consciousness and the same universe conceals Consciousness. It is not a case where one comes first and then the other; it takes place at the same time.

Āvaraṇa power covers Consciousness because of *vijñānarūpiṇi*. This is an interesting word. It means that *āvaraṇa* creates the knowledge of differences

1 see Vivekacūḍāmaṇī 108 - 117

(*viśeṣa jñāna*). It creates variety, provides the knowledge of the names and forms, and therefore makes us see the universe.

We will not be able to see the universe if everything in it is homogeneous; the universe exists because of the differences. The objects of the universe are subject to the three types of *bheda*-s[2]. The universe that I see is a projection and concealment at the same time. This is very important because it takes place simultaneously and so beautifully that people believe the universe to be real. For the one who takes the universe to be real, the projection is indeed very real, *vāstava*.

This *māyā* is called *mahāmāyā* because it can make the unreal look real. The next few verses will use *purāṇic* deities to further elucidate these concepts.

2 see commentary on verse 47 for the discussion of the three types of bheda-s

37

CREATION AND GUNA-S

तमोगुनाधिकविद्यायासादुर्गाभवेत्स्वयम्
ईश्वरस्तदुपहितम्चैतन्यंतदभूद्ध्रुवम्
सत्त्वाधिकाचयाविद्यालक्ष्मीःस्याद्दिव्यरूपिणी
चैतन्यंतदुपहितंविष्णुर्भवतिनान्यथा ॥
रजोगुणाधिकाविद्याज्ञेयासावैसरस्वती ।
यश्चित्स्वरूपोभवतिब्रह्मातदुपधारकः ॥ ८१-८२

tamo guṇādhikā vidyā yā sā durgā bhavet svayaṃ |
īśvaras tadupahitaṃ caitanyaṃ tadabhūddhruvaṃ ||
sattvādhikā ca yā vidyā lakṣmīḥ syāddivyarūpiṇī |
caitanyaṃ tadupahitaṃ viṣṇurbhavati nānyathā ||
rajoguṇādhikā vidyā jñeyā sā vai sarasvatī |
yaścitsvarūpo bhavati brahmātadupadhārakaḥ || 81-82

When avidyā has an excess of tamas, then it manifests itself as Durgā and the intelligence that presides over her is called Īśvara (Śiva).
When avidyā has an excess of sattva, it manifests itself as Lakṣmī and the intelligence which presides over her is called Viṣṇu.
When avidyā has excess rajas, it manifests itself as Sarasvatī and the intelligence which presides over her is known as Brahmā.

At the time *Śiva Samhitā*, perhaps the concept of *trimūrti*-s[1] along with their consorts could have become prevalent. Of course, it is a matter of dispute which of the *trimūrti* represents which *guṇa*. It all depends upon who your *iṣṭa devatā*[2] is. When there is a predominance of one *guna* over the other, then a specific feature is created. When there is *tamas* dominance, *Durgā* is seen and *Śiva* is the intelligence presiding over her. *Sattva* dominance is *Lakṣmī* and the intelligence is *Viṣṇu*; *rajas* dominance is *Sarasvatī* and the intelligence is *Brahmā*.

All these deities have a role to play in creation. *Tamas* is assigned to *Durgā* and *Śiva* because *tamas* is associated with destruction; *rajas* is involved in creation and hence *Sarasvatī* and *Brahmā* are associated with it while preservation is maintenance and balance, and hence *sattva* is associated with *Lakṣmī* and *Viṣṇu*.

1 Brahmā, Viṣṇu and Śiva
2 a term that denotes a worshipper's favourite deity

ईशाद्या सकला देवा दृश्यन्ते परमात्मनि |
शरीरादिजडं सर्वं साविद्या तत्कल्पिता तथा || ८३

īśādyā sakalā devā dṛśyante paramātmani |
śarīrādijaḍaṃ sarvaṃ sāvidyā tatkalpitā tathā || 83

All gods from Śiva etc are seen in the Absolute Self. The bodies etc and everything else are inert, and imagined due to ignorance.

This is another apparently bold verse. All the *trimūrti*-s are not seen apart from the *ātman*. The same idea is expressed in the *Vivekacūḍāmaṇī*,

> *svayaṃ brahmā svayaṃ viṣṇuḥ svayamIndraḥ svayaṃ śivaḥ*
> *svayaṃ viśvamidaṃ sarvaṃ svasmādanyanna kiñcana* ||

> One is oneself *Brahmā*, one is *Viṣnu*, one is *Indra*, one is *Śiva*, and one is oneself all this. Nothing else exists except oneself.

Whatever you see as bodies of inert objects including these gods are products of *avidyā*.

The *Śiva Samhitā* is now going back to the main theme of the text which is *mokṣa* since the subject of creation is going to be concluded. The *trimūrti*-s are not separate from the *ātman*; you are *Brahmā*, *Viṣṇu* and *Śiva*, *Sarasvatī*, *Lakṣmi* and *Durgā*; this is the truth. However, if you are unable to accept this, then the only thing that is left to be done is the worship of the very same *trimūrti*-s for their *anugraha* to assimilate this knowledge.

एवंरूपेण कल्पन्ते कल्पका विश्वसम्भवं |
तत्त्वातत्त्वं भवन्तीह कल्पनान्येन चोदिता || ८४

evaṃrūpeṇa kalpante kalpakā viśvasambhavaṃ |
tattvātattvaṃ bhavantīha kalpanānyena coditā || 84

The wise have thus conceived the origin of the universe in this way. The being and non-being can be in this Brahman only and cannot be conceived elsewhere.

This verse is a reiteration of what has been already presented. It states that the source of creation is indeed *Brahman* and not anything else.

प्रमेयत्वादिरूपेण सर्वं वस्तु प्रकाश्यते |
विशेषशब्दोपादाने भेदो भवति नान्यथा || ८५

prameyatvādirūpeṇa sarvaṃ vastu prakāśyate |
viśeṣaśabdopādāne bhedo bhavati nānyathā || 85

All things manifest themselves as objects of cognition and there arises various distinctions merely through words and names. However, the difference is not real.

All things that are presented as *prameya* (objects of the universe) have no real existence. Because of *Brahman*, everything else exists as *prameya* and it does not exist independently of *Brahman*. What differentiates the *prameya*, which is the universe, from *Brahman* is its names (*śabda*) and varied forms (*viśesa*).

तथैव वस्तुनास्त्येव भासको वर्तते परः |
स्वरूपत्वेण रूपेण स्वरूपं वस्तु भासते || ८६

tathaiva vastunāstyeva bhāsako vartate paraḥ |
svarūpatveṇa rūpeṇa svarūpaṃ vastu bhāsate || 86

Therefore, objects do not exist on its own; it is the Self that makes it so. The nature of objects appears in and through its nature (i.e., the Self).

Nothing really exists except this *param* i.e., *Brahman*. The *svarūpa* (intrinsic nature) of everything is *param*. All cognitions exist in and through this *param*. In every cognition, this *param* exists. It has no death and is free, and hence you are free in every moment. You do not have to search for freedom.

How do you understand a text like *Śiva Samhitā* that aims to present and resolve many ideas? Traditionally it is left to the teacher to assess his students and teach what is needed from a text. Not everything in the text needs to be taught. If you are studying the text on your own, then you should use your own discretion. Of course, this is not the best method. You must look for guidance from a living and available teacher and request that he teaches you. The text is not the primary way to know yourself, but it is the teaching of the text in the hands of the teacher that enables you to know the Self clearly. What the teacher does is that he uses words of the texts in a way that you see yourself as the free Self, *ātman*[3]. A teacher would perhaps use just three verses from a text to teach one student and ten for another because it depends on each of their qualifications and prior knowledge as to what is needed.

एकः सत्तापूरितानन्दरूपः
पूर्णो व्यापी वर्तते नास्ति किञ्चित् |
एतज्ज्ञाने यः करोत्येव नित्यं

3 This method of instruction has been presented in the prose section of the Upadeśasāhasri of Śaṅkarācārya

मुक्तः स स्यान्मृत्युसंसारदुःखात् || ८७

ekaḥ sattāpūritānandarūpaḥ
pūrṇo vyāpī vartate nāsti kiñcit |
etajjñānaṃ yaḥ karotyeva nityaṃ
muktaḥ sa syānmṛtyusaṃsāraduḥkhāt || 87

There is nothing except that One which is eternal, happiness, whole and all-pervading. He who realises this is a mukta, free from the sorrow of death and saṃsāra.

There is a nice term in this verse '*nityaṃ mukta*' which refers to a '*jīvanmukta*'. The definition of a *jīvanmukta* is 'liberated while living'. The word '*ekam*' in the first verse of the text is repeated here as '*ekah*' which refers to *Brahman*. It states that the *ekah* is *satyam*, exists eternally. The next point is that it is *ānanda rūpa*, i.e., it is the nature of *ānanda*. What kind of *ānanda* is this? We discussed two types of *ānanda* – *vṛttimayānanda* and *svarūpānanda*.[4] This *ānanda* refers to the *svarūpānanda* which is limitless *ānanda*.

The whole purpose of understanding *ānanda* is to understand that this reality is *ananta*, limitless. Happiness is always used as a tool to understand limitlessness because in the state of happiness, you do not want a second thing; you feel absorbed. A mind in a state of happiness experiences a *manolaya*, an undifferentiated state. You become very calm and this state is the reflection of my real state – that I do not need a second thing. So every time I am happy, I am sort of having a glimpse of my limitlessness. That is why we always like being happy. Or in other words, the desire to be happy is nothing but the desire to be my 'Self', to know who I am. Every happy state points out this fact to us. The one who does not know this misses it; the one who knows seizes it.

Returning to the topic of *manolaya*; among the three types of *vṛttimayānanda* [5](i.e., *priya*, *moda* and *pramoda*) we do not experience this absorption in the first and second states. It is only in the third state of *pramoda* that we experience this. It is only when you become one with the object that this *manolaya* takes place. That is the reason why you are the happiest when you possess what you want.

Sometimes the thing that brought you happiness at one stage may not bring the same happiness at a later time. This is normal, all objects are like that. You do not have to go about finding a reason for it. For example, when

4 see commentary on verse 58
5 ibid

you were a teenager you may have liked a song and you could have listened to it umpteen times. But listening to the same song right now may not give you the same feeling. You have just grown out of it. This 'growing out' is something that you do not do willfully; it just happens. This is something that we should recognise. It just happens, you cannot choose it. That is why the things that once brought you happiness could not make you happy any more. This is the reason why we are always looking for new experiences. This can be stretched to any experience – from food to music to books. For example, today you are interested in *Vedānta*, maybe after two years it may be something else. The nature of the mind is such that it cannot be always satiated. But the truth is that your Self is limitless.

The *ātman* in this verse is described as *svarupānanda*; it is then described as *pūrṇam* – complete. When something is complete, there cannot be a second thing. When something is whole, there cannot be anything apart from it. The word *pūrṇam* can also be defined as infinite. That which is complete cannot be improved further.

Gaining this knowledge is like knowing that you are the tenth man in the "Tenth Man Story".[6] The *śāstra* states that you do not have to do anything to gain this knowledge just like the tenth man who did not have to 'do' anything to know that he has always been the tenth man. Someone has to only point out to him that he was the tenth man. He was already the tenth man, the *śāstra* only points out that fact to him. He is basically accomplishing the already accomplished.

The *śāstra* states that you are already that which you want to know. If you are already that, you cannot gain it by another experience because the seeker is already the sought. This is the point that the *śāstra* takes a lot of pain to point out. Although it sounds simple, it appears miles away to your understanding; it is so close yet so far away. To close the gap, you need *karma* and *upāsanā* as they are the only ways to tap *Īśvara anugraha*. But for knowing yourself you do not need *karma*.

The next word to be discussed is '*vyāpi*' or all pervasive. Wherever you put your finger on, there *Brahman* is. In fact, it is there in the very finger. That is the part we always miss. It is like whenever your thought reaches out to understand something, there also *ātman* exists. You want to know *Brahman*, there it exists in your thought; you think you know *Brahman*, there it exists too. You think you have understood, there it exists; you think you have not understood, there also it exists. As difficult as it may seem, after knowing

6 see commentary on verse 18 for the story

ātman very clearly, you also need to use the strength of that very knowledge to drop this notional feeling that you do not know the Self adequately.

Nāsti kincit means that nothing else but this exists. That means there is no other second reality. It goes further and states that the one who has this unique knowledge is a *jīvanmukta*; this is a definitive statement. The *Śiva Samhitā* is giving the *jīvanmukti lakṣaṇaṃ*. *Nityam mukta* also means 'ever free'. *Nityam* means eternal or *trikala abhāditam satyam* which means it has neither beginning nor end and is in all three periods of time.

When this teaching takes place at a point in time, this notion that 'I am free' takes place because prior to that, you have not seen yourself as a *jīvanmukta*. So, you may presume that your *jīvanmukti* had a beginning in time. This means that you are not a *nityam mukta*. *Nityam* means there is no past, no present and there is no future. Or rather it pervades through the past, present and future. So *jīvanmukti* or *mukti* is not a state in time but the true nature of yourself even when you were ignorant.

What happens is that at the wake of knowledge, the notion that I am subject to time is not there. When I come to know that I am not subject to time, it is not like the caterpillar to butterfly metamorphosis. It is very important to understand that the *jīvanmukta* is not like the butterfly which was born at a particular point in time. Instead *jīvanmukti* is like the way the wave realises it is water. So even before you realised you were water, you have always been water.

This notion that I came to know that I am a *mukta* must be removed because you are giving importance to a prior state of ignorance. In your understanding, you realise there is no beginning for this Consciousness; there is no beginning to your freedom. The rise of *jīvanmukti* may be in time but you have always been timeless.

The text goes further and states that the knower is free from 1. death, 2. the cycle of birth and death and 3. sorrow. These three words indicate the same thing.

यस्यारोपापवादाभ्यांयत्रसर्वेलयंगताः ।
स एकोवर्ततेनान्यत्तच्चित्तेनावधार्यते ॥८८

yasyāropāpavādābhyāṃ yatra sarve layaṃ gatāḥ |
sa eko vartate nānyat taccittenāvadhāryate || 88

It should be ascertained through the intellect that there is this One in which everything gets dissolved through āropa apavāda.

Āropa apavādābhyām is the same as *adhyāropa apavāda*. The method of *Vedānta* has been restated. By the negation of the superimposition, the whole universe gets resolved in me. The resolution takes place through understanding alone. This reality alone exists and it is seen by the mind as assimilated or established knowledge. By using this method, the whole universe is resolved and not by any other method.

There is the popular notion that the *ātman* is beyond the mind and hence cannot be known by the mind. This is not true. This knowledge gained only through the mind. Self-Knowledge is just like any other knowledge that takes place in your mind. In fact all knowledge is through your mind alone. The verse also states this same point that this knowledge is ascertained though the mind. The *Upaniṣad* too agrees,

manasaivedamāptavyaṃ neha nānā'sti kiṃcana
mṛtyoḥ sa mṛtyuṃ gacchati ya iha nāneva paśyati

By mind alone is this attainable; there is no difference here whatsoever.
Whoso here sees as though different, passes from death to death.[7]

This is a very important point because many modern teachers will request that you go beyond the mind to see this reality when actually it is only through the mind that the reality can be understood. What is beyond the mind cannot be brought within the range of the mind. 'Beyond the mind' means that the *ātman* cannot be objectified, hence *aprameya*. Let the mind be where it is, let the *ātman* be where it is. Let the understanding go beyond the mind by knowing that there is no separation between the mind and the *ātman*. Where the mind is, the *ātman* is there. That is why it is said,

pratibodha viditaṃ matam amṛtatvaṃ hi vindate

When *Brahman* is known in every state of thought, It is
known in reality, because one thus attains immortality.[8]

The meaning is that wherever the mind goes the *ātman* is there. Very astutely, *Śiva Samhitā* points out that the reality has to be understood using the mind and not going beyond the mind. Using the mind, you have to understand that I do not have a mind. This is how you understand this knowledge.

7 Kaṭha Upaniṣad 2.1.11
8 Kena Upaniṣad 2.4

38

BODY IS FOR THE SAKE OF EXPERIENCES

पितुर् अन्नमयात् कोशाज्जायते पूर्वकर्मणः |
तच्छरीरं विदुर्दुःखं स्वप्राग्भोगाय सुन्दरं || ८९

pitur annamayāt kośājjāyate pūrvakarmaṇaḥ |
taccharīraṃ vidurduḥkhaṃ svaprāgbhogāya sundaraṃ || 89

The body is born from the food sheath of the father as a result of past karma. Be it known that the beautiful body is meant for sorrow and experiencing the fruits of one's deeds.

This verse states that the reason why you suffer is not because of your father. The father is mentioned first because conception starts with the father. It is the sperm that moves towards the egg in the womb. Therefore, the first thing that is initiated in conception is the male principle. This is how *samsāra* begins. That is why you have no choice in being born and neither can you choose your parents. The starting point of this birth is the father's body and then to the mother's body. This is the physical cause (*sthūla kāraṇa*). The subtle cause (*sukṣma kāraṇa*) of a birth is one's past *karma*-s.

The verse also makes a sarcastic statement that a beautiful body is experiencing sorrow. Why is the word 'beautiful' associated with the body then? It is mentioned so because it is the very body that experiences sorrow which provides the way out of it. Without this body, you cannot do *śravaṇam*. The body is beautiful but it is ignorantly suffering and enjoying. If suffering is negative, then enjoyment too is negative because suffering wants you to stay away from an object while enjoyment attaches you to it. Both likes (*rāga*) and dislikes (*dveṣa*) will bind.

मांसास्थिस्नायुमज्जादिनिर्मितंभोगमन्दिरम् ।
केवलंदुःखभोगायनाडीसंततिगुल्फितम् ॥ ९०

māṃsāsthisnāyumajjādinirmitaṃ bhogamandiram |
kevalaṃ duḥkhabhogāya nāḍī santati gulphitam || 90

This temple, made up of flesh, bones, nerves, marrow and interspersed with blood vessels etc., is the abode of experiences meant only for undergoing sorrow.

The verse calls the body – *bhoga mandiram* or the temple of enjoyment. There is a sanctum or *daiva gṛham* in all temples. The cave of the mind or *buddhi guhā* is the temple for humans because that is where you see *Brahman* or *ātman*[1]. It is a hidden knowledge. The body is really a temple for the person who sees this reality in his mind. This temple is however made of flesh, bones, fat, muscles etc. But in spite of whatever the body is made of, it is really a temple; a walking temple[2]. The temple is not always open but the deity inside the cave of your mind is always available. You can only close the doors of the temple, but you cannot enclose the deity. Similarly, in our body-mind-sense complex the temple is not always open. When the temple is closed, we are in deep sleep, when the temple is open we are either awake or dreaming. In all the three states the *ātman* is there, just like the deity in the temple. This is a good illustration to see ourselves as a temple.

पारमेष्ठ्यमिदंगात्रंपञ्चभूतविनिर्मितम् ।
ब्रह्माण्डसंज्ञकंदुःखसुखभोगायकल्पितम् ॥ ९१

pārameṣṭhyamidaṃ gātraṃ pañcabhūtavinirmitam |
brahmāṇḍasaṃjñakaṃ duḥkhasukhabhogāya kalpitam || 91

This body (microcosm), known as the macrocosm, created by Īśvara and composed of the five elements is considered to be for the experience of sorrow and happiness.

The verse states that the body made for experiencing *sukha* and *duhkha* is also *brahmāṇḍa*, a macrocosm. The macrocosm is complete and how can it be made to suffer and enjoy. It also makes the point that whatever that is created is made of the *pañcabhūta*-s. The one who does not see oneself as the macrocosm will continue to suffer and enjoy.

बिन्दुःशिवोरजःशक्तिरुभयोर्मिलनात्स्वयम् ।
स्वप्रभूतानिजायन्तेस्वशक्त्याजडरूपया ॥ ९२

binduḥ śivo rajaḥ śaktirubhayormilanātsvayaṃ |
svapnabhūtāni jāyante svaśaktyā jaḍarūpayā || 92

Śiva is sperm and ovum is Śakti. From the union of the two, dreamlike elements arise spontaneously through the inert power of māyā.

Bindu means sperm or semen and *raja* means egg or the procreative fluid of females. The sperm is associated with *Śiva*, the Lord and egg with *Śakti*,

1 see Māṇḍūkya Upaniṣad 3.1.7

2 the Tamil yoga text, Tirumantiram states that human beings are 'walking temples'. see verse 1857

the consort of the Lord. Coming together they create the whole universe. Two definitions of the universe are given in this verse – it is like a dream and it is inert.

It is called a dream not because it is unreal, but because the dream is real until you wake up. Once you wake up, the dream gets falsified. It is not that the world does not exist. It exists like a dream. However, once you wake up, the dream world is gone.

The universe is also *jaḍarūpa* i.e., inert, dependent and has no consciousness of its own. It is not self-shining.

तत्पञ्चिकरनात् स्थूलान्यसङ्ख्यानि समासतः |
ब्रह्माण्डस्थानि वस्तूनि यत्र जीवोऽस्ति कर्मभिः ||
तद्भूतपञ्चकात्सर्वं भोगाय जीवसञ्ज्ञिता || ९३

tatpañcikaranāt sthūlānyasaṅkhyāni samāsataḥ |
brahmāṇḍasthāni vastūni yatra jīvo'sti karmabhiḥ ||
tadbhūtapañcakātsarvaṃ bhogāya jīvasañjñitā || 93

From the combination of the five subtle elements, innumerable gross objects are produced in this universe. Among these according to its actions is the jīva produced. Everything arises from those five elements so that those things called jīva may reap the fruits of their actions.

The *pancīkaraṇam* – evolution of the five elements is the cause of the universe. In this universe, the *jīva* does *karma*-s. Based on these *karma*-s the *jīva* takes multiple births to experience the *pāpa* and *puṇya*. These *pāpa* and *puṇya* are made of *pañcabhūta*-s so that the *jīva* can enjoy them. Therefore, the definition of *jīva* is a person who does *karma* and enjoys the world made of *pañcabhūta*-s.

पूर्वकर्मानुरोधेन करोमि घटनामहं |
अजडः सर्वभूतस्थो जडस्थित्वा भुनक्ति तान् || ९४

pūrvakarmānurodhena karomi ghaṭanāmahaṃ |
ajaḍaḥ sarvabhūtastho jaḍasthitvā bhunakti tān || 94

I make the creation according to the past actions of the jīva. In a state of non-sentience, the sentient experiences all the elements.

The verse is uttered by Lord *Śiva* and he states "I am the giver of the destiny of *jīva*-s" (*karmaphala dātā*). The *jīva* enters the *prakṛti* to do *karma*. *Śiva* states that in conformity with one's past actions, he gives the fruits. This means that all results are the fruits or *phala* of our own actions. Conception is itself a *phala*, birth is a *phala*, living is a *phala*, every speech, every thought and the concept that you exist are all *phala*-s. Everything is given to us through these *phala*-s. The *ahaṅkāra* too is a *phala*. This is one way of neutralising the *ahaṅkāra*, the ego.

From the absolute standpoint, there is no free-will. You believe that you are 'doing' but you are actually doing nothing. Even the body, *ahaṅkāra*, desires etc are all given. Everything that you experience in the body-mind-sense complex has a cause and what you experience is an effect. For example, you desire a *laddū* (an Indian sweetmeat). Where did this desire come? If you keep tracing the desire to the source it goes back to the first *laddū* that someone gave you and why did that person give you this *laddū*? And then you can trace that too. It becomes endless.

Whatever you take yourself to be is just notional. What you refer to as body is an effect for which there is a cause and in turn is an effect to another cause and so on to the first cause. That first cause is *Īśvara* from which 'space' was first created[3]. The other causes and effects are also part of *Īśvara*. That which you call body-mind-sense complex is also in *Īśvara*. Even that *ahaṅkāra* is not yours. There is no such thing as free-will. The will cannot be free because that too is part of a long chain of causes and effects. In fact, that too is *mithyā*.

If you want to see the limitation of free-will, ask the people who suffer from a paralytic stroke, even if they willed it, their limbs cannot be moved.

I cannot even predict what my next thought will be but I am shameless to claim ownership over it. This is something that I must acknowledge – that I cannot predict my next thought. All the things that we have are dependent upon something else. They are entirely not at my disposal and have been given to me by *Īśvara*. He is not only the giver of the experience but also the body-sense-mind complex. We have this notion that "I am doing everything". At the wake of knowledge, this "I am doing everything" notion is dropped. There is no "I" to do something. If everything was indeed part of a long series of causes and effects, you are like a feather in the wind.

Until this so-called *ahaṅkāra* is neutralised, this reality you live in is provisionally real for you. When you know that *ātman*, the force of the *ahaṅkāra* will not be there anymore. *Ahaṅkāra* has its own agenda and plans and when it does not go according to plan, it will rear its ugly head. The moment you realise that you are not the doer; there is a low possibility of it rearing its ugly head. It gets sublated like the snake that has permanently

3 see verse 71

lost its fangs. Its ability is lost because it does not have a sense of doership (*kartṛtvam*) or enjoyership (*bhoktṛtvam*). These two will not be there when you do not see yourself as the doer.

This is one way of neutralising the ego. The *bhakta*-s enjoy such an attitude. They see everything as *Īśvara*'s gift, including the *ahaṅkāra* which loses its ability to sting. That does not mean that people with an inclination towards knowledge cannot see this way. They too could see this through rational analysis, through the understanding that all that I own including my free-will are just effects for which there were a cause.

39

PRĀRABDHA KARMA

जडात्स्वकर्मभिर्बद्धोजीवाख्योविविधोभवेत् ।
भोगायोत्पद्यतेकर्मब्रह्मांडाख्येपुनःपुनः ॥९५

jaḍātsvakarmabhirbaddho jīvākhyo vividho bhavet |
bhogāyotpadyate karma brahmāṃḍākhye punaḥ punaḥ || 95

Bound by their own karma, the jīva-s assume various forms. In this world, they come again and again to experience the consequences of their karma.

Because of my *karma* I take different forms. I have *sancita*, *āgāmi* and *prārabdha karma*-s. *Sancita karma*-s are the sum total of the karmic results that I have accrued over several births; *prārabdha* is the *karma*-s that have caused the current birth while *āgāmi* are the *karma*-s that I am performing in the current birth.

To experience the results of their *karma*, the *jīva*-s are born again and again. The *jīva* that is born again and again is the mistaken, misunderstood *ātman*. This misconception leads to my being born again and again but the potential to understand this knowledge is always there. Ignorantly I am born again and again.

जीवश्चलीयतेभोगावसानेचस्वकर्मणः ॥९६

jīvaśca līyate bhogāvasāne ca svakarmaṇaḥ || 96

When the results of the karma have been experienced, jīva gets dissolved (in Brahman).

The verse states that when the results of the *karma* have been experienced, the *jīva* is absorbed in *Brahman*. What the author means is that when the knowledge takes place and you see yourself as *ātman*, your *āgami karma* drops because there is no doership. You are without an ego (*nirahaṅkāra*). You have no doership so you do not accrue new *karma*-s.

At the wake of knowledge, there is no *sancita karma* – the main account. *Sancita* belongs to the realm of notional reality and when Self-Knowledge takes place, this *sancita karma* drops. At the wake of knowledge, you do not have a body-mind-sense complex. None of it is you. At the wake of knowledge, you also recognise the fact that you never had an *ahaṅkāra*. The *ātman* never performed actions; so, there is no *sancita karma*, *prārabdha* or *āgāmi karma* for the *ātman*, ever.

The *prārabdha* has been discussed previously but it is good reiterate the point at this juncture. People ask if there is *prārabdha karma* for a *mukta* or the *ātman*? The answer to this is a bit tricky. *Prārabdha* means that which has come into force in this birth.

For a *mukta* there is no second reality, there is no *ahaṅkāra* and hence there is no *prārabdha*. However, the onlooker superimposes a *prārabdha* on the *mukta*. But from the *mukta*'s standpoint there is no *prārabdha*. *Prārabdha* is from the point of view of the persons looking at a *mukta*. To say that "I have *prārabdha*" one must have an ego, *ahaṅkāra*, which the *mukta* does not have. The *Aparokṣānubhūti* states,

karma janmāntarīyaṃ yatprārabdhamiti kīrtitam
tattu janmāntarābhāvātpuṃso naivāsti karhicit

That *Karma* which is done in a previous life is known as *prārabdha*. But such *Karma* cannot take the place of *prārabdha* (for a *mukta*), as he has no other birth.[1]

Then why do people talk about *prārabdha* for a *mukta*? Because the onlookers see the *mukta* eating, talking, laughing, dancing etc. and from their standpoint alone there is *prārabdha* for a *mukta*.

The *mukta*'s mind and body will be experiencing pleasure and pain but they have nothing to do with the *ātman* as it is untouched by these. The pain and the pleasure are also *ātman*. One *mukta* may want to get a cure for an illness his body may be suffering from, but another may prefer to suffer through but both of them are free equally. The *mukta* has no notion of doing or not doing. There is no change in the *mukta*. Changelessness is the vision of the *mukta* in spite of all the changes that are happening.

We usually understand the *mukta*'s vision from the standpoint of negation; we try to isolate the different experiences from the *ātman*. But if everything is the *ātman*, what is there to isolate? This is the final lesson that one must learn – there is nothing to isolate, reject or embrace because nothing is separate from the *ātman*. Trying to isolate the second reality from the *ātman* is like removing the pot-ness from the clay. If you understood this, you are free.

The last verse of the chapter is not the *mukta*'s statement. It is the onlooker's

1 Aparokṣānubhūti 92

statement. The question may arise as to what happens to the *mukta* when the *prārabdha* has been experienced and the body falls? As for the ignorant people in *samsāra*, the *sūkṣma śarīra* prepares itself for a new birth or plane of existence (*loka*) based on the past *karma*-s, which one has identified with, as its propellers. For the *mukta*, there is no *karma* and hence no propelling force. The gross body merges back into the *pañcabhūta* and the subtle body comprising of *prāna* and mind disintegrates into the universe as there is no more desire or *saṅkalpa* to be born again. There are no future births either. With this verse, the first chapter of the *Śiva Samhitā* which taught the *yoga śāstra* is complete.

इतिश्रीशिवसंहितायांयोगशास्त्रेईश्वरपार्वतीसम्वादेप्रथमःपटलः|

iti śrīśivasaṃhitāyāṃ yogaśāstre īśvarapārvatīsamvāde prathamaḥ paṭalaḥ|

Thus ends the first chapter of Śiva Samhitā – a dialogue between *Īśvara* and *Pārvati* on the subject of *Yoga*

GLOSSARY

ācārya - teacher
adharma - unrighteous
adhikāra - qualifications, eligibility, competence
adhikāri - a person with adhikāra
adhiṣṭhāna - support, base
adhyāropa - superimposition
adhyāropa apavāda - the principle pedagogy of Advaita Vedānta
adhyāsa - superimposition
adṛṣṭa phala - unseen results
advaita - non duality
advaita Vedānta - the philosophy of non dualism based on the Upaniṣad-s
āgāmi karma - actions performed in the current life
agnihotra - fire sacrifices
agrahaṇa - non-apprehension
aham - I
ahaṅkāra - ego sense
ahimsā - non-injury
ajñāni - an ignorant person
ākāśa - space
alpa - limited
anādi - without beginning
ananta - limitless
anātmavāda - the theory of non-self
anirvacanīya - neither real nor unreal
anityam - impermanent
antaranga - internal
antarātman - inner self
anubandha catuṣṭayam - four fold considerations
anubhava - experience
anugraha - grace
anumāna - inference
anuṣṭhānam - observance

aparāvidyā - inferior knowledge

aparokṣa jñāna - immediate knowledge

apavāda - negation

aprameya - cannot be objectified

artha - wealth, meaning

asamprajñāta samādhi - the highest experience as a result of meditation in Yoga Sūtra

āśrama - stage of life, a place of learning

aṣṭāṅga Yoga - the system of Yoga taught in the Yoga Sūtra

āstika - believer in the Veda-s

āstika śāstra - scripture that considers the Veda-s as a revelation and authority

aśvamedha - a horse sacrifice revealed in the Veda-s

atisulabham - very easy

ātmajñāna - self knowledge

ātmavicāra - self inquiry

ātman - Self

āvaraṇa - cover

avidyā - ignorance

bahīraṅga - external

bhajan - songs of devotion

bhakta - devotee

bhakti - devotion

bhāṣya - commentary

bhoktṛtvam - the sense of enjoyer-ship

bhrānti - delusion, confusion

bhubukṣu - seeker of enjoyments

brahmacāri - a celibate, student

brahman - God without attributes

brahmā - the creator

brahmānanda - happiness of Brahman

brahmaniṣṭha - a person established in the knowledge of Brahman or ātman

brahmavidyā - knowledge of Brahman

buddhi - intellect

buddhi guhā - the cave (core) of the intellect

cakra - wheel

caitanya - consciousness

cārvāka - a materialistic philosophy

citta ekāgrata - one pointed mind

cittaśuddhi - mental purification

dama - mastery of sense organs

deva - god, deity

devī - goddess

dharma - righteousness, duty, order

dhyāna - meditation

duḥkha - sorrow, pain

dṛṣṭa phala - seen result

dṛṣṭi-sṛṣṭi-vāda - a method of teaching in Advaita Vedānta

durgā - a goddess, consort of Śiva

dvaita - duality

dveṣa - dislike

ekātmavāda - a method of teaching Advaita Vedānta

gauḍapāda - the grand-teacher of Śaṅkarācārya, author of the Māṇḍukya Kārika-s

gṛhasta - married householder

guṇa - quality

guru - teacher

hastāmalaka - one of the four disciples of Śaṅkarācārya

haṭha - effort, force, exertion

haṭha Yoga - a system of Yoga that deals with effort, force andexertion

hṛdaya ākāśa - space of the heart, intellect

Indra - a prominent vedic god

indriyā - sensory organs

iṣṭa devatā - a favourite deity

īśvara - God with attributes,

japa - mantra repetition

jagat - universe

jijñāsu - an enquirer

jīva - individual

jīvanmukta - a person liberated while living

jīvanamukti - liberated while living

jīvātma - individual self

jñānakarma samuccayavāda - a theory of combining action and knowledge to attain liberation

jñāna sādhana - a means through knowledge

jñānakāṇḍa - one of the two section of the Veda which deals with knowledge

jñānaYoga - a means through knowledge

jñāna(m) - knowledge

jñānaphala - fruit of knowledge

jñānapravāha - stream of thoughts

jñānasvarūpam - of the nature of knowledge/consciousness

jñānendriya - sensory organs

jñāni - a wise man

jyoti - light

kāma - desire

kāmya - of desire

karma - action

karmakāṇḍa - one of the two sections of the Veda which deals with actions

karmaphala dāta - giver of the results of actions

karmaṭha – a person eagerly engaged in action for gaining artha and kāma

karmin - a person eagerly engaged in action for gaining artha and kāma

Karma Yoga - a means through knowledge, an attitude that prepares one for jñānaYoga

karmayogi - a person observing Karma Yoga

kartṛtvam - a sense of doership

karuṇākara - compassionate one

karuṇāmūrti - a form of compassion

kāśāya - ochre

kāyika - bodily

karmaphạla - result of karma

kṣaṇikavāda - a Buddhist theory of momentariness

kṣatriya - warrior

kūṭastha - unchangeable

lakṣaṇa - definition

lakṣmi - a goddess of wealth, consort of Viṣṇu

loka – plane of existence

lokasangraha - wellbeing of the world

lokāyata - a materialistic philosophy

mādhyamika - a school of Buddhism

mahāprasthāna - the great journey

mahātma - the great self, a wise person

māhāvākya - a great statement, refers to axioms in the Upaniṣad-s

mala - impurity

mananam - reflection, analysis, logic

mānasa karma - mental action

mānasika - mental

manolaya - a state of absorption when happy

mantradṛṣṭā - seers of mantras, people to whom the Veda-s were revealed

mīmāmsa - a philosophy of rituals based on the Veda-s

mīmāmsaka - a follower of mīmāmsa

mithyā - false, dependent reality

māyā - creative power of the universe

moda - one of the three types of happiness

mokṣa - freedom, liberation

mukta - a liberated person

mukti - freedom, liberation

mumukṣu - a seeker of mokṣa

mumukṣutvam - a qualification required for jñānaYoga

naimittika - occasional

naisargika - natural

nāma - name

nāstika śāstra - atheistic texts

nididhyāsanam - a Vedāntic meditation for the removal of opposing tendencies

nirahankāra - without ego

nirguṇa - without attributes

nirvikalpa samādhi - a state of doubt-free knowledge, practice, meditation

nirvikāratvam - without changes, without modification, homogenous

niśtha - commitment

nitya(m) - daily, eternal

nityakarma - daily rites, obligatory rites

nivṛtti mārga - a lifestyle of renunciation, one of two lifestyles taught in the Vedic tradition

niyama-s - observances, 5 or 10 in number

nyāya - analogy, illustration

padmapāda - one of the four disciples of Śaṅkarācārya

pañcabhūta - five elements

pancamahāyajña - the five great duties meant for householders

pancasūnā - the five ways living beings are killed accidentally while performing duties

pancīkaraṇam - grossification of the five elements

pāṇḍavās - the five warrior kings in the epic Mahābhārata

pāpa - sin

paramparā - succession

parāvidya - superior knowledge

parokṣa jñāna - mediate knowledge

pārvati - a goddess, consort of Śiva

patanjali - author of Yoga Sūtra

pāsam - bond

paṣu - animal, individual

pati - lord

pauruṣeya - created by a person

phala - result

prakāśānanda - a teacher of Advaita Vedānta, author of Vedānta Siddhānta Muktāvali

prakaraṇa grantha - explanatory texts

prakriyā - method, pedagogy

prakṛti - nature, material nature, matter

pramāṇa - valid means of knowledge

pramoda - one of the three types of happiness

prāṇāyāma - a breathing technique taught in Yoga

prāṇi - a living thing

praṇidhāna - surrender

prārabdha - the results of actions that operate the current birth prasāda - offering received after having offered to God

pratibhā - insight

pratyavāya doṣa - the defect of non-performance of duties or actions

prasāda buddhi - attitude of Karma Yoga, an attitude of graceful acceptance

prasthāna traya - the three foundations of Vedānta

pratyagātman - inner self

pratyāhāra - a practice taught in the Yoga tradition

pratyakṣa - perception

pravṛtti mārga - a lifestyle of action, one of two lifestyles taught in the Vedic tradition

prayojana - purpose

priya - one of the three types of happiness

punarjanma - rebirth

puṇya - merit, a result of right action

purṇa - complete, whole

puruṣa – person, Brahman

puruṣārtha - goals of life, the Vedic tradition proposes four goals

rāga - like

rajas - one of the three guna-s, activity

rūpa - form

śabda - sound, scriptural teaching

saccidānanda - a definition of Self

sādhaka - a practitioner

sādhana - practice

sādhana catuṣṭayam - four pre-requisites for jñānaYoga or Vedānta

śaiva siddhānta - a school of thought that considers Śiva as the supreme God

sajātiya - of the same breed or type

śakti - power

samādhi - a state of mind, state of knowledge, practice,

sambandha - connection

sampradāya - tradtion

samprajñāta samādhi - one of the experiences as a result of meditation in Yoga Sūtra

sampūrṇa - absolutely complete or whole

samsāra - cycle of births and deaths, a life of constant becoming samśaya - doubt

samvāda - a respectful conversation between two people for the sake of knowledge

sanātana Dharma - a name of Hinduism, eternal way of life

sanātanam - eternal

sancita - the main repository of results of karma from previous lives

saṅkalpa - intention, desire

śaṅkarācārya – Ādi Śaṅkara, the most influential teacher of Vedānta (Advaita Vedānta)

saṇnyāsa - renunciation, monastic life

saṇnyāsin - a renunciate, monk

sarasvatī - goddess of knowledge, consort of Brahmā

sarvajña - all knower

sarvavit - all knower

śama - mastery of mind

samādhāna - one pointed mind

śarīram - body

śāstra - scripture, text

satkarma - good action

sattva - one of the three guna-s, equilibrium, serenity

sāttvika - possessing sattva

satyam - truth, eternal

ṣaṭka sampatti - six fold mental wealth, one of the sādhana catuṣṭayam

savikalpa samādhi - a state of knowledge but lacking clarity

siddhānta - a conclusion, a philosophical psoition

siddhi - mastery

śiṣya, disciple

śiva - God of Destruction,

sevā - worship, service

smṛti - text or memory

śobhana adhyāsa - superimposition of goodness

śraddhā - faith

śravaṇam - listening

śrotriya - a person who knows the Veda-s or the Vedic methodology

sṛṣṭi-dṛṣṭi-vāda - a method of teaching Advaita Vedānta

śruti - the Veda-s

sthitaprajña - a man of wisdom, liberated person

śuddha - pure

sukha - happiness, pleasure

sureśvara - one of the four disciples of Śaṅkarācārya

śūnya - void

śūṇyavāda - a Buddhist theory of void

sūtra - aphorism

svabhāva - nature

svadharma - one's duty

svādhyāya - self study, chanting

svagata - within

svaprakāśa - self illuminating

svarūpa - intrinsic nature

svarūpajñānam - knowledge of intrinsic nature

svarupānanda - happiness arising from its own nature

svataḥ siddha - self established

śvetāśvatara Upaniṣad

tamas - one of the three guna-s, darkness, inertia,

tātparya - aim

tattva nirṇayam - determination of truth

tanmātrā - subtle nature of the five elements

tantra śāstra - another class of scriptural literature

tapasvi - austere person

tejas - energetic, bright

titikṣā - forbearance

toṭaka - one of the four disciples of Śaṅkarācārya

tridhā - three ways

triguṇa - three qualities

trimūrti - trinity

tuccham - non existent

upadeśa - tecahing, instruction

upādhi - limting adjuncts

upaniṣad - the part of the Veda that deals with knowledge and philosophy

uparati - renunciation, completion of duties
upasanā - meditation rites, contemplative rites
uttama adhikāri - very qualified person
vācika - verbal
vāda - position, theory, debate
vaidika - vedic
vairāgyam - dispassion
vānaprasthi - a forest dweller
varṇa - caste, class, vocation
vāsana - mental tendencies, mental impressions
vastradhāri - clothed
veda - the most authoritative scripture in Hinduism
vedānta - a philosophy derived from the final part of the Veda i.e., Upaniṣad-s
vidyā - knowledge
vijātiya - of different breed or type
vijñānavada - a Buddhist theory of reducing reality to thoughts
vikalpa - doubt and thoughts
vikarma - wrong action
vikśepa - projection
viparīta bhāvanā - opposing tendencies
viparīta grahaṇa - misapprehension
viṣaya - object, subject
viṣayānanda - happiness derived from objective experiences
viśeṣaṇam - features, diversity, uniqueness
viṣṇu - God of preservation
viveka - discrimination
vrata - vow
vṛtti - thought
vṛttimayānanda - happiness as a result of thoughts, synonym of viṣayānanda
vyāsa - author of Mahābhārata, Brahma sūtra and the Purāṇa-s
vyoman - space
yama - ethical values
yoga - a system of Hindu philosophy and practice
yogācāra - a school of Buddhism

yudhiṣṭhira - the eldest brother amongst the Pāṇḍavās

yukti - logical reasoning

BIBLIOGRAPHY

Alston, A.J. (1971). *Realization of the Absolute.* United Kingdom: Shanti Sadan

Ashokananda, S. (1988). *Avadhuta Gita of Dattatreya.* India: Sri Ramakrishna Math, 3rd edition

Boetzelaer, J.M.V. (Tr) (1971). *Suresvara's Taittiriyopanisad-Bhasyavartikam.* Netherlands: Leiden University

Bryant, E. (2009). *The Yoga Sutras of Patanjali.* New York: North Point Press

Chinmayananda, S. (1997). *Sadhana Panchakam by Adi Sankara.* India: Central Chinmaya Mission Trust

Chinmayananda, S. (2003). *Aparoksanubhuti: Intimate Experience of the Reality.* India: Central Chinmaya Mission Trust

Dayananda, S.S. (2009). *The Teaching Tradition of Advaita Vedanta.* India: Arsha Vidya Research and Publications Trust

Dutt, M.N. (2012). *Visnusmrti.* India: Parimal Publication

Dutt, M.N. (2008). *The Complete Mahabharata.* India: Parimal Publication

Gambhirananda, S. (1988). *Mundaka Upanisad: with the commentary of Sankaracarya.* India: Advaita Ashrama, 2nd edition

Gambhirananda, S. (1989). *Mandukya Upanisad: with the commentary of Sankaracarya.* India: Advaita Ashrama, 2nd edition

Gambhirananda, S. (1993). *Brahma Sutra Bhashya of Shankaracharya.* India: Advaita Ashrama

Gambhirananda, S. (1985). *Taittiriya Upanisad: with the commentary of Sankaracarya.* India: Advaita Ashrama

Gambhirananda, S. (1986). *Svetasvatara Upanisad: with the commentary of Sankaracarya.* India: Advaita Ashrama

Gambhirananda, S. (1997). *Chandogya Upanisad: with the commentary of Sankaracarya.* India: Advaita Ashrama

Gambhirananda, S. (1998). *Kena Upanisad: with the commentary of Sankaracarya.* India: Advaita Ashrama, 3rd edition

Gambhirananda, S. (1999). *Aitareya Upanisad: with the commentary of Sankaracarya.* India: Advaita Ashrama, 2nd edition

Gambhirananda, S. (2000). *Isa Upanisad: with the commentary of Sankaracarya*. India: Advaita Ashrama, 3rd edition

Gambhirananda, S. (2000). *Katha Upanisad: with the commentary of Sankaracarya*. India: Advaita Ashrama, 2nd edition

Gambhirananda, S. (2006). *Bhagavad Gita: with the commentary of Sankaracarya*. India: Advaita Ashrama

Jagadananda, S. (1941). *Upadesa Sahasri*. India: Sri Ramakrishna Math

Katti, S. (2012). *My Humble Understanding of Spirituality*. USA: Createspace

Madhavananda, S. (Tr) (1965). *Brhadaranyaka Upanisad: with the commentary of Sankaracarya*. India: Advaita Ashrama, 4th edition

Madhavananda, S. (1991) *Vivekacudamani*. India: Advaita Ashrama

Maheshananda, S., Sharma, B.R., Sahay, G.S., Bodhe, R.K., Jha, B.K. and Bhardwaj, C.L. (Tr) (2009). *Siva Samhita: A Critical Edition – English Version*. India: Kaivalyadhama S.M.Y.M. Samiti

Mallinson, J. (2007). *The Shiva Samhita: A Critical Edition and an English Translation*. USA: YogaVidya.com

Mokshadananda, S. (1996) *Jivan Mukti Viveka*. India: Advaita Ashrama

Mukerjee, Radhakamal. (2009). *Astavakragita: The Song of the Self Supreme*. India: Motilal Banarsidass

Muktibodhananda, S. (1998). *Hatha Yoga Pradipika*. India: Bihar School of Yoga

Natarajan, B. (Tr) (1991). *Tirumantiram. A Tamil Scriptural Classic*. India: Sri Ramakrishna Math

Nikhilananda, S. (1990). *Vedanta-Sara of Sadananda*. India: Advaita Ashrama

Nikhilananda, S. (Tr) (2000). *The Mandukya Upanisad with Gaudapada's Karika and Sankara's Commentary*. India: Advaita Ashrama

Olivelle, P. (Tr) (2000). *Dharmasutras: The Law Codes of Apastamba, Gautama, Baudhayana, and Vasistha*. India: Motilal Banarsidass

Olivelle, P. (Tr) (2006). *Manu's Code of Law: A Critical Edition and Translation of the Manava-Dharmasastra*. India: Oxford University Press

Panoli, V. (2006). *Prasthanatraya (6 Vols)*. India: Mathrubhumi Grandha Vedi

Piparaya, R.K. (2003). *Ten Upanishads of Four Vedas*. India: New Age Books

Radhakrishnan, S. (2006). *The Principal Upanisads*. India: HarperCollins Publishers India

Sarup, Lakshman (Tr) (1967). *The Nighantu and the Nirukta, the oldest Indian treatise on etymology, philology and semantics*. India: Motilal Banarsidass

Sastri, S.S.S. (Tr) (2003). *Vedantaparibhasa*. India: The Adyar Library and Research centre

Satchidanandendra, S.S. (1999). *Minor Works of Sri Sankaracharya*. India: Adhyatma Prakasha Karyalaya

Shastri, J.L. (Tr) (1957). *Garuda Purana*. India: Motilal Banarsidass

Singh, J. (2002). *Vijnanabhairava or Divine Consciousness*. India: Motilal Banarsidass

Sinh, P and Vasu, R.B.S.C. (Tr) (2004) *The Forceful Yoga: Being the Translation of Hathayoga-Pradipika, Gheranda Samhita and Siva Samhita*. India: Motilal Banarsidass

Sivananda, S. (2000). *Jnana Yoga*. India: Divine Life Society

Swahananda, S. (Tr) (1967). *Pancadasi of Sri Vidyaranya Swami*. India: Sri Ramakrishna Math

Tapasyananda, S. (2007). *Srimad Bhagavata (4 Vols)*. India: Sri Ramakrishna Math

Tattvananda, S. (2002). *The Quintessence of Vedanta of Sri Sankaracharya*. India: Sri Ramakrishna Advaita Ashrama

Tattvavidananda, S. (2005). *Vedanta Dindimah by Sri Sankaracarya: with the commentary Tattvaprakasika*. India: Brahma Vidya Kuteer

Joshi, K.L., Bimali, O.N. and Trivedi, B. (Ed) (2006).112 *Upanisads (2 Vols)*. India: Parimal Publications

Tejomayananda, S. (1994). *Tattva Bodhah*. India: Central Chinmaya Mission Trust

Tejomayananda, S. (2001). *Acarya Sankara's Drg Drsya Viveka*. India: Central Chinmaya Mission Trust

Venis, A. (Tr) (2008). *The Vedanta Siddhantamuktavali of Prakasananda*. India: Chaukhamba Orientalia

Venkataramiah, M. (2003). *Talks with Sri Ramana Maharshi*. India: Sri Ramanasramam

Venketasananda, S. (1993). *Vasistha's Yoga*. USA: State University of New York Press

Wilson, H.H. (2011). *Visnu Purana*. India: Parimal Publications

INDEX